WESTERN TIBET AND THE BRITISH BORDERLAND

Kailas (21,850 feet)

The Heaven of Hindus & Buddhists, and the Axis of the Universe.

WESTERN TIBET AND THE BRITISH BORDERLAND

THE SACRED COUNTRY OF HINDUS AND BUDDHISTS

WITH AN ACCOUNT OF THE GOVERNMENT, RELIGION AND CUSTOMS OF ITS PEOPLE

BY

CHARLES A. SHERRING, M.A., F.R.G.S.

INDIAN CIVIL SERVICE, DEPUTY COMMISSIONER OF ALMORA

WITH A CHAPTER BY

T. G. LONGSTAFF, M.B., F.R.G.S.

MEMBER OF THE ALPINE CLUB

DESCRIBING AN ATTEMPT TO CLIMB GURLA MANDHATA

WITH ILLUSTRATIONS AND MAPS

GYAN

Published by

GYAN

Gyan Publishing House
5, Ansari Road
Daryaganj, New Delhi-110002
Phone: 011-47034999, 9811692060
E-mail: books@gyanbooks.com

Distribution Network
gyanbooks.com
India, USA, Canada, UK, Australia, France

ISBN : 978-81-212-4213-4 (PB)
First Published, London, 1906

2nd Impression 2020

Printed at: Gyan Press, Delhi.

Western Tibet and the British Borderland
Author: Charles A. Sherring

DEDICATED

BY KIND PERMISSION

TO

THE RIGHT HONOURABLE

LORD CURZON OF KEDLESTON

G.C.S.I., G.C.I.E.

PREFACE

At a time like the present when, owing to freer access to the country, books on Tibet are becoming multiplied and the reading public is beginning to appreciate the homely truth which tells us that "of making many books there is no end; and much study is a weariness of the flesh," it is not too much to say that the general information on matters Tibetan is wonderfully advanced in comparison with what it was even five years ago. In fact, so far have matters gone along the whole line of Tibetan exploration, that the public expects nowadays something which is decidedly new and distinctly additional to what has already been so ably put before it by writers in the past. It is therefore to a more highly enlightened and more exacting reader that an author has nowadays to address himself, and year by year the task will become more difficult. What has been the charm of the past is not to the same extent the charm of the present: what was once novel in the paucity of literature has now become familiar owing to the numerous books lately published which have become the classics of Tibetan research.

It is, then, with the greatest diffidence that I present

this venture to a critical public, and my apology is that the subject has been but little dealt with by previous writers, and that the information gathered on the spot does add, however inconsiderable the addition, something to that vastly interesting mass of knowledge which is the delight of those interested in comparative religions, ethnology and political science, while I trust this book will also find favour with the geographer and the lover of tales of travel. For there is a portion of Western Tibet and the British Borderland, full of holy lore, which is most sacred to the Hindu and Buddhist, where there is a romance of legends and myths and where quaint customs and manners appeal to the poetry that runs in all men's veins. It is in regard to these subjects that I ask the reader to give a patient hearing, and to bear with whatever crudeness the narrative reveals in the telling, remembering in charity that life on the border is not the school for literature which the metropolis affords, and that words written amidst daily duties, while travelling in some of the wildest landscapes known to mankind, where tempestuous rain and freezing winds dull the mind and numb all thought, can never bear the rounded rhythm and the equal pose of those of the writer who enjoys an undisturbed comfort and a facility of seeing books of reference, which are the pleasures of civilisation.

The object of this book is entirely non-political, and most carefully have all matters controversial been omitted, as is befitting a Government servant whose appointment and duties preclude him from entering upon such subjects.

I would also mention that there is an account of a climb on the highest mountain in Western Tibet by Dr. T. G. Longstaff, and (although I am wholly ignorant of mountaineering myself) I think I may venture to say that this description of a climb with Alpine guides should prove of extreme interest to all mountaineers and all good sportsmen, who are capable of appreciating pluck and endurance, while the fact that the climbers reached an altitude which is amongst the highest ever hitherto attained adds an additional zest to the tale. This is the first occasion on which a Tibetan mountain has been attacked according to approved modern methods.

I take this opportunity of thanking Dr. Longstaff for his kindness in allowing me the use of so many of his photographs: out of the one hundred and seventy-five illustrations sixty-four are his. The rest with the exception of six are mine, including the panoramic views, which are a special feature of this book.

To those interested in geography there are two illustrations of special interest: first, the panoramic view of the two lakes Mansarowar and Rakas showing the low hills separating the two with Kailas in the distance (*see* p. 261): and secondly the panoramic view of the whole length of the channel between these two stretches of water, showing the lakes at each end (*see* p. 271). Every reader can now solve for himself those problems which have engaged the attention of the public for a century, viz., as to whether there is any, and if so what, connection between the two lakes.

I am much indebted to Messrs. Lawrie and Co., photographers, Lucknow, for the great pains they have taken over the photographs.

C. A. SHERRING.

CAMP TANAKPUR,
Jan. 21, 1906.

CONTENTS

LIST OF ILLUSTRATIONS

MAPS AND SKETCHES

WESTERN TIBET AND THE BRITISH BORDERLAND.

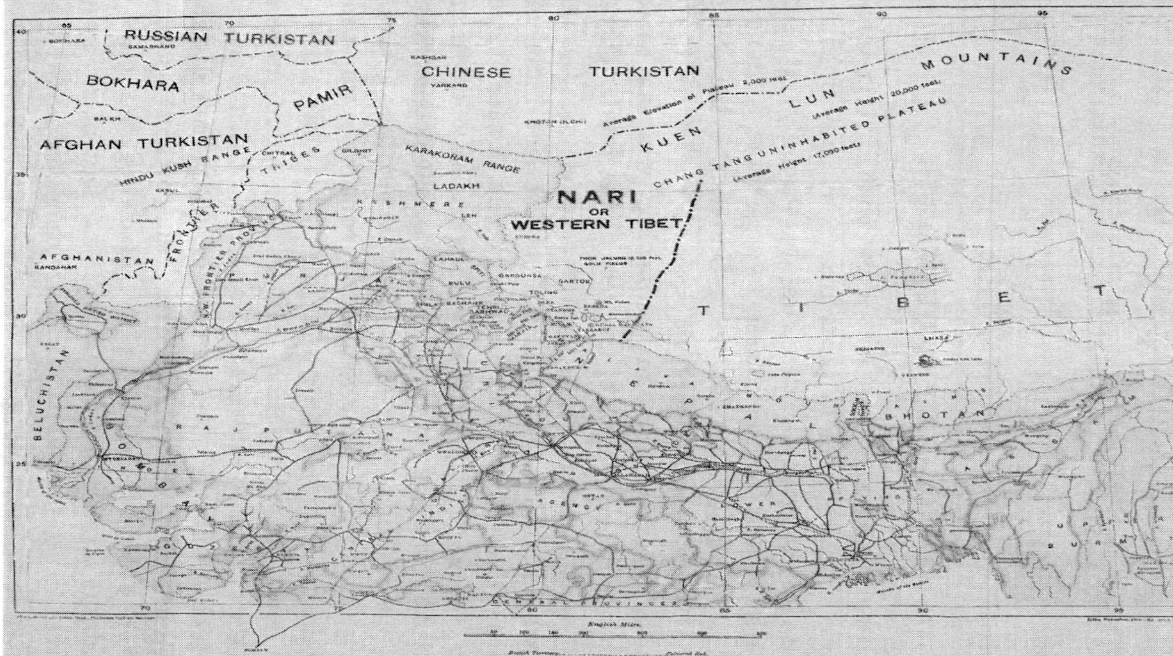

CHAPTER I

INTRODUCTORY

A GLANCE at the map will show that British territory only touches Tibet in three places, viz., at Spiti in the Kangra District of the Punjab, secondly, at British Garhwal and Almora, these two districts forming part of the Kumaon Division of the United Provinces of Agra and Oudh, and, thirdly, at Assam, where the Brahmaputra enters the Indian Peninsula; whereas throughout the entire length of the rest of the border there are either protected Native States, such as Cashmere, Bashahr, Tehri Garhwal, and Sikkim, or independent States like Nepal and Bhotan. The Assam border is at present of little use to us owing to the wildness of the country and the savage character of the people, whereas Western Tibet, with which British territory comes into actual physical contact, is of enormous importance, while it may be safely said that it is difficult to find in any other portion of the earth a more interesting country than Western Tibet and the British Borderland which adjoins it. Geographically, this portion of Tibet is the nearest to Russian territory, and, although separated from Russian Turkistan by chains of the most forbidding mountain ranges, still the fact of its position gives it great political importance. But, above all else, it is interesting for its place in religious thought, for it is in this part of Tibet that we find Mount Kailas, the Heaven of Buddhists and Hindus, answering to the Olympus of Homer. This sacred spot is at present visited by some hundreds of pilgrims annually, but, with improved communications, these hundreds should become thousands in the near future, and the ultimate effect of this increase in the number of pilgrims should be very great.

This part of Western Tibet and the British Borderland is a country most sacred to Hindus and Buddhists, and appealing as it does with its awful solemnity and weird grandeur of landscape to all that is romantic in the human soul, it is clothed the while to the eye of faith with a garment of mystery which makes it the fit abode of the great gods of Hinduism and Buddhism. In India, the great Buddha has left associations which cling to numerous spots: at Gya he obtained Nirvana; at Benares he preached his doctrine of sorrow and showed the path leading to its cessation; at Taxila in a previous birth he accomplished the perfection of charity, when he gave his own head and distributed his flesh and blood to a tigress and her seven cubs; but it is to Mount Kailas that the Tibetan points as the home of his gods and the axis of the universe. To the Hindu, death at Benares ("Holy Kashi") is the supreme desire of the pious mind, and hundreds, aye, thousands, go there to await their end in this *sanctum sanctorum* with a cheerfulness which sees beyond the grave. Prag (Allahabad), where the Ganges and Jumna meet the third invisible stream of Sarasvati, and Hardwar, which marks the spot whence the sacred stream of Ganges leaves the Himalayas, attract their millions of earnest pilgrims; but it is to Kedarnath and Badrinath in the everlasting snows that they point as the home of their gods, where Shiva lived, and Krishna dallied with the cow-herd maids, and to Mount Kailas, the heaven of Shiva and the goal of all happiness.

Waddell, in his "Buddhism of Tibet" (p. 81), writing of the belief of the Tibetans regarding their heaven, says: "And in the very centre is the 'King of Mountains,' Mount Meru (Kailas), towering erect, 'like the handle of a mill-stone,' while halfway up its side is the great wishing-tree, the prototype of our 'Christmas-tree,' and the object of contention between the gods and the Titans. Meru has square sides of gold and jewels. Its eastern face is crystal, the south is sapphire, the west is ruby, and the north is gold, and it is clothed with fragrant flowers and shrubs." Here also are the Holy Lakes of Mansarowar and Rakas, so eloquently described in the "Ramayana" in the passage given below (*see* pp. 36, 37).

JAGAT SING, POLITICAL PESHKAR

The British territory, which adjoins this part of Tibet, is the Kumaon borderland, which is to the Hindu "what Palestine is to the Christian, the place where those whom the Hindu esteems most spent portions of their lives, the home of the great gods, the 'great way to final liberation.' This is a living belief, and thousands every year prove their faith by visiting the shrines of Kedarnath and Badrinath. To many the fruition of all earthly desire is the crowning glory of a visit to the sacred places, by which the sins of former births are cleansed, and exemption from metempsychosis obtained. Each rock, or rivulet, is dedicated to some deity, or saint, and has its own appropriate legend. Nature in her wildest and most rugged forms bears witness to the correctness of the belief, that here is the home of the 'great god'" (Atkinson's "Himalayan Districts").

Apart from their religious attributes, this part of Tibet and the adjoining block of the Himalayan range, full of snow peaks and giant mountains, are unrivalled in the whole world for sublime grandeur, for, in the small area of a strip thirty miles wide along the Kumaon border, there must be some eighty peaks above 20,000 ft., and standing out boldly above their setting are Nanda Devi, 25,689 ft., the highest mountain in British territory throughout the world, and her sister Kamet, 25,373 ft., her rival in elevation and beauty, while north of this mass of grandeur lies the tableland of Tibet, of an average height of 13,000 to 15,000 ft. above sea level, and dominating all her fellows is Gurla Mandhata, a gigantic pile, the highest peak of which is 25,350 ft., visible as a landmark for very many miles.

This beautiful country, full of sacred associations, and replete with nature's greatest and most awe-inspiring marvels, is inhabited on the British side by a race named Bhotias, who, intrepid traders as they are, yearly endure vicissitudes of climate and dangers of mountaineering which win our admiration for their manly qualities; while at the same time, they are a people who absorb our interest owing to the extremely quaint manners and customs which still find a place amongst them in these lonely hills. And beyond them live the Tibetans, of whom hitherto so little has been known, with their mysterious religious rites of prayer-wheels and prayer-flags, their monasteries full of lamas, and their wizards, who drink blood in cups made of human

TAHSILDAR KHARAK SING, FORMER POLITICAL PESHKAR (IN FRONT)

skulls, and eat human bones and skin, and conjure the spirits of the "vasty deep" by means of trumpets of human thigh-bones and other implements of their black art.

Having had the good fortune to be posted officially in the Almora district for some time past, I have been often thrown in close contact with the interesting people who live in these grand mountains, and have been able to study some of their ways, and to get an intimate knowledge of the life and problems of the frontier. This information has now been supplemented by a trip in Western Tibet.

On this expedition, in addition to my usual staff, I was accompanied by Dr. T. G. Longstaff, of the Alpine

RAI SAHIB PUNDIT GOBARIA
A rich Bhotia trader, one of the interpreters

Club, who had with him two Alpine guides, Alexis Brocherel and his brother Henri Brocherel, of Courmayeur in Italy, and also by the Tahsildar Kharak Sing Pal, formerly for ten years Political Peshkar on the frontier, with his brother Jagat Sing, the present Political Peshkar. Both these latter are cousins of the Rajbar of Askot, whose territory of Askot is so situated as to command all the principal passes into Tibet, as well as the Kali River, which is our frontier against Nepal.

HARARA SUSPENSION BRIDGE, BETWEEN ALMORA AND ASKOT

This book has been written with the hope that the information acquired during past years may prove of interest and use to others who may be brought into contact with this part of the world, or whose sympathies have been drawn towards those mysterious marvels of the Forbidden Land which have attracted the minds of so many.

THE ESCORT OF ARMED POLICE

CHAPTER II

ASKOT AND THE ABORIGINAL RAJIS

THE most picturesque, as well as the most interesting, spot, from which to commence this narrative, is Askot, distant some seventy miles from Almora and ninety miles from Taklakot, the latter being the first large town one meets on entering Tibet, where there is the seat of a Jongpen and a large monastery ruled by a powerful lama. The most direct approach to Askot from the plains of India is along a fairly good road running parallel to the frontier of Nepal, the large mart of Tanakpur, which is at the foot of the Himalayas, being only some eighty miles distant; should at any time the forty miles intervening between Tanakpur and the railway at Pilibhit be linked up, Tibet would be directly brought into close contact with some of the large cities and manufacturing centres of India, such as Delhi, Cawnpore, and Lucknow, and indirectly with Calcutta and Bombay. In the afternoon after our arrival the Rajbar of Askot paid us a formal visit accompanied by his two eldest sons. He is a fine specimen of a native gentleman, and has always received the greatest consideration at the hands of Government. He claims descent from the Kings of Katyur, who ruled from Kabul to Nepal, and who have left a memento of their name in that portion of the Almora District which is known as Katyur. Askot, as I have said, commands the roads leading to the principal passes into Tibet, while, from its position on the borders of Nepal, it is of the greatest importance in our relations with that country. The present Rajbar is an Honorary Magistrate with powers in criminal work of awarding imprisonment up to six months and of fining to a maximum of two hundred rupees. He enjoys universal respect, and takes great pains to keep his family from that stagnation which is the ruin of so many of the Indian nobility. His two eldest sons (he has five sons and five daughters) are being educated at Allahabad, and, to ensure proper supervision of the best kind, they are residing in the Oxford and Cambridge Hostel, where the University influence of England can be brought to bear upon them.

One day we went to see the so-called "wild men" (Ban Manus) who live quite close to Askot town, though I had seen them before, and had, in fact, during the cold weather camped quite close to their dwellings. They live in a valley some two thousand feet below the town, and in the heat of the end of June the descent into such a furnace was quite a consideration. However, we started at three in the afternoon, to get as much of the cool of the day as possible, and descended rapidly to the stream in the valley. The difference of temperature in these valleys as compared with the hill tops has often been remarked by travellers, but I think nothing, apart from actual physical experience, would have borne the fact home to our party. Longstaff and his two men were in perfect physical training, having just come from a trip of considerable hardship, and yet they felt the heat terribly. When we arrived at our goal, we found one old man present at the huts, while all the others were in the woods, and until these appeared we sat down in the shade away from the piercing rays of

Kharak Sing   Jagat Sing

Kharak Sing's father   The Rajbar   The Rajbar's eldest son

ASKOT

the sun, which seemed to cut into us, and two of our attendants fanned us with an impromptu fan made of a sheet held between them, as we all felt so terribly exhausted from the heat. At length eight men and one woman came, and later on two children, but Longstaff had to make several attempts to photograph

RAJIS, OR RAWATS

them before he succeeded, for every time he stood up he nearly fainted from the heat.

The above description will convey some impression of some of the difficulties of touring in the hills in the hot weather, and of the heat we endured at times. The climate of the higher levels is very pleasant, but the heat of some of the valleys is almost intolerable.

We sat and had a long talk with these interesting people, and, to break the ice (purely metaphorical in that warm spot), smoked and offered them the contents of a tobacco-pouch, but they suspected the tobacco; however, without more ado, they put it into an ordinary hookah-bowl and placing a hot coal on the top solemnly handed it to one of our servants to smoke first. Without question they suspected something wrong, but our attendants, who knew them well, speedily dispelled their fears. In a few minutes the hookah was passed

RAJIS, OR RAWATS

from hand to hand and Players' Navy Cut was duly appreciated.

These wild men, clad in the scantiest loin-cloth, claim royal origin, and in the East one is never surprised at such apparent anomalies. Does not the Brahman chuprassi claim that he is a deity? and do his wages of six shillings and eight pence a month prevent his being invariably called "Maharaj"? These royal wild men, when visiting the Rajbar of Askot, sit close by his side and call him " younger brother," and his Rani " younger sister," while they love to pose as of elder royal stock, nor will their royal dignity permit them to salute any man great or small. They are known as Rajis, or Rawats, and speak an aboriginal language, which is

RAJIS, OR RAWATS

believed to be of the Tibeto-Burman family, but this point will shortly be made clear by Mr. Grierson, who is in charge of the Linguistic Survey of India, and to whom specimens of their dialects have been submitted. Similar aborigines are found also in Doti in Nepal, and these Askot men admit that they are all of the same race. They have very little hair on the face, though beards can be grown among them, but they are always thin, and the general appearance of the face is hairless, while the type appears to be Mongolian.

This party of Rajis was composed of eight men, four

women and some children, and these formed two families (dharas). It is difficult to enter into domestic details with the royal wild men without giving obvious offence, but there can be no doubt that polyandry is practised, though publicly it is denied—in fact, this is notorious scandal among their neighbours. Marriage must take place outside the "family" (dhara) and only when the young lady is of age, and has reached a marriageable state. Child marriage is unknown and highly disapproved. The inclinations of the bride are not consulted, but, with naïve simplicity, the only formality is the fixing of a date with her parents, and then she is fetched away by the bridegroom and his party. If the groom is a man of means, he pays five shillings to six shillings for her to her parents, and the wedding is complete. There is no ceremony of any kind whatever, except that her parents give the wedding breakfast, nor are even the services of the priest required. There is a priest (whom they call Dhami) who acts for all the Rajis in the Askot district; we did not see him as he was at this time living on the other side of a neighbouring hill, where there were other Rajis. This priest is one of themselves specially appointed, and the priesthood runs in the family. I have not been able to discover any gods of their own apart from the local deities Khudai and Malikar Jan, whom they worship in common with Hindus. They have no idols amongst them, and they do not worship the other deities of Hinduism except on one day, *i.e.*, on the festival of Nanda Devi, the goddess who presides over the highest mountain in the British Empire, when they sing and dance, forming two rows facing each other, and move round in a circle. The curious point is that they move from left to right in the exactly opposite way to that in which Tibetans twirl their prayer-wheels, and in which the Hindus turn when they bathe in sacred rivers.

On the birth of an infant they dispense with the

ON THE WAY

services of a midwife ; the mother always goes through her time of trial alone, unless, which is frequently not the case, there are other married women near by, who can conveniently attend her. For two months after child-birth they drink no water from the hands of the mother, considering her to be unclean. The ceremony of naming the child is certainly peculiar. On the fifth day the priest appears and works himself into a religious frenzy, and it is popularly supposed that the god takes possession of his human frame. In the midst of his ecstatic trance he names the child. All children have two names, one Hindu such as Mohan Sing, Deb Sing, &c., and the other in the aboriginal tongue, *e.g.*, Dharemia, Sistia, &c.

It has been said that the Rajis bury their dead,* but these men certainly nowadays practise cremation, whatever their former practice may have been, and the spot chosen is always on the bank of some stream. They employ no mourning ceremonial whatever, except that they fast on the day of death, and the next day eat rice instead of ordinary food.

They are extremely particular as to the water they drink, never drinking from anywhere except at the actual source of the spring, and all river water they refuse absolutely, fearing contamination. They do not carry these sanitary precautions as far as their dwelling-houses, for the smell round their abodes is simply appalling, and in person these aborigines look as if they had never washed in their lives. They live in stone houses, nicely built, and have a few fields of cultivation adjoining. They keep a few cattle, and eke out their livelihood by fishing and trapping. They never use a net, or a rod, to catch the fish, but always rely upon getting them by tickling with the hand as the fish lie concealed behind some rock. They showed us a fish eight inches long which had just been caught. They have never used for the destruction of big game, bows and arrows like the Bhotias, whose national weapons they once were, but always rely on snares, the common trap being a very heavy stone poised upon sticks, which give way as soon as the animal approaches

* *Cf.* Atkinson's "Himalayan Districts," xi.-367.

B

for the bait, and they have killed tigers and every description of animal by this simple contrivance. They make a very common bait for deer by saturating a particular spot with urine, and when they see that the deer are

THE FOAMING KALI, OR SARDA

drawn to this place by the saline deposits in the ground, in fact, when the spot has become a "salt-lick," they erect a heavy stone delicately balanced on sticks ready to fall on the next comer.

The royal wild men are not nearly so shy now as they were some thirty years ago. They will even go for medicine to the Rajbar, who has always shown them great kindness, and will sell wooden bowls to the

ROPE BRIDGE AT DHARCHULA BETWEEN BRITISH TERRITORY AND NEPAL

LONGSTAFF IN THE CRADLE

traveller, but the nomadic spirit seems to be unquenchable, and nothing will keep them in one place long. They are here one day and gone the next, and nobody knows their movements. Nor can they ever forget their royal descent. When we parted ours were the only salutations.

As we left Askot the Rajbar was very anxious for Longstaff to give his professional advice about a stroke of paralysis which had overtaken his uncle, the father of Karak Sing. The old man was placed under the shade of a tree on the road, and Longstaff very carefully overhauled him and explained at length the exact working of the electric battery, which Karak Sing had very dutifully bought, and which must have cost a large sum as it was a good one. The scene was a pretty one. A large crowd of villagers watched the application of this European cure, and, of course, little boys and girls were crawling everywhere where they should not, and in the centre sat the dignified old man in his dandy, with the Rajbar standing by his side, while Western science was explained to sons, who with gentle hands applied the battery: and all around us the grand mountains towered overhead, and the surging river Kali rushed on its course.

As we began our descent to the river we very soon felt the heat, for the road descends to the glacial stream of the Gori, and then runs along a hot, confined valley to the junction of this river with the Kali. This spot of the junction is a particularly sacred one, and in winter, *i.e.*, when the water in the Kali is low, there is a small bridge built across the river to enable traders to pass, and devotees to frequent the shrine which stands on the narrow tongue of land between the two rivers. Our British boundary on the Nepalese side is the Kali river, which is known as the Sarda in the plains, and over the entire length of its course, except near its source, the Kali is unfordable, being throughout a tearing, raging torrent. The only suspension bridge, which was built by the British, is at a spot some thirty miles below

NEPALESE LIEUTENANT AT DHARCHULA

Askot, and that is so constructed that, by removing one bolt on the British side, the whole bridge can fall into the river. This bridge takes one's thoughts back to the early part of the nineteenth century, when we had only just wrested Kumaon from the Nepalese and both parties were anxious to secure themselves against invasion. The only other bridges are the one which we had just reached, a frail edifice of beams (two logs laid side by side), lodged on piles of stones, and a third which we came to at Dharchula. This place is the winter headquarters of the Political Peshkar, the residence of two missionary ladies, and the cold weather rendezvous of very large numbers of Bhotias; while on the Nepalese side there is a court house, a gaol and the residence of the Nepalese Lieutenant, who is in civil and criminal charge of this part of the country. The bridge connecting the two sides here is composed of one

NATIVE CROSSING ROPE BRIDGE

rope! The ordinary native climbs over by the help of his hands and feet, being kept from falling into the abyss of angry waters by a noose of rope round his body, to which is fixed a bar of wood to counteract the friction. Longstaff and I have been on this rope-bridge, but neither of us could persuade the other to adopt the native method. The more sedate cradle appealed very forcibly to us.

We halted at Balwakot, twelve miles from Askot and at Dharchula ten miles further on, but our stay at both places was of the shortest, owing to the great heat, which is most oppressive in this long valley of the Kali river. Further, we were much troubled by mosquitoes and sand-flies, and at Dharchula we had scorpions, only one of which, however, did any harm. In the cold weather, when my wife and I were camping here, although we had scorpions in our bedding and under our

NATIVE CROSSING ROPE BRIDGE

pillows, and the servants were continually finding them in their quarters, we had all escaped in the most fortunate way, but this time one stung the cook on the forehead in two places. He had a sleepless night from pain, but in the morning a couple of injections of eucaine by Longstaff brought immediate relief. This fact is of interest because there are some who say that scorpions and snakes lose their venom in the hills, but the reverse is my own experience; certainly one servant of mine at Binsar would have actually died from snake-bite, had it not been for instant application of the knife and the usual remedies.

There is no relief from the warmth of this hot valley of the Kali until one reaches Khela, which is 5000 ft. in elevation, and is about thirty miles from Askot. Here we rested to let the whole camp thoroughly recover from the effects of the great heat we had passed through.

Last year there were some villages near Khela, at least 9000 ft. up on the sides of the Chipla

CRADLE ON ROPE BRIDGE

mountain, which were terrorised by a man-eating tiger. Fifty years ago, tigers were very common even in the high hills, and were a positive nuisance in the lower altitudes, and we read of the great havoc that they used to commit. At the present time, however, owing to the increase of population and the general spread of cultivation, they have become rare in the hills south of Almora and Ranikhet, and are practically unknown at altitudes of 9000 ft. A man-eater, therefore, on the slopes of Chipla (13,000 ft.) created great consternation. He started by carrying off a poor old woman, who was cutting grass in a lonely spot. He was distinctly seen and very half-heartedly pursued, so he got clear away with his prey. The news spread over the countryside and no villager felt safe in these mountain solitudes. He next attacked a party of men who were cutting high crops in a field, carrying off an old man who was a little removed from the others. The alarm was so great that no pursuit was attempted, but the headmen of the

NATIVES OF THE UPPER HILLS

neighbouring villages became painfully alive to the stern reality that, at whatever cost, this pest must be exterminated, otherwise no one's life would be safe for a moment. It is customary for the women and children of these hillmen to wander alone, or in groups of two or three, anywhere and everywhere, as there is generally no fear of attack from wild animals. On the following day, there were gathered together a hundred grim men, armed only with axes and stones—for they had not a gun among them. The men of this part are brave and hardy: they differ from the men of the lower hills in that they wear a black blanket as their sole covering, neatly folded round and across their bodies and fastened by two great iron or copper skewers. On that particular day they meant to kill, whatever the cost.

Soon after the search began, a bone of the deceased was found, all that was left of the old man, about the size of a man's hand. Cautiously and stealthily the pursuit was continued, and fortune favoured the brave, for the tiger was found asleep under a rock. At once each man dropped silently into the cover of the brushwood, and piled a heap of stones near to his hand, while one of the most trusted of the party was commissioned to stalk to the top of the rock and drop a huge stone on the sleeping brute. So well was the work done that the stone fell true on the back, and immediately with a roar the wounded tiger sprang up, and, seeing the attackers, who leaped from their cover, charged the line. But a hundred men, desperate as to consequences, throwing stones with might and main, are not to be awed, or turned from their purpose, lightly. The stones broke the tiger's teeth, and went into his mouth, and his body was a mass of wounds. Turning he tried to escape, and took his pursuers up hill for a mile, but wherever he turned, and whatever he did, he could not escape the pitiless rain of missiles. The blow on his back, first given, effectually checked his speed, and finally, worn out, he came to bay under a great cliff. The rest was easy. He was immediately hemmed in, and the stones were showered on him thicker than ever, hurled with redoubled energy. As he sank down the villagers rushed in and despatched him with axes. I was fortunate enough to be in the neighbourhood a day or so later, and saw the skin and the skull. The mangy skin had not been pulled out, and so had dried into creases, but measured close on nine feet, while there were great cuts in it where the axes had done their work. Almost all the teeth in the skull were broken, an eloquent testimony to the accuracy of the stone-throwers. Evidently, the tiger was a very old one, and had become a man-eater when unable to catch other prey.

NATIVES OF THE UPPER HILLS

A crowd of the villagers who had taken part in the fray carefully and with the greatest detail explained the whole episode, and by means of rocks and boulders fought the good fight once again.

Longstaff was kept busy dispensing medicines and prescribing for the sick, who flocked in from all sides. One of the commonest complaints was the following: A man, otherwise hale and hearty, would stagger up with one hand tenderly patting the region of the "lower chest" and would pitifully shake his head from side to side, while with his other hand he would ceaselessly

OUR CAMP. ALEXIS AND HENRI UNPACKING

grip at some imaginary enemy in the air. The writhing fingers, and the whole attitude, spoke more eloquently than any school-boy to the family physician after the gaieties of Christmas week. The remedy, very potent, but the more appreciated for its potency, was monotonously the same—calomel and colocynth are tenderly remembered in these parts.

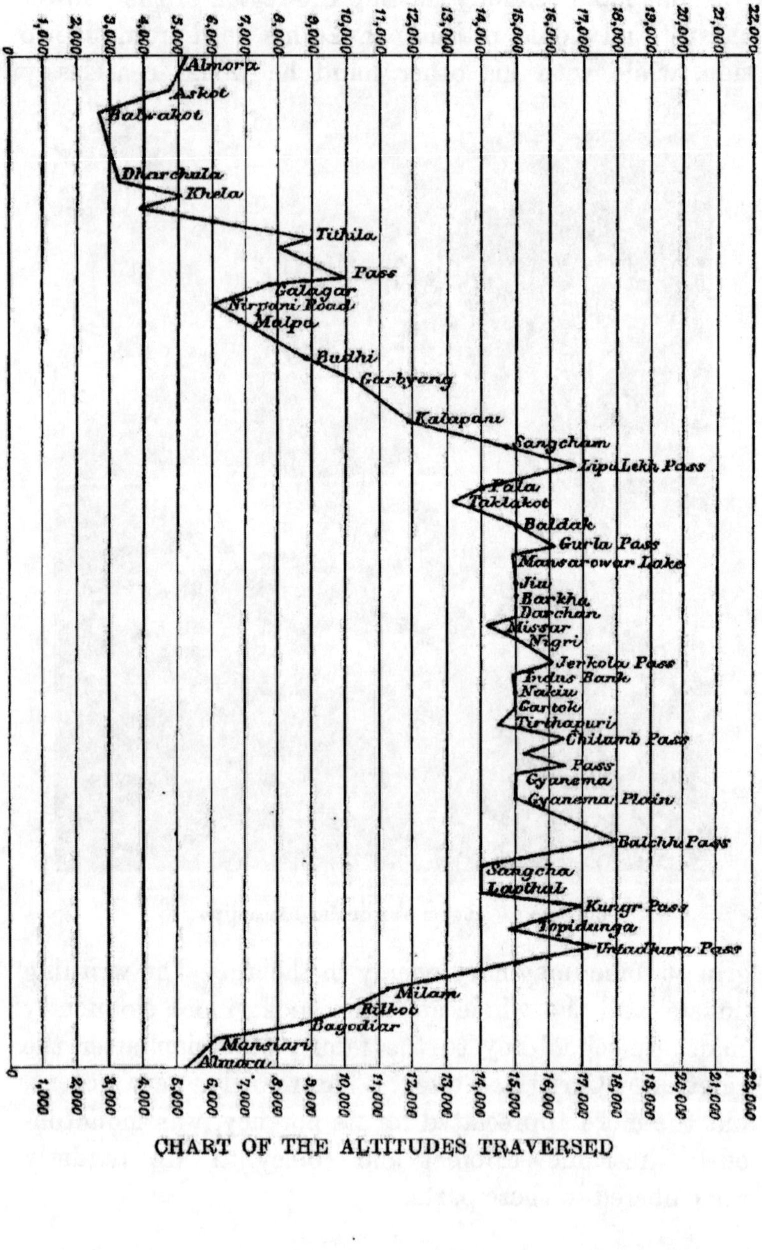

CHART OF THE ALTITUDES TRAVERSED

CHAPTER III

LEGENDS OF THE HOLY LAND

FROM Khela one looks across a valley to that block of the Himalayan range which, full of snow peaks and giant mountains, is unrivalled in the whole world for sublime grandeur. In the small tract of country reaching from Nepal on the east to the native State of Tehri on the west, and of a breadth of thirty miles along the Tibetan border, there are grouped mountains which collectively can find no comparison in any part of the globe. In this small space there must be some eighty peaks of 20,000 ft. and over, and studded in their midst, like diamonds amongst pearls, are some of the highest mountains in the world. Beyond these comes the lofty tableland of Tibet, with Gurla Mandhata and the Kailas Range standing out clear above their fellows, while Tise, or "the" holy Kailas peak, full of majesty, a King of mountains, dominates the surrounding country. And withal the sacred and religious associations of this interesting country, ever present in the minds of Hindus and Buddhists, make one realise, in the words of Holy Scripture, that "The place whereon thou standest is holy ground."

The plateau of Tibet adjacent to the British border varies from 13,000 to 15,000 ft. above sea level, and standing clear above the highest part is the mountain range of the Gangri or Kailas peaks on the south-east of Gartok, rising to a general elevation of some 4000 ft.

NANDA DEVI (25,689 FT.) AND THE EASTERN PEAK (24,379 FT.)

THE TWO PEAKS OF NANDA DEVI AS SEEN FROM AN ALTITUDE OF 20,000 FT. ON THE SOUTHERN RIDGE OF THE LOWER PEAK

above the plateau, that is, to 19,500 ft. of absolute elevation above the sea. "The" peak of Kailas, that is to say, the famous holy mountain, 21,850 ft., known to Tibetans as Tise, dominates the rest of the ridge by a clear 2000 ft., standing out majestically like a cone and visible from a very considerable distance. The only rival that can bear comparison with the Holy Mount is Gurla Mandhata, 25,350 ft., called by the Tibetans Memo, or Memo-Nam-Nyimri, which is one of the highest mountains in Tibet. Between these two lie the Rakas Tal and the Mansarowar Lake (respectively Lagang and Mobang of the Tibetans), 14,850 and 14,900 ft. above sea level: and there is no more sacred spot in all Hinduism, or Tibetan Buddhism, than the country so enclosed.

Further south, the principal line of water-parting along the Tibetan and British frontiers is a ridge of great altitude, the mean elevation being upwards of 18,000 ft. above the sea, and the highest peak, Kamet, reaching an elevation of 25,373 ft. At no point is it possible to enter the British territory of Almora and Garhwal without rising to 16,750 on the Niti Pass or 16,780 ft. on the Lipu Lekh Pass, whereas the other passes range from 17,590 ft., viz., the Untadhura, to Mana, 17,890 ft., and Neo, 18,510 ft., and the Lankpya, 18,150 ft., while the road over many of the passes is rendered very dangerous owing to the presence of glaciers and hidden crevasses, traders frequently tying poles to their persons to prevent total destruction in the event of a fall into some concealed crack.

Both in Almora and Garhwal the most important of the masses of snowy mountains are found in groups along a line from twenty to thirty miles south of the above water-parting, with which they are connected by lofty ridges covered with perpetual snow, whilst they are separated from each other by deep gorges, which lead up to the main passes into Tibet, and form the main trade routes between India and Central Asia. The chief of these groups is that of which Nanda Devi is the culminating peak, 25,689 ft. above the sea, the highest

Alexis Henri

THE NORTHERN BARRIER OF THE PINDARI GLACIER (NEAR NANDA KOT) AS SEEN FROM THE NORTH

mountain in British territory throughout the whole of our Empire. The great ridge of Trisul, which nowhere throughout a length of ten miles is less than 20,000 ft., is connected with Nanda Devi, but advanced about ten miles in front of it to the south-west, its three peaks, 23,406 ft., 22,490 ft. and 22,360 ft., standing out as a landmark of the most striking beauty from an immense distance. The highest of these, viz., the western, has three other peaks, all over 20,000 ft., to the north and south of it, while the eastern peak is connected with

Nanda Devi by peaks of 21,858 ft., 21,624 ft. and 24,379 ft., and close to these is Nanda Kot, 22,530 ft. To the north-west of Nanda Devi we have Dunagiri, 23,184 ft., and again east and north of this we have five other peaks varying from 20,754 ft. up to 23,220 ft.

During June of this year (1905) Longstaff and his two Italian guides explored the three large valleys on the east of Nanda Devi and Nanda Kot. They successfully crossed two hitherto unattempted snow passes of about 18,000 ft. over both of which they had to carry their own impedimenta, as the climbing was of too severe a character to be attempted by their Bhotia coolies. They also made an attempt on the eastern peak of Nanda Devi: the actual climbing lasted three days and entailed two bivouacs, the last being on the actual watershed between Garhwal and Kumaon at an altitude of over 19,000 ft. The attempt had to be given up owing to the great length of the climb, and the difficulty of themselves carrying more than three days' food. In the same month they attempted Nanda Kot, but were turned back about a thousand feet from the summit by the risk of starting an avalanche. Judging from Longstaff's experience on Gurla Mandhata, detailed by him in another chapter, their discretion was probably justified.

To the east of the Nanda Devi group we have the Pancha Chuli, of "Five Peak" range, the summits varying from 19,923 ft. up to 22,661 ft., and still further east another range with many peaks over 20,000 ft. Whereas west of the Nanda Devi group we have the sacred Badrinath, Kedarnath, and Gangotri mountains, and others, which, falling within an area of twenty-six miles from north to south and thirty miles from eas to west, present a panorama of lofty peaks whose grandeur baffles description, for we have in this small area four peaks above 23,000 ft., nine above

Alexis and Henri

BIVOUAC ON THE RIDGE OF NANDA DEVI AT 19,100 FT.

22,000 ft., eleven above 21,000 ft. and eight above 20,000 ft.

It may well be said that there is no place in all this fair earth of ours which can compare with the marvellous beauty of these everlasting snows. The Hindu sage who penned the following words, with all his glowing imagery, has scarcely overrated what all men must find beyond the power of adequate expression:

"He who thinks on Himachal (*i.e.*, the Himalayan snows), though he should not behold him, is greater than he who performs all worship in Kashi (Benares), and he who thinks of Himachal shall have pardon for all sins,

NANDA KOT AND ITS GLACIERS, TAKEN FROM AN ALTITUDE OF 20,000 FT. ON NANDA DEVI

and all things that die on Himachal, and all beings that in dying think of his snows, are freed from sin. In a hundred ages of the gods I could not tell thee of the glories of Himachal, where Siva lived and where the Ganges falls from the foot of Vishnu like the slender thread of a lotus flower. I behold Mansarowar, and there in the form of a swan dwells Siva. This lake was formed from the mind of Brahma: there dwell also Mahadeo and the gods. When the earth of Mansarowar touches any one's body, or when any one bathes in the lake, he shall go to the paradise of Brahma, and he who drinks its waters shall go to the heaven of Siva and shall be released from the sins of a hundred births, and even the beast who bears the name of Mansarowar shall go to the paradise of Brahma. Its waters are like pearls. There

NANDA DEVI (LEFT) AND EAST PEAK (RIGHT) AS SEEN FROM NANDA KOT

is no mountain like Himachal, for in it are Kailas and Mansarowar. As the dew is dried up by the morning sun, so are the sins of mankind dried up at the sight of Himachal" (Ramayana).

It is interesting to note the steps by which this region came to occupy its present position in the religious life of the Hindus, for it is not on the main route by which the

Aryans entered India, and there is no obvious reason why it should have taken to itself the honour of a pre-eminently first place except on account of its surpassing beauty and striking characteristics. For the Aryans, following the route generally adopted in every successive invasion, came from Baktria over the Hindu Kush, and down the Kabul valley of Afghanistan, until they finally crossed the Indus. However, from the earliest times the Himalayas were regarded by Hindus with awe, and were shrouded with majesty, and it was said by them that Sanskrit had been preserved in great purity in these northern regions, especially in Cashmere and Badrinath. This latter place had already some centuries before the Christian era acquired a reputation for sanctity and as a place of learning. The blessed abode of continual happiness was said to be in these grand mountains. "The people are liberal, prosperous, perpetually happy and undecaying. In their country there is neither cold nor heat, nor decrepitude, nor disease, nor grief, nor fear, nor rain, nor sun" (Ramayana)—a description which Kumaon has taken to itself—and, the same epic poem adds, "where the mongoose sports in a friendly fashion with snakes, and tigers with deer." From the earliest times we find that the place is considered holy ground, the well-loved home of the gods, containing many places of pilgrimage. Krishna stood at Badrinath a hundred years with arms aloft, on one foot, subsisting on air, with his outer garments thrown off, "emaciated and with veins swollen," a not very unnatural result.

To quote from Atkinson's "Himalayan Districts" again:

"It is not difficult to picture the Aryan immigrants arriving at the Ganges and sending some adventurous spirits to explore its sources. After traversing the difficult passes across the snowy range and the inclement tableland of Tibet, they discovered the group of moun-

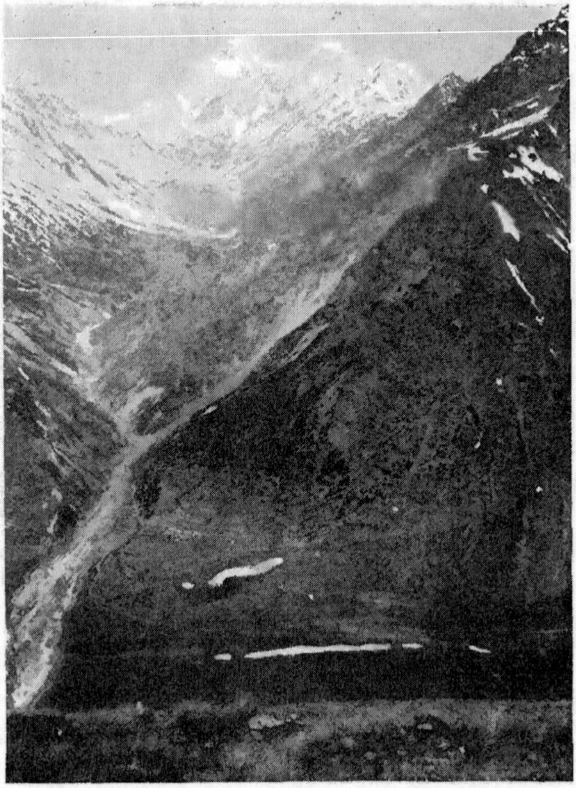

EAST PEAK (LEFT) AND NANDA DEVI (RIGHT), AS SEEN FROM THE EASTERN SIDE OF THE MILAM VALLEY

tains called Kailas, and the lakes from which flowed forth the great rivers to water and give life to the whole earth. The rugged grandeur of the scene, the awful solitude and the trials and dangers of the way itself, naturally suggested to an imaginative and simple people that they had at length rediscovered the golden land, the true home of their gods whom they had worshipped, when appearing under milder forms, as storm, and fire and rain in the plains below. In the course of time, Brahmanical innovations caused the worship of the Vedic gods of natural forces to give place to a system, where the intervention of a sacerdotal caste between the worshipper and his creator was essential. Brahma of the Vedas gave place to Brahma, Vishnu, and Siva, the triad of the new revelation, who took possession of the Himalayas," and Mount Meru became the Olympus of the Indian gods.

Mount Meru is described with a wonderful fulness and detail, but there is apparently little doubt that there is a mingling of facts true of the country to the north of Cashmere with facts true of the country north of Kumaon. In some accounts Mount Meru clearly indicates the group of mountains to the north and west of Cashmere, and in others those in the neighbourhood of Kailas and Lake Mansarowar. But whatever may have been the original meaning of the description, there is no question that all local traditions fix the spot as lying directly to the north of the Almora district, and this is the universal belief amongst all Hindus at the present time.

When Brahma formed the desire that the universe should be created, he instantly assumed the visible form of Vishnu. The whole universe was covered with water, on which Vishnu floated sleeping on a bed, which rested on a serpent. From his navel sprang a lotus from which issued Brahma, who then created the seven great island continents, of which Jambu is one. In the centre of Jambu is the glorious mountain Meru of various colours ; on the east it is white like a Brahman (priestly caste) ; on the south it is yellow like a Vaisya (trader) ;

The path winds along the precipice

ON THE ROAD TO TIBET. A REPAIRING GANG AT WORK

on the north it is red like a Kshattriya (warrior); and on the west it is dark like a Sudra (servile caste). Four mountains form buttresses to Meru, and on each of these stand severally a kadam-tree (*anthocephalus cadamba*), a jambu-tree (*eugenia jambolana*), a pipal-tree (*ficus religiosa*) and a fig-tree (*ficus Indica*). There are also four great forests and four great lakes, one being Lake Mansarowar, called Mobang or Mapan by the Tibetans, and the gods drink their waters. "There are the regions of paradise (Swarga), the seats of the righteous and where the wicked do not arrive even after a hundred births; there is no sorrow, nor weariness, nor anxiety, nor hunger, nor apprehension: the inhabitants are exempt from all infirmity and live in uninterrupted enjoyment for ten or twelve thousand years. Devi never sends rain upon them, for the earth abounds with water. There is no distinction or any succession of ages" (Hindu Shastra).

Compare with this Homer's account of Olympus, Odyssey vi. 42:

"Olympus, where, as they say, is the seat of the gods that standeth fast for ever. Not by winds is it shaken, nor ever wet with vain, nor doth the snow come nigh thereto, but most clear air is spread about it cloudless, and the white light floats over it. Therein the blessed gods are glad for all their days" (Butcher and Lang).

And Tennyson's, "The Passing of Arthur":

> "The island valley of Avilion,
> Where falls not hail, or rain, or any snow,
> Nor ever wind blows loudly; but it lies
> Deep-meadowed, happy, fair with orchard lawns
> And bowery hollows crown'd with summer sea."

The Buddhism of Tibet was obtained from India,

and, therefore, it is only natural to find that this country of Kailas and Mansarowar, which is the heaven of the Hindus, should be regarded as most sacred by the Tibetans, and we are then not surprised to see that the Tibetans call Mansarowar "Rimpoche" or "the holy lake, and look upon Kailas as the Paradise of their gods." The Bhotias also, who are a Mongolian living on our borders, have been so far influenced by the Buddhist and Hindu veneration accorded to this country, that they too have themselves attached great religious importance to it, and consider it as their own heaven, in which dwells Brahma the omnipotent. Waddell in his "Buddhism of Tibet" writes regarding the Tibetan belief: *

"Each universe, set in unfathomable space, rests upon a warp and woof of 'blue air,' or wind, like crossed thunderbolts, hard and imperishable as diamonds, upon which is set 'the body of waters,' upon which is a foundation of gold, on which is set the earth, from the axis of which towers up the great Olympus-Mount Meru, 84,000 miles high, surmounted by the heavens, and overlying the hills. In the ocean around this central mountain, are set the four great continental worlds, all with bases of solid gold in the form of a tortoise. And the continents are separated from Mount Meru by seven concentric rings of golden mountains, the inmost being 40,000 miles high, alternating with seven oceans of fragrant milk, curds, butter, blood or sugar-cane juice, poison or wine, fresh water and salt water. And in the very centre of this cosmic system is 'the King of mountains,' Mount Meru, towering erect 'like the handle of a mill-stone,' while half-way up its side is the great wishing-tree, the prototype of our 'Christmas-tree,'

* *Cf.* pp. 77, 81.

and the object of contention between the gods and the Titans. Meru has square sides of gold and jewels. Its eastern face is crystal (or silver) the south is sapphire or lapis lazuli stone, the west is ruby, and the north is gold, and it is clothed with fragrant flowers and shrubs."

The Tibetans believe that the Titans, or ungodly spirits, were originally gods, but were expelled from heaven, and now occupy a position at the base of Mount Meru, *i.e.*, Mount Kailas, intermediate between heaven and earth. The Titans spend their existence in constant war with the gods, and, in the intervals, in dallying with their wives, the object of their warfare being to seize some of the precious fruit of the great tree of the concentrated essence of earth's products, whose branches are in heaven, but whose roots are in their own country. Against them the army of the gods is directed by the great Tibetan war-god, Gralha (or Mara), the god of lust and desire, who holds a place higher than Brahma himself, and is in very truth the king of heaven.

Returning to the Hindu stories of heaven, we find that on the summit of Meru is the city of Brahma and thousands of great gods are in his beautiful Court, and there dwell the seven Rishis, or Sages, created by Brahma, who form the stars in the constellation of the Great Bear. The holy river of Ganges issuing from the foot of Vishnu and washing the moon, falls here from the skies, and after encircling the city of Brahma divides into four mighty rivers, flowing in opposite directions. These are (1) on the north the Indus—Tibetan, Sing Chin Kamba, which means lion's mouth, so-called from the valour of the men through whose territory it passes; (2) on the east the Sanpo or Brahmaputra—Tibetan, Tamjyak-Kamba, or horse's mouth, from the excellence of the horses met with in its course; (3) on the west the Sutlej—Tibetan, Lang Chin Kamba, or bull's mouth, from the violence of its stream; (4) on the south the Karnali—Tibetan, Mapchu Kamba, or peacock's mouth, so-called from the beauty of the women in those coun-

NANDA KOT (22,530 FT.)
Alexis and Henri in Foreground

tries through which it flows. This remarkable river, which is one of the sources of the Ganges, rising considerably north of the Himalayan Range, makes a breach in the massive bulwark of that chain, and flows through Nepal, subsequently joining the Gogra east of Lucknow, and finally uniting with the Ganges.

The Indus rises in the Kailas Range, and while one of the streams, which forms the southern source, flows along the southern slopes of that range, past the vice-regal capitals of Western Tibet, viz., Gartok and Gargunsa, the other, and northerly, branch starts north of the range, and passes through miles and miles of rich gold-fields, of which, perhaps, Thok Jalung is the best

Alexis and Henri

PINE-TREES.

known, until it finally unites with the sister stream and flows past Leh and close to Gilghit.

Although the garden of Eden was never in this part of the world, yet it is impossible not to note the wonderful analogy of the two descriptions :

" And a river went out of Eden to water the garden ; and from thence it was parted, and became into four heads. The name of the first is Pison : that is it which compasseth the whole land of Havilah, where there is gold ; And the gold of that land is good : there is bdellium and the onyx stone. And the name of the second river is Gihon: the same is it that compasseth the whole land of Ethiopia. And the name of the third river is Hiddekel: that is it which goeth toward the east of Assyria. And the fourth river is Euphrates" (Genesis ii. 10–14).

It was in the holy mountains of this part of the Himalaya, that the great god Shiva is described as having dallied with the wives of the seven Rishis, or Sages, who are the stars of the constellation Ursa Major, and for this he was cursed with the curse that his Ling should fill the whole earth. He accordingly flung down his Ling on these very mountains, and hence the origin of phallic worship, for now in every temple and shrine, throughout the length and breadth of India, the Ling of the god is worshipped. Subsequently, Shiva Mahadeo (*i.e.*, mighty deity) married the daughter of Himachal, and his nuptial attire is truly awesome in its details. "Then Mahadeo smeared his body with ashes, and threw over his shoulders the skin of a deer, and adorned himself with snakes instead of jewels, and took the Trisul, or trident, in his hand, and wearing a necklace of dead men's skulls, and seated on a bull, came to the marriage." And so the legends and tales go on, quaint in themselves, yet of absorbing interest, when we realise that these form the mantle of mystery which for ever hangs round these sublime mountains, in the minds of the millions of worshippers who live in every part of India. Selecting some of these that are the more fascinating, we read that Himachal is the giver of the four great gifts of virtue, wealth, desire, and absorption, or death, and is the home of mines of gold and other metals, tigers, deer, all kinds of birds, wild men, and herbs good for medicine. In Mansarowar Lake, we are told, is a golden Ling, and the great grey royal goose with red legs and bill dwells on its waters. Shiva is described as saying: "I dwell everywhere, but Himachal, (*i.e.*, the mountain of Kailas,) is my peculiar seat, and there I dwell for ever. There is no mountain like Himachal: look upon him and receive whatever you desire."

The Lake of Mansarowar was created by a mental effort on the part of Brahma at the request of the Rishis, or Sages, who were engaged in mortification and prayer on Kailas, and who found it irksome to go to some considerable distance to perform the daily ablutions which are the most necessary portion of a devout Hindu's life. By the creation of the lake, close to the foot of the holy mountain, the Sages were enabled to curtail the time spent in travelling to and from another distant lake, and to devote it to further meditation, and worship of the golden Ling, which rises from the lake.

There is a pretty story of the earth and a raja, who was the incarnation of Vishnu. She went to him one night as a woman, and said: "I have not seen a man as beautiful as you, and so I come to you, seeing your beauty. I have left all other rajas, my former husbands, for they have ascended in old age to paradise (Swarga), but I remain still young. I will have you for my husband." He said: "If I die, my wife must burn on my death as Suttee." She replied: "When I too become old, I will burn with you as Suttee." However, when the raja reached old age, and the time of his death approached, the earth was still, as ever, young, and refused to die as Suttee. On this the raja pursued her and caught her at Mansarowar, and decapitated her, but, behold, she could not die, for the earth must needs ever be young.

A careful and authoritative account is given in the Hindu scriptures as to the manner in which the pilgrimage to Kailas and Mansarowar is to be performed. The start is to be from Tanakpur at the foot of the hills, where Almora and Nepal are divided by the Kali,

OUR CAMP. SHEDS MADE OF BOUGHS FOR SERVANTS AND PONIES
Alexis and Henri in Foreground

or Sarda, River, and which it is hoped will soon be the terminus of a railway from the main line forty miles distant. The pilgrim must travel due north to Champawat, the capital of the ancient Chand Rajas of Kumaon, now bereft of its past time glories, and worship on a hill at Cherrapani, where there is a beautiful fruit estate owned by the Raja of Nahan, and bathe in the river at the old cantonment of Lohaghat, where, till recently, Goorkha troops formed our advanced outpost against Nepal. Thence he must go to the Sarju River, famous among anglers for its fish, and on to Jageshar, in whose shrine, buried amongst time-honoured deodars, are the original fragments of Shiva's Ling, and thence to the mountain of Dhuj, 8300 ft., which towers above the adjacent hills, and on the way he must bathe in the Ramganga River, which rivals the Sarju for its fishing. He must not omit to bathe at the junction of the glacier-fed Gori with the black Sarda, here called Kali, and to reach this spot he must pass through Askot, the capital of the Rajbar, descendant of the Katyur Kings, who reigned from Kabul to Nepal. Then passing through the country of the Bhotias, viz., Chaudans and Byans, he is to worship, at Kalapani, the springs, which the devout Hindu considers the sources of the river Kali, and most sacred to the goddess of that name. From this spot the Lipu Lekh Pass conducts the pilgrim by an easy route to Tibet, where he should visit the sacred monastery at Khojarnath, and thence to go to the Holy Lake of Mansarowar, past the mountain of Gurla Mandhata. Here he must offer water to the *manes* of his ancestors, and bathe, and worship Shiva in the name of the royal swan. He is further to walk round the lake, visit the adjoining Rakas Tal, circumambulate Kailas, and bathe in all the neighbouring streams.

As a matter of fact, notwithstanding the above commandment, what usually happens is that pilgrims meet in their thousands at Hardwar, which is a most sacred spot, for the sacred Ganges here leaves the hills, and when the fair which occurs annually at the beginning of the hot weather is over, the pilgrims decide on a tour in the cool of the hills, as a pleasant escape from the heat of the plains, and passing through Garhwal visit the shrines of Kedarnath and Badrinath, whence they can, should they be so venturesome, approach Kailas and Mansarowar from the west over the Niti Pass. Others prefer to take a direct route from Hardwar over the Lipu Lekh, or the more difficult Untadhura Pass, into Tibet. It is a common practice to go by one of these routes and return by another, and very frequently the pilgrims observe the rule, which is so common in many parts of the world, and is found with us in the passing of wine, of going from left to right, as this is considered lucky and correct (sulta), whereas the reverse is objectionable (ulta).

The peculiar sanctity of Kedarnath lies in the fact that it was here that the great god Shiva took refuge when flying from the Pandavas in the form of a buffalo, and being hard pressed he dived into the ground, leaving, however, his hinder parts on the surface, an object of adoration for ever afterwards. Notwithstanding this humorous incident, Shiva is at all times a grim god, a god who inspires terror, and with whose worship there has been associated every form of debauchery, lust, and cruelty. He is the Mahadeo, or God Omnipotent, and to him is given a wife who bears divers names as she answers to various conceptions, *e.g.*, Kali, goddess of death and blood, and in their abominable rites the Tantrik sect adore her with every form of obscenity, licence, and brutality. It is the Ling of Shiva which is worshipped throughout the length and breadth of India, and it is to this phallic worship that men and women flock everywhere—

which cannot but have a degrading effect upon the morality of the nation. To propitiate this great god men perform unheard-of austerities. Near Kedarnath there is a celebrated cliff from which pilgrims used to leap as an offering to Shiva, but the practice has been forbidden by the British Government, and now does not find any votaries. It is one thing to give oneself as an offering when an excited crowd applauds the act, and the mind is in an ecstatic frenzy, but it is quite another to commit suicide in cold blood, alone and unseen. A similar result has followed the prohibition of Suttee, and now it is an almost unheard-of thing for the widow to cast herself on the flames of her husband's funeral pyre. It was in former days also customary for pilgrims, who desired to give their lives to Shiva, to wander into the higher snows, and there to perish from cold, hunger, and exposure. It is popularly believed that Shiva reveals himself to the eye of faith on these lofty mountains, and there are sounds—which are curious, but attributable to avalanches, falling trees, or rocks—which make the rustic mind fancy that the gods are, indeed, the residents of these hills.

Opposed to the grimness of Kedarnath are the genial surroundings of Badrinath. Here, there is a thermal spring which gives forth thick smoke, or steam, of a strong sulphurous smell, and the water is so hot as to be scarcely endurable to the touch, until the temperature has been reduced by an admixture of cold water from another spring. In the bath so formed pilgrims of both sexes bathe indiscriminately. The shrine is consecrated to Vishnu, and the place has enjoyed a reputation for sanctity and learning from the earliest times. The god Vishnu is the type of all that is best in

A RUGGED LANDSCAPE NEAR THE LIPU LEKH PASS

Hinduism, and the worshippers of this god number amongst them most of those who wish to throw off all the impurities and extravagances of the debased religion which are so common in India.

This part may well be closed with an extract from Atkinson's "Himalayan Districts." * "The importance of the Kumaun Himalaya, in the history of religion in India, is mainly due to the existence therein of the great shrines of Badrinath and Kedarnath, containing forms of Vishnu and Siva, which still hold a foremost position in the beliefs of the great majority of Hindus. To them the Kumaun Himalaya is what Palestine is to the Christian, the place where those whom the Hindu esteems most spent portions of their lives, the home of the great gods, the 'great way' to final liberation. This is a living belief, and thousands every year prove their faith by visiting the shrines. The later devotional works are full of allusions to the Himalaya, and wherever a temple exists the celebrant sings the praises of Kedarnath and Badrinath. To many the fruition of all earthly desires is the crowning glory of a visit to the sacred places, by which the sins of former births are cleansed, and exemption from metempsychosis obtained. Each rock and rivulet is dedicated to some deity, or saint, and has its own appropriate legend. Nature in her wildest and most rugged forms bears witness to the correctness of the belief that here is the home of the 'great god,' and when, wearied with toiling through the chasms in the mountains which form the approach to the principal shrines, the traveller from the plains is told to proceed in respectful silence lest the god should be angered, he feels 'the presence.' And should the forbidden sounds of song and music

* *Cf.* p. 703–xii.

arise, and the god in wrath hurl down his avalanche on the offenders, then the awe-stricken pilgrim believes that he has seen his god, terrible, swift to punish, and seeks by renewed austerities to avert the god's displeasure. All the aids to worship in the shape of striking scenery, temples, mystic and gorgeous ceremonial, and skilled celebrants are present, and he must indeed be dull who returns from his pilgrimage unsatisfied."

CHAPTER IV

A GENERAL DESCRIPTION OF THE BHOTIAS

On our journey from Askot to Khela we had followed what is the prescribed route for Hindu pilgrims, as found in their sacred books, and it was impossible, therefore, not to enter in some measure into those feelings of the devotee which he must necessarily experience as he nears the wonderful country so sacred to his gods. Khela itself is about 5000 ft. high, and, on leaving it, one descends over one thousand feet, and then begins to climb what is veritably "the steep ascent of heaven"; for one rises 5000 ft. in direct ascent to the next camp at Tithila, which is situated in what may be called, "The Holy Land," as described in the last chapter. This is Chaudans, the country of the Bhotias, and one immediately realises that it is a different country, inhabited by a totally different people, whose faces, religion, dress, and surroundings are entirely at variance with all that is to be found further south.* We are amongst Mongolians, amongst women who, like the little Japanese, laugh at everything and everybody, and do not rush away to hide, or draw their veils over their faces as the Southerners: we are amongst prayer-flags, chortens, and prayer-poles, where stone pillars fend off spirits and ghosts from the homestead, where men whistle to the sheep

* For further details *vide* "The Bhotias of Almora and British Garhwal," by the Author (Asiatic Society of Bengal Memoirs, i. 8).

and goats which carry precious burdens on their backs, and sneeze at the ponies or mules which they ride, and where yaks and jibboos replace the homely cattle of the lower hills. It is a strange country which charms

PRAYER-FLAGS AND CHORTENS OF BHOTIAS

at first sight, and for which one forms a singular attachment, that never grows cold.

The mass of the population of the Almora and Garhwal districts belongs to the Khasia race, and speaks a dialect of Hindi closely related to the language of Rajputana. The root Khas, or Kho, is found in the names Khophene, Khoas, Khoaspes, given to the rivers of the Kabul valley by classical writers, and also in the words Hindu-Kush and Kashgara and Kashmir (Cashmere).

"We may connect with them Kissia mentioned by

BHOTIA WOMEN : PRAYER-POLES AT THE BACK

Herodotus as an old name of Susa, and Strabo also calls the people of Susa, Kissii, whilst Diodorus and Quintus Curtius mention the Kossaei amongst the principal troops of Darius at Arbela. We may also connect with their name the Caucasus of Pliny, and the Kasian mountains of Ptolemy, as well as his Kasia Regio. The Khasiyas were the principal inhabitants

BHOTIA WOMEN

THE JEWELLERY IS OF SILVER. NOTE THE MUSK-DEER TUSHES ON THE RIGHT SHOULDERS. THE BOOTS ARE OF TIBETAN MAKE AND ARE CALLED BAUKCH. THEY HAVE ROPE SOLES

of the regions to the west of Kashmir, of Kashmir itself, and of the hill country as far as Nepal, and of a considerable part of the plains: and, though now possessing a national existence in Kumaun alone, can still be traced from the sources of the Kabul River to the Teesta by Darjeeling." *

The Khasias are certainly Aryans, and are closely connected with that branch of the great Aryan race which entered India in Vedic times, and has spread itself over the great Gangetic valley and elsewhere, notwithstanding that the religious books of the Hindus speak of them with contempt, the simple reason for this being that they had not adopted all the Brahmanical ritual and the complicated system of caste which these holy books approve. They are undoubtedly Hindus just as much as their brethren of the plains, but, to remove all occasion for contempt at the hands of the scoffer, they are yearly taking the greatest possible pains to conform in the very smallest details with the current ritual and customs of their brethren of the plains.

A very extraordinary thing about the Khasia race is that it is found in many parts of India, and in some places the members of that race have become Buddhists, while in others they stand as the followers of the holy faith of Islam, and again in others they are Hindus.

On the north side of the Himalayas are the Tibetans, while throughout the length and breadth of our own hills the population is either Khasia (this is the majority) or imported from the plains, but along our very border, inhabiting the giant mountains which separate us from Tibet, is the race of Bhotias, which is certainly

* *Cf.* Atkinson's "Himalayan Districts."

one of the most interesting of all the numerous peoples of India, and which forms the connecting link between the two countries of India and Tibet through the medium of trade.

Just as the Tomos of the Chumbi Valley, who are a

A LADEN JIBBOO (A CROSS BETWEEN A YAK AND A COW)

blend of Tibetan and Bhotanese, are the intermediaries of trade between Darjeeling and Tibet, so the trade with Western Tibet has been carried on for centuries past by a clique, and so jealously have the members of this clique guarded their monopoly that up to the present no other persons have been permitted to enter into competition with them. We name these traders "Bhotias," following the example of the ordinary hillman of Kumaon, but they themselves are not in all cases willing to be known by this appellation. Bhot, or, more correctly, Bod, is really the same word as Tibet. In the records of the Tartar Liaos in the eleventh century the name is written T'u-pot'e, in which the latter syllable represents Bod. The Chinese character for "Po" has also the sound "Fan," and with the addition of "Si," or western, the portion of Tibet to the north of Kumaon is called Si-fan, and the people Tu-pote. The Tibetans give themselves the name of Bodpa generally throughout Tibet, meaning thereby "inhabitants of Bod." Further, they sometimes call the country near Cashmere by the name To-Bod. Now, this latter was the part of Tibet with which Europeans first became acquainted, and, obtaining the name through the Cashmere word Tibbat, or Tebet, we have accordingly given the name Tibet generally to the whole territory. On the other hand, the hillmen of Kumaon call the country inhabited by the Bhotias of their hills Bhot, and Tibet itself Hundes, and the Tibetans they call Huniyas. It cannot be too carefully pointed out that the term Bhotia, as applied in this book, does not relate to the inhabitants of the independent State of Bhotan, nor to the Bhotias of the parts round Darjeeling, who are in reality Tibetans but pass currently by this name, nor to Tibetans at any time, although the term Bhotia is frequently applied to them in Western Tibet by the general public of Tibet.

The Bhotias of our hills are found in that very tract of country which has been described above as being so very sacred to the Hindus, viz., all along our Tibetan border, from Nepal on the east to Tehri State on the west, for a distance, roughly speaking, of thirty miles south of the border-line. They are to be found at the mouths of all the passes into Tibet. Those by the Mana Pass, near the holy temple of Badrinath, and those by the Niti Pass are known as Tolchas and Marchas, whereas those by the Untadhura Pass, in Johar, are Shokas (otherwise called Rawats), and amongst them there are also some Tolchas and Marchas. All these compose the western division of the Bhotias,

MEN OF EASTERN BHOT

who are in their own estimation superior to all other Bhotias, with whom they will not eat or marry, and whose ordinary language they cannot talk, as they have forgotten it. South of the Johar Bhotias are the Jethora Bhotias, who do not trade but are cultivators. These have a Tibeto-Burman dialect of their own (called Rankas or Shokiya Khun), and consider themselves the first settlers (Jeth means elder brother), and, as such, far superior to all other Bhotias, though, as a matter of fact, they are severely left alone by the others of their race for no apparent reason, as they seem particularly harmless. Lastly, there are the eastern Bhotias, living in the pargana of Darma, which is sub-divided into three pattis, or sub-divisions, viz., Darma patti, the inhabitants of which use the Neo, or Darma, Pass, and Chaudans and Byans pattis, whose residents use the Lankpya Lekh, Mangshan and Lipu Lekh Passes, and frequently also the Tinkar

BHOTIAS. PRAYER-FLAGS IN THE TREE

Pass of Nepal. These are much more backward than the others, and their customs are, therefore, all the more interesting: they have a Tibeto-Burman dialect of their own, and are much nearer akin to the Tibetans. They are looked down upon by the other Bhotias, because of their primitive ways, and, although all Bhotias call themselves Hindus, the knowledge of the eastern Bhotias about Hinduism extends to little more than the name, whereas the western Bhotias, and Jethoras, have made some progress in Brahmanical rites and customs. All Bhotias everywhere are divided into two castes, viz., Rajputs, or upper class, and Dumras, or low caste. This accounts for primitive customs even amongst the western Bhotias, for, although the upper class clings more and more to Hinduism, the Dumras are still partial to the old ways.

In the matter of dress there is a great difference between the western and eastern Bhotias. The men, it is true, generally dress in woollen-stuffs of home manufacture, their garments being the coat, trousers, and cap familiar among hillmen, with the very general addition of a long frock-coat, while their shoes are the same as are worn everywhere in the hills, though sometimes they take the form of woollen boots of chequered colours, which come from Tibet and are soled with rope very ingeniously and finely plaited. These boots are called Baukch, or Babch, and are found everywhere, except among the Jethoras, who do not visit Tibet. They cost three to four rupees a pair. The women, on the other hand, are different from the ordinary hill women. The western women wear a skirt, coat, shirt, and waistcoat, and finally a headgear, which goes one to one and a half yards down the back, and with which the face can be covered. The Hindu custom of "purda," *i.e.*, covering the face, is extending, but happily the practice of close seclusion at home so dear to Hinduism is unknown. However, "purda" is so far practised that the elder brother never sees the face of his younger brother's wife, nor does he ever speak to her, or go into the same room with her. Gold ornaments are very common with the women of the west, whereas they are unknown among their eastern Bhotia sisters, except in a few of the very richest families. The eastern women wear a short-sleeved coat (Chung), which reaches down to the ankles, and is fastened round the waist, a skirt (Phu or Bala) which is fastened round the waist by a long sheet (known as Jujang), a cap (Chugti) on the head, and after marriage a much larger cap of thicker cloth (known as Chukla). In case of mourning the Chukla is worn inside out. The hair is plaited into a tail which comes down to the

WOMEN OF EASTERN BHOT

shoulder blades, and in Chaudans a little lower. The front hair is plaited into slender threads (Tzi) which are very carefully arranged on both sides of the face, and a silver chaplet invariably holds the plaits in place (known as Anjang). Long woollen boots imported from Tibet (Baukch) complete the description. Richer women wear in addition two sleeves (Rakalcha) which are pulled on over the arms, while all women wear large quantities of beautiful silver jewellery, some of which hangs down in long tapering chains almost as far as to the knees.

The eastern Bhotias often have curious names:

such, for example, as (names of animals) Mushiya (mouse), Kukuria (little dog), Hansu (swan), Maina (bird), Bandar, or Bandaru (monkey), Bila (cat), Nikhi (dog), or the girl's name Wombari (Wom = bear, Bari = wages); or, to avert the jealousy of the gods,

WOMEN OF EASTERN BHOT
(Note the Musk-deer Tushes as Ornaments)

evil names, as Dam (let the scoffer note that this means blacksmith), Pang (a Tibetan), Chora (a slave), Khyembo (a Tibetan word meaning a wanderer), Dola (a beggar). Tibetan names are not uncommon, such as, Chhiring, which is derived from Chhi = life, and ringbo = long.

The question of taking food with certain persons, and not with others, which is of absorbing importance to the ordinary Hindu, is treated in some respects very seriously—for instance, the western Bhotia Rajputs do not eat with Bhotia Dumras—and in other respects very lightly—in that they are quite willing to eat with cow-killing Tibetans, although the killing of the cow is the most heinous offence known to Hinduism. Bhotias do no care, as a rule, to partake of the Tibetans' food, solely because the latter are abominably filthy in their habits, and generally eat rice and meat which is only half-cooked, while Bhotias, who are of much better social condition, and enjoy greater material prosperity, look with contempt on such poor food; but, supposing that the food is properly treated and rationally prepared, all Bhotias will willingly join Tibetans at a meal. The Johari Rawats profess not to eat with Tibetans, but only to drink tea with them. As a matter of fact, the beverage called tea contains in it, besides tea, large quantities of butter, salt, flour and sometimes flesh, so that the above professions of the Rawats are scarcely true. In Johar, with the pride of new converts to Hinduism, the men in every family eat first, and then the women, the leavings being always for the women and children, whereas in Darma pargana there is still found the old-fashioned politeness, which shows some regard for the feelings of the gentler sex, and which acknowledges no custom of eating leavings, for in all families men, women, and children all sit down and eat together. Further, throughout all the domestic details of life the eastern Bhotias invariably put women in a high place, in this way differing radically from Hindus, who regard her as a chattel, and Buddhists, who let her rank among dogs.

To understand the political history of the Kumaon borderland, we must remember that the country now occupied by the Bhotias, who are loyal British subjects, belonged originally to Tibet until the time that Garhwal became consolidated under the chiefs of Srinagar and Kumaon of the famous Chand dynasty. It was in 1670 A.D., that one portion of these so-called Bhotia mahals was conquered from Tibet, while the remainder of the tract was only conquered when the Gurkhas ruled over Kumaon a hundred years ago. The latter took the tract, in which lies our best pass, viz., the Lipu Lekh in the Almora district, from the Jumlis of Nepal, who at that time occupied it, and not directly from the Tibetans; and when the British, after the Gurkha War, took over the rights of the vanquished, this very tract came also into the British Empire.

The Bhotias are of Tibetan origin, though they themselves have still current among them the belief that they were originally Hindus. It is true that Tibetan and Chinese histories do speak of Rajput colonies in Tibet in the earliest times, but, whether Hindus or not, there is no doubt that they are Mongolians, for their features betray them, and they eat and drink freely with the Tibetans. So great an influence has this practice of eating and drinking together had on their method of trade that it is commonly said that the Tibetans will only trade with those persons with whom they can eat, and as this preference creates a monopoly in favour of the Bhotias, the latter are very eager to spread this belief. As a matter of fact, other hillmen have had, at times, the right to trade in Tibet, and have been perfectly willing to pay all trade dues so as to be allowed to go on trading, but so bitter in their jealousy have the Bhotias been that, up to the present, no other person, be he ever so willing to pay, has had the privilege of trading. Further, so far has the monopoly system been carried, that there are regular and systematic "house-connections" (in the business sense of the word), and a Bhotia may only trade with his correspondent, and *vice versa*, and certain Bhotias only may go to certain markets. At one time only the Johar Bhotias could go to Gartok, but now all Bhotias have had that right for some years past; again, there has always been bitter jealousy when Bhotias visited marts to which they were supposed not to go, and such offenders have been beaten and robbed in the past, and formal complaints made about them to the Tibetan authorities. Lately, there has been a burning question pending as to whether certain Johari Bhotias could, or could not, trade with the Tibetans of the Jiu monastery, which is a sacred spot on the Mansarowar Lake. Often in the British courts Bhotias have sued each other and obtained decrees, as to who had the preferential right to trade with a certain Tibetan, and the feelings of the Tibetan correspondent concerned have never been consulted. There have been signs, though faint, that this system of correspondents and special markets was breaking down; for instance, Taklakot has had such an enormous increase of trade within the last twenty years that it has been carried on there in the open market, as well as with correspondents, while the eating of food there has been frequently done away with, although the drinking of tea has been a *sine qua non*, as in Japan.

Some of the Bhotias understand the Tibetan language easily, others with difficulty, though all learn the language for trade purposes. The Bhotias have always had a language of their own, very much akin to Tibetan: some of them have forgotten that language, and others understand each other with the greatest difficulty. They are daily becoming more and more Hinduised; they add "Sing" to their names; practise formal ablutions (which many of them require sadly); some follow the Hindu rites and customs as to birth, marriage, and death ceremonies, and all are seeking after a higher respecta-

OUR ROAD ALONG THE KALI RIVER OVERHANGING A SHEER PRECIPICE

bility. Some of the Bhotias of the more distant valleys still retain their pristine religion and customs; they worship the great god Gabla for prosperity in business, and Kebang-Rangchim, who is both male and female, and sacrifice a goat covered with red earth to the deity Chan for mountain sickness, invoke Sain to show them where a lost sheep or goat may be, and worship the goat-herd brothers Siddhua and Biddhua to restore health to their ailing flocks. In those lonely valleys there is still the romance and poetry of life: each tree has its god, each bush its spirit; precautions are taken to exclude malevolent ghosts from the house

THE LEAFY MONTH OF JUNE

by turning a basket upside down and sticking twigs in it and leaving it on the outer wall; and, if a man dies away from home, a clue of worsted is laid on the ground from the spot of death to the house to lead the spirit home. Women, too, have the greatest liberty; they can, amongst the eastern Bhotias, pick and choose their own husbands, and matrimony is compulsory for none. Such liberty contrasts strangely with the rigorous and insistent law of Hinduism, which requires a man to have a son to perform his funeral ceremonies, and so save his soul from hell, and compels matrimony for a girl before puberty on pain of everlasting disgrace to herself and her family: nay, so far do the orthodox "strain at a gnat and swallow a camel," that they formally celebrate the rites of wedlock of their dumb, blind, idiot, and otherwise incapable children by putting forward as the other party to the ceremony a pitcher of water, or a pipal-tree! *Fiant noces, ruat cœlum!* (*cf.* Mayne's Hindu Law, pp. 10 and 105.) On the other hand, amongst the eastern Bhotias in all their villages, there are many men and women who are unmarried, and a rich man, though ever so desirous of wedlock, has often been known to go wifeless, because of an offending eye, or a nose which was not acceptable. The Bhotia maid has to be wooed and won, and if her heart is not in the arrangement, no marriage takes place. Such is the race of Bhotias who have for centuries fought with the inclemency of the weather, conquered all difficulties of the road, and mastered the loftiest and most perilous passes. They have had a monopoly of trade, and richly have they deserved it for their great fortitude. Soon must that monopoly pass from them, as good roads take the place of execrable tracks, and the sheep and the goat as beasts of burden are supplanted by the mule and the pony, and civilisation with its bustle and competition enters as a discordant factor into the even tenor of their way.

CHAPTER V

THE RELIGIONS OF THE TIBETANS, HINDUS, AND BHOTIAS COMPARED

ONE of the things that strikes the observer most about these eastern Bhotias, though it really holds good with the other Bhotias also, who have only lately issued from their seclusion and become Hinduised, is, that they have been so little affected by their surroundings to the north and south. Being Mongolians, we should naturally expect them to have much in common with the Tibetans, especially in their religion, but the reverse is the case. Similarly, their freedom from Hindu influence in the past is due to the fact that, up till quite recent times, certainly within the last fifty years, they have had a terrible dread not only of the plains but even of the lower mountains. They disliked leaving their homes and mixing with strangers, and it was only when the middle-man in trade began to make exorbitant profits that they broke through their prejudices and went further afield. They can now be found in all parts of India, such as Calcutta, Delhi, and Cawnpore, while one man in Garbyang said he had been twice to Bombay with a friend "just to have a look at the place," and to see the big ships, and he further informed me that he had had a "sail" (using this very word) on a boat in the harbour.

But it is more difficult to understand their freedom from Tibetan influence, for they have been ruled by

A LANDSLIP. A TEMPORARY PATH DOES DUTY FOR THE ROAD

the Tibetans for many centuries. The inaccessibility of their mountain home is one reason that accounts partially for their immunity. The earliest introduction of Buddhism into Tibet dates from the year 641 A.D., but as it is certain that the Bhotias migrated into Bhot at a period prior to this, it is necessary to see what religion was current in Tibet before Buddhism became the state doctrine.

Laotse founded in China between the years B.C. 604–523 a sect whose doctrines have received the name of Taoism, which spread rapidly into Tibet. The members of this sect were indecent in their dress, and grossly atheistical in their principles, but shamelessly gave themselves the name of "Pure doers," and were known in Tibet as Pon (the "pure"), or Bon. Their tenets were in many ways a mere Fetishism and resembled Shamanism, consisting of the worship of monstrous idols, whose loathsome features were revolting in the extreme. The worshippers employed diabolical masks of men and animals and trumpets of human bones, and practised rites of incredible ferocity, such as human sacrifice and other cruelties, and mingled with the whole such indecent immorality, lust, and mummery that the religion can fittingly bear but one name, viz., that of devil-worship. The inhabitants of Tibet appear to have been savages pure and simple, with a reputation amongst the neighbouring nations for cannibalism and rapacity, combined with a total ignorance of the gentler arts of civilisation. It is interesting to note that the language of Tibet was not in pre-Buddhist times reduced to writing, and that, so far as I have been able to ascertain, the peculiar dialects of the Bhotias, which are undoubtedly of the Tibeto-Burman family, and which are now occasionally found written in the Hindi character by missionaries and others, have never in the past been expressed in letters. There can be no question that the Hindi letters do not adequately correspond to the sounds in these Bhotia dialects, and that the only alphabet which is able to meet all their requirements

TIBETAN MASKED DANCERS

is the present Tibetan character. Now, this is all the more remarkable as we know that the Bhotias are an intelligent and mercantile race, and that writing must have been of primary necessity to them in their trade dealings, and that, therefore, it must have been a serious drawback for them to be unable to make use of some alphabet to express the sounds of their own language. In my opinion, this fact can only be accounted for on the theory that the Bhotias left Tibet before writing was introduced into that country about 650 A.D., and that the physical difficulties surrounding their home in the giant mountains of the Himalayas were so great that they have been left, ever since, untouched by the influences at work on both sides of them, viz., in Tibet and India. It is nothing but their seclusion among these vast mountains that can account for the fact that they have among them none of the doctrines of Buddhism, or the common practices of Lamaism, and that Hinduism has been till quite recently an unknown religion, and that their own language has never been reduced to writing. Further, I consider it wonderful, and I think the reader will agree with me as he reads their customs and habits, that we can find among them so little of the degrading immorality and demon-worship of the Bon faith, which must have been in vogue in Tibet before the time of their immigration, and I think it speaks volumes for their national character that, although they have been for centuries in constant touch with Tibet for business purposes, they have never absorbed into their own simple religion the extravagances and demonology of Lamaism.

OUR ROAD ALONG THE KALI RIVER

After the Hindus entered India, the simple teaching of the Vedas and the simple state of society underwent a change, and there were set up hosts of gods, which could only be worshipped through the Brahman priests, who acted as mediators between gods and men. Thus arose a peculiar caste of priests, which not only arrogated to itself the first place in society, but claimed even the title of divinity, and to this present day the Brahman, however humble in circumstances, is popularly regarded as an emanation from the deity. Buddhism was a protest against caste privileges, ritualism, and priestly tyranny, and answered the worship of a multiplicity of gods, extending to thousands, nay, millions, by the atheistic doctrine which denied that there were gods. For years Brahmanism and Buddhism contested the field for supremacy, and in time the former gave place to the latter, which became the Catholic faith of India and was prevalent in these Himalayan tracts. But the seeds of destruction had already been sown which sapped the purer Buddhist faith, and eventually led to its final overthrow by Brahmanism. What has been described above as the Bon religion of Tibet had its counterpart in India in the horrible and diabolical worship known as the Tantrik cult, which revelled in obscenity, immorality, lust and all forms of wickedness, and even in murder and human sacrifice, setting up for itself goddesses of revolting form and abominable character, such as Kali, Durga, and others. They say that the five M's summarise their doctrines: Meat of fish, Meat of flesh, Madness of wine, Mating sexually with women, and Mystic mummery.* Those human blood-hounds, the Thugs, who, till recent years, formed a secret society

* *Cf.* Monier Williams' "Hinduism," p. 127.

for the perpetration of murder as a divine obligation, winning favour with the gods, and who, known to each other by secret signs and passes, would combine to waylay the belated or weary traveller, and strangle him on his lonely way, or in his cups, never failed to worship with every obscene rite, and satanic ritual, the goddess of death, whose lust for blood remained ever unappeased. This Tantrik religion entered into Brahmanism and Buddhism, and, in their eager rivalry for supremacy, both these religions stooped to admit what they fundamentally abhorred, and thus both religions fell from their high estate of purity, with the result that Brahmanism became an easy victor over Buddhism, which was expelled from India in the twelfth century, the victorious Moslem invaders of India assisting in the expulsion. How else could it be? The faith that denied all gods took to itself the host of Hinduism and the Tantrik cult, and forthwith its foundation was struck away when the Brahman priest stepped in ever ready to act his ancient *rôle* of mediator between gods and men.

OUR ROAD ALONG THE KALI RIVER

It was this degraded form of Buddhism that was introduced into Tibet by the sovereign who, himself an unbeliever, found himself wedded to two Buddhist princesses, and discovered, like many other husbands, the force of conjugal pressure which urges to conversion to a better life. This King Sron Tsan Gampo sent a messenger from Tibet to India who, in 650 A.D., approximately, returned and converted the land to Buddhism of the Indian type, and introduced an alphabet modelled on the Hindi characters of that period, and published the first literature of the Tibetan language. These efforts were supplemented a century later by the reigning monarch of that time, who called from India the famous Guru Padma-Sambhava, who forthwith on his arrival stopped human sacrifice and cannibalism amongst the Bonpas and introduced what is now known as Lamaism, and this teacher has since been deified and receives in many quarters even greater worship than Buddha himself. He was a native of Udyana, or Urgyan, to the north-west of Cashmere, a country famous for its magic, wizards and exorcists, and was himself a proficient exponent of the black art. He was welcomed by the Tibetans with open arms, as they felt themselves surrounded by demons of the most terrible description from whom they sought emancipation. This he willingly gave them by vanquishing all the Bon devils of the country by means of his magic arts until they (the devils) cried for mercy, when he allowed them to be freely incorporated into the national orthodox faith on condition that they should be subject to his power, and they in turn were to be properly fed and propitiated. And so arose the priest class of the Lamas, an institution contrary to the whole spirit of Buddha's teaching, who learn in monasteries the whole duty of propitiation and exorcism, and are ever ready to lend their aid (for a consideration) to the laity to rid them of all the foul fiends that dog them during this transitory life and that of the world to come, be it in heaven, or hell, or transmigration. Thus the ignorant masses are burdened with an incubus which wrecks the whole happiness of their lives. It is true that they feel they have the devils always with them, whether in life or in death, in sleeping or in waking; but the Lamas, with their ceaseless demands for donations, never allow the people to forget that they have them too; and doubtless the next historic question to be settled in Tibet will be, which of the two the laity prefers.

Subsequently there were reactions to a purer and nobler faith, and the great reformation, introduced by Tson-Kapa in the fifteenth century, led to the formation of the Gelug-Pa sect, or the established Church of Buddhism, to which the Dalai Lama himself belongs, and which is generally known as the "yellow caps," in contradistinction to the Lamas of the then prevalent Lamaism, who are known as "red caps," whereas the adherents of the Bon faith are "black caps." The "yellow caps" hold the entire secular government of the country in their hands, but have much degenerated from the temporary purity of the reformation.

Now, the Bhotias know nothing of Buddhism, or Lamaism, for they have no lamas in their own country, and although they are not atheistical, still they are not a people addicted to idols, like the Hindus or Tibetans. It is true they worship the Ling of Hinduism, and in many places stones are set up to represent the local deity, but we do not have idols of Ganesh, the elephant-headed god of wisdom, or Hanuman, the monkey-god, or Krishna dallying with scantily clad, sensual-looking maidens, or of the many other gods of Hinduism

A MOUNTAIN TORRENT

which are noted for their lust or ferocity. Nor do we find the gods and demons of Lamaism. They have no images of Buddha, or of Bodhisats (*i.e.*, saints, who are on the high road to becoming Buddhas in future transmigration), whether in their mild type or in their character of angry or ferocious gods; they do not attach any particular sanctity to the lotus flower, nor do they use the prayer-wheel; nor are the Tibetan tutelary or country gods, local gods and genii represented by them in the terrifying shape of idols and pictures so general in Tibet. The peculiar service of the Lamas, vividly recalling the gorgeous ritual of Roman Catholicism, composed as it is of prayers, wearing of sumptuous vestments, adoration of images, ringing of bells, burning of candles on terraced altars, dispensing the so-called Eucharist of Lamaism, the elements being consecrated bread and wine, or the weird rites resembling the Mumbo Jumbo worship of Africa, viz., wearing of horrible masks, devil-dancing, drinking of blood in human skulls, using trumpets of human bones and other uncanny ceremonial, are not found among the Bhotias at all, nor have they priests, or Lamas, to interpret the Tibetan faith. As for the Tibetan shibboleth "Om Mani Padme Hung"—"Hail! Jewel of the Lotus flower (the Dalai Lama) Hail!"—which is universally repeated in Tibet and, without which, and the prayer-wheel, the spiritual life of that country would apparently come to a standstill—it is not even known in Bhot, and certainly no special efficacy is attached to it. Had they ever been incited by the desire to imitate the Tibetans, there is no doubt that they could have found the means to do so, but we find that they have preferred an exactly opposite line of conduct. It is true that the Bhotias, when visiting or trading in Tibet make a point of worshipping the deities of that country, no doubt in order to make quite sure that their spiritual affairs have received every possible advantage, and similarly they reverence the gods of Hinduism when they descend to the lower country inhabited by Hindus, but they do not bring these gods of the outside countries into their own. This statement must be a little modified now that they are beginning to call themselves Hindus, and to adopt the customs and manners of Hindus. But still the visible objects of their religion and their ritual are of the simplest.

Landon in his "Lhasa"* writes of Central Tibet: "Invariably there will be found outside a house four things. The first is the prayer-pole or the horizontal sag of a line of moving squares of gauze; the second is a broken teapot of earthenware from which rises the cheap incense of burnt juniper twigs—a smell which demons cannot abide; the third, a nest of worsted rigging, shaped like a cobweb and set about with coloured linen tags, catkins, leaves, sprigs and little blobs of willow often crowning the skull of a dog or sheep. The eyes are replaced by hideous projecting balls of glass and a painted crown-vallary rings it round. Hither the spirits of disease within the house are helplessly attracted, and small-pox, the scourge of Tibet, may never enter there. Last of all is the white and blue swastika, or fylfot, surmounted by a rudely-drawn symbol of the sun and moon. This sign marks every main doorway in the country."

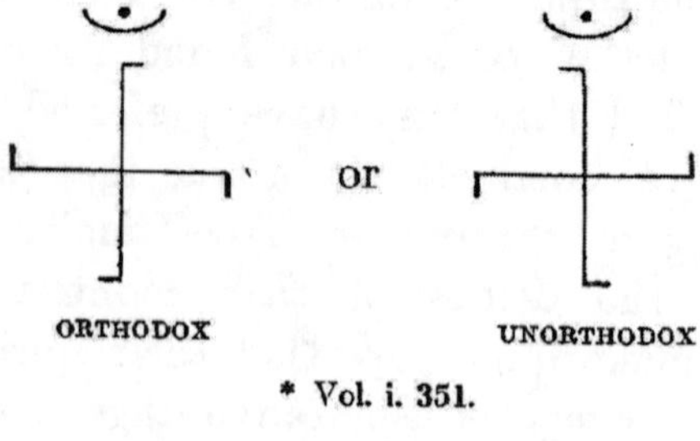

ORTHODOX or UNORTHODOX

* Vol. i. 351.

The left hand swastika is considered orthodox and the right hand unorthodox, though both are found frequently together in Central Tibet. The left hand orthodox symbol is obtained from the Hinduism of India, where it is very common in houses and elsewhere, while the unorthodox is the peculiar symbol

WOMEN OF EASTERN BHOT
(Note the Ornaments of Musk-deer Tushes)

of the black cap Bonpas of Tibet. But the remarkable thing is that none of the four above signs are found among the Bhotias, except the first, viz., the prayer-flag pole and the prayer-flags, which are seen, not in front of every house, but occasionally in the villages.

Apparently there is a considerable difference in the customs of Central Tibet, regarding which Landon writes, and those of Western Tibet adjoining our borderland. At Taklakot, and throughout the parts of Western Tibet visited by us, the four signs which are noted as invariably present in Central Tibet were all conspicuous by their absence, except the first, viz., prayer-poles and lines of moving squares of gauze. We never saw broken teapots full of burning juniper, or

GRAND, BUT DESOLATE

worsted rigging on the skulls of dogs, or sheep adorned with hideous projecting eye-balls; and as for the fly-foot cross, it took us ever so long to explain to the Lama in charge of the monastery at Taklakot, with careful diagrams, what was meant, and he seemed never even to have heard of it, and certainly attached no importance to it. We never saw it anywhere, not even in the important monasteries of Taklakot and Khojarnath, and certainly never in the villages. To this there is one exception: it was found by us in the Jongpen's fort at Taklakot, and no one could explain it, and all seemed surprised to find it there at all. These are some of the differences between the Western and Central parts of Tibet, and others will be noted elsewhere, one of the principal being the death ceremonies.

There is one very marked difference in the two races, and that is that the Tibetans are polyandrous, whereas the Bhotias are not, although they retain some vestiges of polyandry, *e.g.*, on the death of the elder brother his wife becomes the wife of the younger. In my opinion, the physique of the women of the two races, when compared, very clearly indicates the baneful results of polyandry. The figures of Tibetan women lack that vigour which is noticeable among the Bhotia women, suicide is not uncommon among them, and families are small, while many women resort to convents or take the vow of chastity, and the population is dwindling; whereas Bhotia women are remarkable for their gaiety of spirits, instances of girls becoming nuns for religious motives are almost unheard of, and there is certainly no reason to believe that the population is decreasing. Between 1872 and 1892 the population in Johar increased by 13·75 per cent., whereas in Darma pargana, in the same period, the increase has been by 93·12 per cent. No doubt one chief cause of the decrease of population in Tibet is that so many men become Lamas and take the vow of celibacy, but that polyandry and promiscuity are principal factors there can be no doubt. It has been noticed in our own hills that where polyandry has existed the result has been small families with males preponderating. In Atkinson's "Himalayan Districts" * the following occurs: "It is remarkable that in Western Tehri and Jaunsar Bawar, wherever polyandry exists,

A TYPICAL BRIDGE

there is a striking discrepancy in the proportions of the sexes amongst young children. Thus in a village where there were upwards of four hundred boys there were only one hundred and twenty girls. In the Garhwal hills, however, where polygamy is prevalent, there is a surplus of female children."

* *Cf.* vol. xii. p. 256.

CHAPTER VI

SUPERSTITIONS

THE eastern Bhotias erect shrines, called Saithans, for their gods in some quiet place outside the village, or in a grove or by the road side in a shady nook, and in their devotions wholly dispense with the services of the priesthood, some elder of position taking the leading part.

The western Bhotias employ Brahmans as priests, and are year by year being further enmeshed in the toils of Hindu ceremonial ritual, while the low caste Bhotias of all parts of Bhot universally employ the sister's son for all priestly functions. The Saithan, or god's place, is a little chamber a yard in length and the same in breadth and one or two yards in height, in which there is a white stone, viz., the familiar "ling," and on the top of which there is a small branch of a tree adorned with narrow strips of white cloth (Daja) which flutter in the wind. However, most frequently we find no shrine, but instead a simple stone, and by it a prayer-pole or Darcho (a tree trunk with a few branches left on the top) fixed in the ground with streamers (Daja) floating from it. The general form of worship consists in the cooking of cakes or rice, and preparation of dough cones or "dalangs," which are offered with liquor. The "dalang" is so typical of all Bhotia ceremonies that it merits description. Sattoo or flour is made from parched grain, and this sattoo is worked into a cone of dough one and a half feet high, pointed at the top and large at the bottom, and from the sides of this cone

SHRINES AND PRAYER-POLES
NOT GROWING TREES AS MIGHT BE SUPPOSED

stand out spikes of sattoo from the base to the vertex. The "dalang" occupies a leading place in all social rites, and so important is it that the binding part of the marriage ceremony consists in the bride and bridegroom breaking a "dalang" and eating it. In this connection the following quotation from Waddell's "Buddhism of Tibet" is very important (p. 297): "Another food-offering to the gods is a high, conical cake of dough, butter and sugar, variously coloured, named 'Torma' or z'al-ze', that is 'holy food.' It is placed on a metal tray supported by a tripod. To save expense a painted dummy cake is often substituted." When

SHRINE AND PRAYER-POLES

all is ready, small pieces of food are broken off and thrown with both hands towards the seat of the god, bits of cloth are torn up and similarly thrown, liquor is sprinkled with two pieces of grass, one in each hand, towards the same spot, and sometimes the worshippers offer burning lights. Meanwhile a man brings water in a glass, and puts into it an old coin, which must on no account ever afterwards be spent, and also a sprig from the Dhupee tree. Fresh streamers are tied on to branches and put over the shrine, and prayers are offered, while goats and sheep are often slaughtered in numbers. A man sprinkles water on the victim, and as soon as it shakes its body to throw off the drops every one realises that the deity has accepted the sacrifice, when immediately its hair is pulled out in tufts and thrown towards the shrine, the animal being subsequently despatched. Fresh blood is taken from its breast by tearing open the skin, and is sprinkled on the "ling" inside the shrine, while the horns are cut off and placed on the shrine with some of the brains mixed with rice. When the skin has been removed the liver, diaphragm and lungs are taken out reeking, and are carefully examined by the diviners for portents as to the future. The art of divination is in great request, but diviners are few, and amateurs are chary of meddling with the terrible possibilities of the unknown. These rites are faithfully carried out before the Bhotias make their annual exodus to the lower hills for purposes of trade and to escape the cold, and again on return from below to their homes after trading in the plains. Formerly the liver was torn from the living animal, but at the present time this barbarous custom has been given up and the internal portions are only removed after death, but while they are still reeking hot, and often many animals are slain before the desired signs are apparent.

The Bhotias are a hard-working, practical race, but withal most superstitious. They are always at work, both men and women, and in their idlest moments are still spinning thread for weaving, and in all their business are most capable and clear-headed. Still, this is the race that is in the clutches of a superstition that permeates the whole life. They attribute all sickness to evil spirits; they place an axe at the door of a house where any one is seriously ill; when they take a sick man to see a European doctor they fasten a sickle round his waist to fend off the evil one; a returning traveller before entering his village confines thorns and nettles under stones, thinking that in this way he has laid the evil spirit, and this practice is common at the heads of passes, near dangerous bridges, or in

WEAVING: THE USUAL OCCUPATION OF THE WOMEN

difficult places. For the cure of sickness these people resort to burning and bleeding in a manner that makes the civilised beholder sick to look at, and these barbarous remedies are made more effective by incantations. They no longer believe that a thunderstorm will take place if they discharge fire-arms or rub their metal vessels clean with earth in the usual manner (a belief that at one time made the inhabitants of Darma patti notorious for their filthiness, for they cleaned their vessels on their wearing apparel instead, and never washed themselves or their garments), but they do believe that they must fire off guns to prevent the blacksmith Kaliya from seizing the deities of the sun or moon at the time of an eclipse, and their other beliefs are on a par with this.

In all villages we find prayer-poles, analogous to those of Tibet; the incantations also have their counterpart in that country, where the Lamas powerfully advocate the efficacy of spells against the demons of the spirit world, while, strange to say, the Tibetans at Taklakot object to interference with thunderstorms during the rains, and strictly forbid the firing off of fire-arms, a prohibition which was known in Darma in years gone by, but which has now, together with the prohibition of rubbing metal vessels with some hard substance, completely disappeared. The Bhotias are superstitious, and, of course, as superior Europeans, we smile at their fears and ridicule their dread of a spirit world, which to them is a stern reality; but should we gauge them from an Oriental standpoint, I think we shall find them no worse than many other Asiatics.

Let us take one instance that actually happened during our tour. With our party there was a native of position, a man who is a gentleman of good family and superior education; he can talk and write English and has mixed freely with Europeans, and one would credit him with a certain superiority as regards superstitious credulity. He had the misfortune to have a fall from his pony when we were at Askot, as the pony put its foot on a treacherous bit of ground which gave way under its weight. He was badly bruised and complained of pains in his legs, and Longstaff bandaged one leg, which was cut. After leaving Askot we went through trying changes of climate:

first of all terrific heat in the low valleys, then rain, bitter winds and cold, while at Tithila, 9000 ft. up, the weather was particularly unpleasant. Then, as we marched to Galagar over a pass 10,000 ft. high, we had drenching rain all day, and this was followed

A TYPICAL BIT OF ROAD ALONG THE KALI RIVER OVERHANGING A PRECIPICE

by a very moist night. Again, as we marched on to Malpa, and Budhi, 9000 ft. high, the rain and damp continued and affected many in the camp, who contracted fever. On reaching the plateau of Garbyang, 10,300 ft. high, we had a driving wind with mist and more rain, while the cold after the heat of the valleys seemed to eat into one's very bones. Very unfortunately, this native gentleman had fever with ague pains and a severe chill on the chest, all of which were perfectly natural considering the trying weather we had had. At Garbyang he was so ill that he had to take to his bed, and we began to doubt if he could ever be well enough to go with us into Tibet, for Longstaff diagnosed the case as rheumatic fever. He was perfectly willing to take European medicines, but . . . and there was a very great but . . .

A VERY STEEP AND ROUGH ASCENT ALONG THE KALI RIVER
(Photographed from below)

There is a Bhotia (popularly christened "Lama") who lives at Tinkar, just across the border of Nepal opposite Garbyang. This man is wholly ignorant of medicine and never pretends to employ drugs, but is proficient in the use of spells and incantations. When the nephew of Pundit Gobaria, the local millionaire, had such terrible rheumatism in his legs that he was unable to walk, this "Lama" effected a cure, simply by spells, in one day. Not only has he a great reputation in these parts, but this gentleman himself had been once previously treated by him with success, for some years ago, at Taklakot across our border in Tibet, when he had been suddenly attacked by a pain in his abdomen and a fainting sensation in the head, the "Lama," who chanced to be there at the time, cured him by incantations in one night, and he became quite well. So on this present occasion, being ill with fever and ague, he was perfectly willing to use European medicines, but the faithful "Lama" was also summoned. The diagnosis proved that, when the fall had taken place, a wind (Hawa) had struck the patient, and this had been made more serious by the fact that a demon on the road had overlooked him. This demon is abroad both by day and night, and generally rides some steed, and is always accompanied by a dog with a bell fastened round its neck. The cure lay in enchantments, the rubbing on of butter over which a spell had been cast (I saw the butter), the use of mesmerism, in which the Lama was a proficient by popular report, and massage of the limbs from the upper part of the body down towards the legs. Last, but not least, there was fetched a white goat, and the pain and the devil were massaged down to the foot, and thence into the goat, which was then immediately removed to some distance. The subtle humour of the situation lay in the fact that the "Lama" subsequently ate the goat!

The whole of the above took place as described, for we were frequently seeing the patient, and there can be no question that, for the time being, the pain was removed and the fever reduced, the patient becoming immensely better, although subsequently there was a relapse. Now no preaching in the world will persuade the camp that there is no potency in spells; they have seen with their own eyes, and against this reasoning what arguments will prevail?

ALONG THE KALI RIVER

To Garbyang there came a havildar, a non-commissioned officer in the army, who went out shooting and saw a phantom girl, whom he chased attracted by her beauty, and every time he tried to catch her she became a rock in his embrace. He was led by this siren on to a terrible precipice, and in the darkness that came on he lost his way, and a search party had to be sent out to find him. All this story was carefully narrated to us, with the details of names, dates, &c., and the actual precipice pointed out.

But apart from the story of the havildar, my own syce, a hillman who attends my pony, has actually seen two ghosts, with one of whom he held a long conversation. He was then serving in the plains at Saugor, and coming back between twelve and one at night to the mess he met another syce calling loudly for his father. The ghost said he was the son, and had come from Satara in the Bombay presidency to find his father, and could not find him. My syce told him that he had not seen him, and bade the ghost to keep quiet or else he would have him locked up as a bad character. The ghost then departed, wailing for his father, and my syce went to the watchman and reported the matter, saying there was a suspicious character hanging round the mess. He was told in reply that what he had seen was a ghost, which had often been encountered, the facts being that the father had been ill with plague and his son had been sent for from Satara. On his arrival the son found the father dead, and died himself from plague two days later, and ever since then had haunted the place as a spectre.

This syce drove the lesson home one day when we were passing a Mahomedan cemetery half a mile outside Almora town, where there lives a famous ghost of a Mahomedan, and so terrible is this spectre that death is the reward of him to whom he shows himself. As we passed by I noticed a fresh corpse by the cemetery bound ready for cremation at the Hindu burning ghat, and saw the syce stop and question the bearers. He informed me that, the evening before, two Hindus, father and son, returning from Almora town, had been

"WHERE THE AWFUL SOLITUDE OVERWHELMS THE MIND"

NEAR THE LIPU LEKH PASS

benighted at this haunted spot and spent the night near the cemetery. During the night the son rose and, going forth in obedience to a call of nature, saw the dreaded ghost, returned gibbering with fright and died in the morning, although apparently up till then in perfect health. To speak with levity about ghosts and haunted spots in the presence of death and a heart-broken father was out of the question, but this anecdote shows the wonderful hold that the spirit world has upon the hillman's mind, even in the very precincts of Western civilisation and of a military cantonment full of troops. And this is the case not only with the uneducated but with those also from whom we should expect something better. The reader can now, perhaps, understand how it was that when, two years ago, a leopard entered in broad daylight a house quite close to the law courts at Almora, and the Joint Magistrate rose from trying a case and shot it in the ordinary course of events, returning afterwards to continue the legal argument, native opinion pointed out that the leopard had really personified a deity, and had come to visit its temple near the place where it was shot, and that the wrath of heaven would certainly descend in consequence of the death. And so, sure enough, when cholera broke out in the town shortly after, and many people died, there were hundreds, and among them the educated, who saw cause and effect quite clearly.

When this is the state of mind of the ordinary hillman, even though well educated and familiar with Western ideas, what can be said of the Bhotias, who live in the wildest surroundings, where the awful solitude overwhelms the mind and fantastic forms and eerie sounds seem to speak of an ever-present spirit world, and to compel men to see the supernatural in every bush, and rock, and avalanche; where the soft soughing of the breeze is the divine music of heaven and the shrill blast of the tempest the unholy carnival of monstrous fiends; where the gathering gloom of evening reveals a lurking spirit at each bend of the path, or a demon, scarce concealed, behind each boulder; and as the shades of night engulf the lonely traveller, what heart so strong as not to dread the following spectre that dogs the steps and seems ever ready to drag the timid mortal into the yawning abyss where, thousands of feet below, the hungry river fights the opposing rocks?

CHAPTER VII

BHOTIA MARRIAGE CUSTOMS

ANOTHER noticeable thing, as one travels through Eastern Bhot, is to see the extraordinary familiarity between men and women. Although marriages are occasionally arranged through the parents of the parties concerned, yet practically the universal custom of the three pattis Darma, Byans and Chaudans is to arrange marriages at the Rambang, which is the village club, and generally a very disreputable place. The Bhotias of Johar and Niti look down upon the Rambang, and will have nothing to do with it in their own country, having given it up many years ago, still they are quite willing to avail themselves of the Rambang when they visit the pargana of Darma. In every village a house or some spot is set apart, which is called Rambangkuri, or place of the Rambang, at which men and women meet and spend the night singing lewd love songs, and drinking and smoking. Married and unmarried men go there, also single women, and married women up to the time that their first child is born. Girls start to go to the Rambang from the age of ten years, and practically never sleep at home after that age, the result being that a virtuous girl is scarcely known in the pargana of Darma. As is to be expected, a system such as this leads to the freest intimacy, and one sees a man walking about with his arm round a girl's waist both under the same covering shawl, a practice common in Europe but rare in the East: modesty is unknown and there is a boldness

EASTERN BHOTIA WOMEN

The jewellery is all silver; rupees are frequently strung together as ornaments. Note the musk-deer tushes on the shoulder of the girl on the right. The Baukch long boots are of chequered cloth above with rope soles below

in the faces of the women. Intentional miscarriages of illegitimate children are not at all uncommon.

Large villages have more than one Rambang, and, as the avowed object of these Rambangs is to arrange marriages, only those persons resort there who can marry one another, such as the boys of a neighbouring village, or, if of the same village, only those who are not relations. When a resident of a distant part of

SHEEP CARRYING GRAIN IN BAGS

the country comes to a village, travelling on business, he would not dream of asking his friends to give him food and shelter, for this would be regarded as a disgrace; he must wait to be invited by them first. However, if he goes to the Rambang he is sure of a hospitable welcome. In this way the Rambang is a great convenience, but it can only be used thus by persons known in the village; a stranger is unwelcome without an introduction.

When the Bhotias are travelling or go to their winter quarters one of the first considerations is to set apart some spot for the Rambang. If girls wish to invite the boys of a neighbouring village to meet them, they wave long sheets, one girl holding one end and another the other end. This waving can be seen for miles, and is really a very pretty custom. It is also used in bidding farewell to friends and lovers, and is frequently accompanied by whistling, two fingers being placed in the mouth as in the familiar London catcall. Boys and girls are both adepts at this whistling, and it is the usual method employed by the boys of inviting girls to come out of their homes. On hearing the whistles the girls take a little fire and issue forth from their houses and proceed with the boys to the chosen spot, and, if they are old friends, they sit side by side round a blazing fire, otherwise all the boys sit on one side and the girls face them. Often the girls dance, and sometimes the boys, while singing, smoking and drinking are continued until they are all weary, when sleep brings quiet to the scene.

The Bhotia songs, called Bajyu, or "old-fashioned," are the general favourites with the elders, and are always sung by the company with a fervour that shows how keenly all appreciate the formidable vicissitudes of climate and the terrible hardships of mountaineering, or the brave deeds of their ancestors, which are faithfully portrayed in them. These songs of a bygone time, composed in the Bhotia language, are now supplemented by others in the ordinary hill dialect, of which those called Timali most closely resemble, in their serious nature, the old Bajyu, whereas the gay Tubaira

(Tu = fleeting and Baira = a song) is full of levity, hilarity and wantonness.

The Bhotia is a wise and cautious trader and circumspect in all his dealings, and it is not to be supposed that he allows the passion of the moment to override the value he attaches to a powerful alliance through matrimony with a rich neighbour's family, and therefore in almost all cases a young man takes his parents, friends and relations into his confidence with regard to the object of his affections, and it is only if the arrangement appears to be a satisfactory one that they advise him to make an offer of marriage. And we must remember that the young ladies of these parts are allowed full liberty in exercising a preference, and further, if they do not find a wooer, they have the certain prospect of remaining unmarried all their lives. In every village there are women who have grown old and have never known wedlock, and similarly there are men who fail to find a mate owing to some physical defect or bodily infirmity. I know one of leading position and great wealth who perseveres in wearing an outrageous dark blue monocle, a ceaseless source of merriment to the fair sex and an impassable barrier to matrimony.

After due consideration the young man, either personally or through his friends, offers the girl a sum of money, varying from six shillings to six pounds, bound up in a piece of cloth. Generally the young lady is not directly approached, but the gift is handed over to her intimate associates (popularly called Taram, which means, literally, a key) and they promise to exercise their influence with her. Her answer is not obtained without a family consultation of her relations, and should the match appear a suitable one the gift is retained, otherwise it is returned. In the case of acceptance the Tarams always pose as having been indispensable.

In fixing a day for the marriage Monday is carefully avoided, as that is universally considered an unlucky

TIBETAN WOOL FOR THE CAWNPORE MARKET

day, and although the date thus fixed is well-known by both families, a pretence is always kept up that the girl's parents are not going to let her go willingly. Therefore, when the bridegroom (Byolishya) leaves his house to fetch his bride (Byolo), his father summons his son's friends (called Dhami) to a feast quietly at night, and subsequently they are despatched by him with secrecy during the dark hours in the company of his son to the bride's village. Arrived at the village they go to the Rambang, where they find the bride and her bridesmaids (shyasya), with whom they consort for a time, and then carry off the bride in their arms. They convey her only a short way, in order to keep up the semblance of forcible removal, and then wait and call the bridesmaids, and with them proceed home-

A TYPICAL BRIDGE

wards until they reach the groom's house, outside which they all sit down. Each one of the groom's women relations brings them a glass of liquor to show the pleasure felt at the marriage, and, in the names of all the gods, they drink to future happiness. On entering the house the first part of the binding ceremony of marriage is performed by the elders of the village, who produce two "dalangs" or cones of dough, two glasses of liquor and rice, and, calling all the gods to witness, break off the tops of the "cones" and give them to the bride and bridegroom to eat and the liquor to drink. Feasting now commences, which lasts cheerfully for a fortnight, each family of relations taking it in turns to entertain the bridal party, and liquor is drunk until, as a Bhotia described it, a man "is bathed in drink," and the whole village

ALMOST PERPENDICULAR DESCENT ALONG THE KALI RIVER

becomes a pandemonium of drunken men and women. Then follows the second binding ceremony, namely, the formal rite of Datu, when small pieces of the cone are broken off and put in a dish, and the couple are made to exchange by giving a piece with one hand and taking with the other. This ceremony, done before the gods, with the elders and bridesmaids as witnesses, ties the final knot of wedlock.

This is known as a Patham day, that is, the releasing of a girl from her house, and the local blacksmith claims a gift, which takes the form of money or a blanket. The bridesmaids are then allowed to go, but the groomsmen, who have by now become their firm friends, take them into their charge and feast them for some days, and, before saying good-bye, they combine in erecting as a sign of the marriage a " Chandan," that is, they place two long poles (Darchos) in the ground and fasten a rope between them, and on to the rope they tie all sorts of things, such as caps, books, mirrors, streamers of different colours of cloth, scissors, &c., and no one would dream of removing any of them. Subsequently it is a point of honour for the bridesmaids to invite back the groomsmen, a few at a time, and return their hospitality in their own village.

Keeping up the semblance of a forcible removal, envoys are sent to the father of the girl to persuade him to accept what cannot be mended. This he readily does, and the final stage is reached when the bridegroom pays the bride's " mother's milk money," viz., nine shillings and four pence, and also a little money to the father.

It sometimes happens that a girl is carried away in reality by force from the Rambang, but unless, and until, she eats " dalang," "datu," and drinks liquor with her captor she is not considered to be married to him. If she is conniving at the elopement against the will of her parents, and formally eats and drinks the ceremonial food, in process of time her relations are compelled to accept the inevitable. There have been instances when three parties of boys have been determined to carry off the same girl and have blocked all the tracks, the girl being finally taken off across an almost impossible mountain slope, but such cases are not the common practice of the people, just as in England runaway matches are not unknown, but Heaven

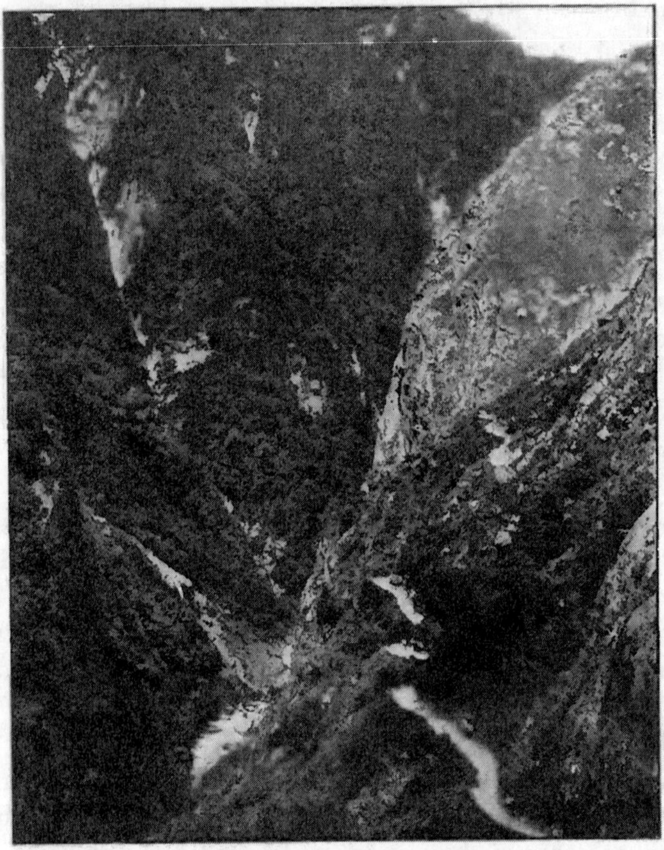

OUR ROAD ALONG THE KALI RIVER

forfend that they should be considered the rule! Widow marriage, in the sense of a marriage with all the honour and dignity of a first marriage, is unknown. However, it is a common practice for widows to go and live with other men, but the unions thus created never occupy the same rank in popular estimation as an ordinary marriage, although no disfavour is shown, such as outcasting from food or drink.

Divorce exists, and the form of divorce is simplicity itself. A man tells his wife to go, and she leaves him. If she wishes to live with another man the union is not known as a true marriage, although the man in question has to pay for her to her former husband, who on his part gives a relinquishment. In divorcing a woman the husband gives her a piece of white cloth. The cloth is invariably white, the idea being to give her, and her children by any subsequent marriage, purity and legitimacy, and until the cloth is given no divorce has taken place; in fact, should a man elope with another man's wife he is shoe-beaten and his goats and sheep stolen from him with their packs, while the children are considered illegitimate. The husband, or any of his close relations, can so treat the erring man or any of his close relations—a practice which might, with the greatest advantage, be adopted in Europe. The children are known as Teliyas until the second husband has held a formal meeting of village elders in the presence of the first husband, and an official account has been taken of the original husband's marriage expenses, and these have to be made good, and it is only then that the white cloth is given, which sets the woman free. An accompanying final ceremony is the waving of a live and screeching fowl round the heads of the woman, the man, and the village elders, much to the amusement of the bystanders. There is no means by which a wife can claim a divorce, and if a man takes a second wife, and refuses to release the first, there is no way in which he can be compelled to release her, however unhappy she may be, and she cannot marry again unless she has been properly released. However, in common practice a second wife is only taken with the concurrence of the first, generally in cases of sterility, or on the definite understanding that the first wife will be released. Human nature is the same all the world over, and in dealing with the frail sex the lord of creation, man, has found it more to his comfort and composure of mind to consult his better half, or halves, about an addition to the number of wives before taking the fatal step than to act regardless of feelings, for the shrewish tongue of fragile woman is more than a match for the burly strength of a gay Lothario.

CHAPTER VIII

TIBETAN AND BHOTIA DEATH CEREMONIES

WHERE the resemblance between the Tibetans and Bhotias is most apparent is in the comparison of the death ceremonies of the two races. There can be little doubt that both have as a common foundation the old Bon practices, although each has in some measure made alterations and additions from the early rites that must have been general before the Bhotias migrated from Tibet. For the following Central Tibetan death rites I am indebted to Waddell's "Buddhism of Tibet."* After the death the corpse is left undisturbed until the soul-extracting Lama arrives, as it is feared that otherwise the soul might leave the body in an unorthodox manner and become the prey of some demon. After ejecting weeping relatives, and closing all doors and windows, the Lama chants directions for the soul to find its way to paradise, and in order to extract the soul he seizes and pulls out some of the hair of the corpse, and thus the liberated spirit passes through a minute perforation of the skull. The spirit is then further directed how to avoid the dangers which beset the road to paradise, and is bid god-speed. Meanwhile the astrologer Lama has prepared a horoscope, clearly indicating the persons who may touch the corpse, and the date and mode of burial; and also pointing out the

* P. 488.

remedies to be employed by the survivors who came in contact with the deceased just before his death, in order to avoid unpleasant consequences from the death-demon's visit. The corpse, having been tied

A ROUGH AND STEEP ASCENT
(Photographed from below)

up in a sitting posture, is placed in a corner of the room not already occupied by the house-demon, and friends and relations are summoned, who loiter in and around the house whirling prayer-wheels and enjoying the boundless hospitality of the household. The deceased is always, at every meal, offered his share of the day's food, including tobacco, &c., and his own bowl is kept filled with beer and tea, and is set down beside the corpse. This practice is continued till the forty-ninth day from death, as his spirit is free to roam about for this maximum period. To feed the *manes* of the deceased a sacrifice for the dead is offered,

ROUGH GOING

by calling all the hungry demons by means of a small gong struck by a horn, and throwing a cake and rice into the nearest stream.

All night and day Lamas sing the litany for sending the soul to paradise, and read over the corpse directions as to how to avoid pitfalls and ogres, and to find the white path which alone leads to a good re-birth. Throughout there is a blending of ideas as to the future life: it may be heaven, and it may be hell, and again there is the re-birth of transmigration. Before removing the corpse from the house an especial feast of delicacies is set before it. Then a Lama ties one end of a long white scarf to the corpse and, holding the other end himself, walks in front of the corpse-carriers blowing a trumpet made of human thigh-bone and beating a drum. He frequently looks back to invite the spirit to accompany the body, which, he assures it, is being led in the right direction, and chants a liturgy for general edification. After the corpse comes the rest of the procession. The corpse is disposed of by cremation or burial, or is exposed to be devoured by vultures and dogs, but there still remain the rites for expelling, from the house and locality, the demon who caused the death.

To do this a toy tiger is fashioned out of grass and mud plaster, and a toy figure of a man is placed on his back, and to lead the tiger is a man with a bird's head, and to drive it another with an ape's head; finally around these figures are placed all kinds of food, wine and coins. After the sun has set, when alone demons can take their walks abroad, the neighbours and the members of the household, armed with swords, knives, &c., wildly cut the air, assisted by the Lamas beating drums and cymbals and blowing trumpets, and by these means formally eject the demon with cries of "Begone!" The small figures are then carried away from the house and placed, if possible, where four roads meet. Meanwhile, to make doubly sure that the demon has really left the house, a Lama remains behind and makes frantic passes in the rooms, mutters spells, and throws hot pebbles roasted in the fire into all the corners of the dwelling. Besides all this a lay figure of the deceased man is made, and dressed in his clothes and a paper-mask put for his face, and all sorts of food and drink are placed before it. A share of each meal is given to it daily until the end of forty-nine days, when the paper-mask face of the figure is burnt and the figure dismantled. The ashes

ALMOST PERPENDICULAR DESCENT. NOTE THE SADDLE

of the mask are mixed with clay to form miniature caityas, or death monuments, some of which are carried to a neighbouring hill and deposited under a projecting ledge of rock to shelter them from the rain, while the deceased's clothes are given to the Lamas, by whom they are sold. If the deceased has left a widow, or widower, the survivor is free to re-marry after one year.

In comparing the practices thus narrated with those existing in Western Tibet, *i.e.*, at Taklakot,

Gartok, Gyanema, Kailas, Mansarowar and the adjoining parts, we find that the ceremony of dressing up the lay figure is entirely unknown and never practised by Tibetans, except those who have settled down in our territory and have come under the influence of Bhotia customs. The non-Hinduised Bhotias always practised this custom, and also many of the rites above detailed, and in these respects much resemble the Tibetans of Central Tibet whom Colonel Waddell has described; but the fact of this disagreement as to the lay figure between themselves and the Tibetans on their border is one amongst many reasons for holding that there is no close alliance between the Bhotias and those residents of Tibet who live closest to them. The Hindus of our hills have a custom which bears some slight similarity to the ceremony of the lay-figure. In cases where the body of a deceased person cannot be recovered, or death has taken place at a distance, they make an image of grass of the dead and cremate it with the ordinary ceremonial, and thus they open the way for the annual death ceremonies of ancestors, which can, after the above rites, be performed in the usual manner. Without these rites a Hindu's soul will assuredly go to hell, and to save him from such terrible calamity two things are indispensable: firstly, a son to perform them; and secondly, a due performance.*

Further, the Tibetans of this western portion have four ways of disposing of the corpse, the attendant astrologer Lama telling them exactly which one to employ. There is cremation (Phukant), interment (Gadant), and also the placing of the body in some place, a high hill or elsewhere, to be eaten by dogs,

* *Cf.* Mayne's "Hindu Law," pp. 8 and 105.

vultures and birds of prey (Khawant). The Parsis of Bombay, who are fire-worshippers, have an analogous custom in the exposure of their dead on the top of the grim Towers of Silence, where the vultures speedily pick the bones clean of all flesh. The object that the Parsis desire to attain by this quaint practice is to insure that their elements of earth, air, fire and water should not be defiled as they would be if burial or cremation or casting in the river were adopted. Similarly orthodox Parsis do not smoke, as they do not wish to pollute their element of air. Reverting to the Tibetans of Western Tibet we find that the fourth method of disposing of the corpse is to cut the flesh and bones into thousands of fragments and to throw them into the river (Urant).

A variation is to bury the corpse for a week or a fortnight, and then after disinterment to give it to the fowls of the air, or cutting it piecemeal to cast the fragments into the water. The bodies of persons who have died of any serious disease are invariably buried, or thrown into a pit and covered over with earth. In all principal respects there is practical agreement between the customs in force in this part of Western Tibet and those of Central Tibet mentioned by Colonel Waddell, the Lamas invariably posing as indispensable for a good re-birth, or the finding of the way to heaven, and of absolutely primary importance in securing the transfer of the soul from one part of hell to another more favourable quarter, or its transmigration from some inferior animal to a higher plane of existence. In the words of the Tibetan proverb : "Without lamas god is unapproachable."*

* For further details *vide* "The Bhotias of Almora and British Garhwal" by the Author. ("Asiatic Society of Bengal Memoirs," i. 8.)

The ceremonies of the Bhotias compare strikingly with the above.

In regard to funeral customs a distinction is drawn between little children and grown-up persons, the line of separation being the permanent teeth. As soon as the milk teeth are being replaced by the permanent ones a child passes from the one category to the other. Little children are wrapped in wool and buried facing the east, the head being to the north and the feet to the south, and little is done in the way of ceremonial, though should the child be on the point of getting its second teeth children of a similar age are feasted on boiled rice. The dead body of a grown-up person is placed in a white cotton bag (Katro) with the knees touching the chin, and not at full length as is the practice of the Hindus; further, the bag is sewn with thread spun contrary to the usual way. The bier is the same as that used by Hindus, viz., two poles with slats of wood across. The corpse is then placed on the bier, with the face to the east, and is carried head foremost in the procession. To the front of the bier is fastened a piece of white cloth, cotton if the deceased is a man and woollen if a woman (the latter being specially prepared by the women folk for themselves), which is carried by the deceased's women relations on their heads in front of the bier, their Chuklas, or head gear, being turned inside out. The cloth is known as Am Lugara, Am meaning a way and Lugara cloth, the signification being that the spirit or soul of the deceased can be thus easily guided forth. The Chinese have a somewhat similar practice and use a white banner. The procession is led by a young boy or girl, with fire in the hand for the funeral pyre, next come the women holding the Am Lugara, then the bier carried by four men relations, and finally the villagers with fuel for the cremation. On the way to the pyre all men relations walk with their caps doffed.

"BLEAK, BARE AND RUGGED." NEAR THE LIPU LEKH PASS

The burning-place is usually on the bank of a river, and the pyre is formed of a stone enclosure. The clothes worn by the deceased at the time of death are placed among the faggots, and the corpse having been put on the top, with face towards the east, by one of the mourners, the bag is cut at the face and a piece of precious metal, such as gold or silver, or even a pearl, is placed in the mouth, the corpse being supposed to become "Sudh," or purified, thereby.

On the following day men and women proceed to

the burning-place and pull down the enclosure, and wash the place and remove one of the burnt bones. The men doffing their caps and the women turning their head-dress (Chuklas) inside out, solemnly bear the bone enclosed in an iron or tin box to the place (each village has one or more) of dead men's bones. To screen the spot from the vulgar gaze, curtains are erected on both sides of the place, and two girls, one with a cup of flour and the other with a jug of water, sprinkle on the ground, while the men dig a hole and put the bone with its case into the ground. After this four reed sticks are put up at the four corners, four feet apart, like boundary pillars, and the tops are joined by three threads of different colours, viz., red, white and yellow. Next, immediately above the interred bone, a forked stick is placed in the ground, and from one arm is suspended a pair of new shoes if the deceased is a man and a pair of long boots (Baukch), if a woman, and from the other arm is suspended a gourd full of water. Below the gourd is a plate with flour covered with butter, and as there is a small hole in the bottom of the gourd water drops continually on the food beneath. This custom is borrowed from the Hindus, who always hang in a pipal tree (ficus religiosa) a pitcher of water, prepared with a hole and a rag in the bottom in such a way that water falls in drops from it, and thus they hope to quench the thirst of the departed spirit, whose mouth is so small that it can take no larger draught, the spirit being but the size of a man's thumb.* That night there is given a funeral feast, and very special provision is made for the soul of the deceased. A stone is placed

* *Cf.* Monier Williams' "Hinduism," p. 65. The Tibetans have a similar belief.

upon two sticks, outside the house, and a little cooked rice is put on it, and the elders of the village make special prayer, beseeching old souls, called Yishimis (Yi = old), not to appropriate the food for themselves and thus deprive the deceased. Great care is taken to renew the food thrice daily before the family takes its own food, and it is not until the Dhurung, or death ceremony, has taken place that this giving of food ceases. From this day onwards up to the Dhurung ceremony all singing is stopped among relations, and men may not wear a turban or a ring on the right ear (the left is immune), nor may they shave or crop the head: similarly the girls who are related to the deceased have to eschew rings on the right hand and allow two frontal hair plaits (Tzi) to hang down on each side of the face, and sometimes they go the length of putting off all jewellery for three years with the exception of a coral wreath and a bracelet.

If the deceased has succumbed to some infectious disease, such as small-pox or cholera, the corpse is not burnt but buried, or is thrown into the water, and in this case no bone is retained, except a tooth to be put in the place of dead men's bones. Such a horror have they of leprosy that, if the deceased has been a victim to this dread disease, they simply cast the corpse into the water and retain nothing, not even a tooth. In the pattis of Byans and Chaudans cremation follows death immediately, but in Darma patti burning takes place only in the month of Kartik, *i.e.*, once in the year, and the corpses are interred in the ground during the interval and are exhumed in Kartik for cremation. This is a filthy and most insanitary practice and resembles the Tibetan customs. The Bhotias of Darma pargana all speak of the funeral ceremonies as Gwan, but they are known amongst the western Bhotias by the term Dhurung. They were undoubtedly practised in the past by all Bhotias, even in Johar, Niti and Mana, but at the present time the

TYPICAL COUNTRY ABOVE THE TREE LEVEL. NEAR THE LIPU LEKH PASS

western Bhotia Rajputs have entirely abandoned the custom, which is only followed in those parts by the Domra Bhotias. For the performance of the Gwan the members of the family summon the village elders to fix a date, and some time during the waning moon is chosen. In the ceremony of the Gwan an animal is always made to represent the deceased, and is called Ya; in some places a yak is always chosen, and great care is taken to see that its forehead, back and tail are marked with one continuous blaze of white, but elsewhere the influence of Hinduism has made the people give up yaks (except the Domras) on the ground that they are cows (and to Hindus cow-killing is anathema), and sheep and goats are selected instead. The selection is left to the spirit of the deceased, which marks its approbation by making the approved animal shake its tail while the relations throw rice on it. The sex of the animal follows the sex of the deceased. An indispensable part of the ceremony is the presence of a Seyaktza, who is an old man well versed in the lore of the future world, and it is his duty to instruct the spirit of the late deceased (Nushimi, Nu = new) as to the paths it should follow, and the dangers it should avoid, in reaching heaven.

The Gwan ceremony lasts four days. The principal duty on the first day consists in the taking of the Ya to a spot outside the village by the relations, who also take with them a suit of clothes and a few ornaments, and having reached the given spot the deceased's clothes are tied on to the Ya. Then grains of barley are thrown on the Ya, and it is solemnly stated that the Ya represents the deceased, and old spirits (Yishimis) are besought not to take the food of the lately departed spirit (Nushimi). After this a solemn procession is formed, in exactly the same way as when the corpse was taken out for cremation, the Am Lugara, or white-cotton cloth, being fastened to the horns of the Ya. Also a tablet of accounts is drawn up, written with wet flour on a wooden slat, showing, for the edification of the dead, exactly how much flour and other things have been used in entertaining the guests for his benefit. The Bhotia, being a man of business, likes to have no possibility of the least misunderstanding between himself and the ghost as to the exact amount that has been spent, fully knowing that the ghost, also a man of business, will thoroughly appreciate the arithmetic.

The second day is like the first, but on the third

NEAR THE LIPU LEKH PASS

day they take the Ya and go to the place of dead bones (Ya shyam) where the deceased's bone is lying in the casket. Great care is taken to ensure privacy by again putting curtains on both sides while the case is being taken from the ground, and, when extracted, the case is immediately placed inside so-called "ghost-boots," which have been made during the preceding night. These "ghost-boots" (Shimi Babch, or Baukch) are some six inches long,

[NOTE.—Much fuller details are to be found in "The Bhotias of Almora and British Garhwal," by the Author. ("Asiatic Society of Bengal Memoirs," i. 8.)]

being simply a round cylinder of cloth with a leather sole, the whole very diminutive and very coarsely prepared.

After this a procession is formed as on the other days, and on reaching the village the Ya is fed, and the bone in the ghost-boots, together with the deceased's clothes, is brought into the house. Then the Seyaktza, versed in the knowledge of the spirit world, gives his advice to the departed soul, nor must the old man relax for a moment during the whole of that day, and all that night, be sleep never so importunate.

Then comes the weird ceremony of the formal dance, executed by all the men of the village (they are called Garkhal) in a long row. They come dancing up to the deceased's house and are feasted, contributions of food being levied from all relations, if the people of the house are not rich enough to incur this expense. As this dance proceeds, metal dishes and cooking utensils are taken out of the house and beaten by the men, while the girls carry torches in their hands, and finally all the dancers go round in one direction and the others in the opposite direction, beating the vessels and holding torches.

The last day is Ya Pongmo (rooting up of the Ya), on which they get rid of the spirit of the deceased. The venerable Seyaktza having finished his last words of advice to the soul, the lay figure is taken out and the clothes removed and put on the Ya, and a man leads forth the Ya to a distant spot from the village, and on this occasion all the villagers beat the poor victim to drive it away and chase it to prevent return. In Chaudans it is allowed to roam free on the mountains, but elsewhere low caste Bhotias, or Tibetans, speedily despatch it and eat the flesh. So pleased are the villagers that the spirit has departed that they return singing and dancing, and after this men and women shave, cut

BUDHI CAMPING-GROUND. THE ROAD COMES DOWN THE HILLSIDE

their hair, wash their heads and wear rings on their ears and hands. As to the bone, half is taken and buried in some lofty spot and the other half is taken to some sacred place, such as Kailas or Mansarowar, by one of the household, who remains unkempt until he has deposited the bone in its final resting-place. Formerly in the patti of Darma if any onlooker wished his descendants to note that he desired his own obsequies to be performed on a magnificent scale, he blew a trumpet and announced the fact publicly, and woe betide any heir who failed after that to do all honour to the spirit of the deceased. A widow throughout the whole of Bhot leaves off all jewellery for a year or more, and also the nath or wedding nose-ring.

Such are the death ceremonies of the Tibetans and Bhotias, and the most superficial observer cannot help noticing the wonderful resemblance between the two.

Whatever the history of a race, and whatever the changes in life due to migration and a variation of surroundings, practices such as these, which relate to some of the most important events of life, date back to the early times when the race lived in another home amongst other neighbours, and a comparison in these later days, between tribes with kindred customs and languages, alone can read the page of history, which otherwise would remain inscrutably closed.

CHAPTER IX

A TIBETAN TRADE ROUTE

To resume the narrative of our expedition, along the route from Askot to the Lipu Lekh Pass the very worst part of the road is the Nirpani, or waterless, track. This name was given to it many years ago when there was great difficulty in obtaining water along the route, as the road was carried over the tops of mountains and along dangerous cliffs. The present track, bad as it is, is a great improvement upon the old state of affairs. We marched from Tithila, 9000 ft., over a pass of 10,000 ft. to Galagar, about 8000 ft. in height, where we had to leave our ponies, as it is quite impossible to convey them over the Nirpani track quickly. The Bhotias, it is true, get their ponies across by much holding of the head and tail, and sometimes by carrying, the animals being slung on a pole with feet tied, but the loads have to be removed and the whole proceeding takes a long time. The path descends sheer down many hundreds of feet, and the stones of which it is composed, when in the form of steps, are easy to travel over, but when they become a confused heap there is a very little foot-hold for any animal except sheep and goats, and the incline is frequently one in one. I have photographed a kid with its mother on this inhospitable track, the kid having just been born on the verge of a terrible precipice, and at one of the worst places along the whole route. The Bhotia herdsman gave the poor mother half an hour's rest, and then drove the whole herd on, while he carried the kid in his arms.

The opposite bank of the river on the Nepal side is so

KID BORN ON A PRECIPICE OF 1000 FT. SHEER DROP ALONG THE NIRPANI TRACK (MOTHER LYING DOWN IN CENTRE)

close at times that one can frequently get a shot at ghural, a deer of the chamois tribe, grazing quite unmindful of the traffic which is going on across the raging stream. But having shot the deer it is always hard, though generally quite possible, to recover the body. As the Nepalese do not favour bridges it is exceedingly difficult for a coolie to get across the stream, and when he has actually crossed he is liable to find the cliffs so precipitous that he is compelled to spend much time in going even a short distance.

Girl

THE SCHOOL AT GARBYANG. ONE GIRL ATTENDS IT WITH THE BOYS

Two days are often spent by coolies before the deer is brought into camp, while on this present occasion the one we shot was brought to Garbyang in three days, as it fell in a particularly difficult spot. We camped at Malpa by the side of the river, and at Budhi, before we finally reached Garbyang, both short marches, but the exceptionally trying wet weather and the bad road made short marches a necessity for the party. This part of the road is on the point of being immensely improved, and the new alignment has been actually marked out. When the work is finished this route ought to be one of the very easiest into Tibet. The only difficulty is the Nirpani track, otherwise the road throughout its whole length, from Tanakpur in the plains to Taklakot in Tibet, can be easily made, with a little expenditure, into a first-class bridle-path.

Garbyang is a very important place, being the headquarters of the Political Peshkar during half the year. It is also a great trade centre and has a fine school. Approaching from Budhi, by a very steep ascent, one comes on to a plateau which is well over 10,000 ft., and here there are holes made in the ground where a large quantity of grain is stocked. The reason is that the Dokpa Tibetans, who are very rich, and have only yaks and big Tibetan sheep, never care to descend lower than 10,000 ft. with their goods for fear of endangering the health of these animals, which are so accustomed to the rarefied air that they die when brought out of it. So here, at what may be called the Gates of Garbyang, there is a centre for the exchange of goods, and grain is buried in the ground for months without fear of thieves, being protected from the damp by the bark of the birch tree.

At the entrance to Garbyang there are three big

THE MEETING OF THE WATERS: KUTI YANGTI (LEFT) AND KALI (CENTRE) RIVERS. THE LATTER IS OUR BOUNDARY AGAINST NEPAL (RIGHT)

stones, erected with due solemnity, to keep spirits and ghosts from entering the town, and near by is another pillar, whose grim memories still strike terror into the villagers. In the old days the Tibetan Jongpens used to use this stone as the whipping-post for the administration of justice—a fact which brings home the close connection in the past of this part of the country with Tibet.

Opposite Garbyang on the Nepalese side there is a cave near the village of Chhangru which is of quite remarkable interest. It is about 1200 ft. above the village, the climb being very steep and difficult, as there is no semblance of a path, and we had to go through thorns and bushes when we ascended to it last year. In old days it used undoubtedly to go back for a long distance into the mountain, but as one of the sides has fallen in the cave has been considerably shortened. We found it full of dead bodies of men, women and children, the hair and flesh in some instances being wonderfully preserved owing to the extraordinary dryness of the interior. It appears that this cave was unfortunately ransacked by thieves some years ago and much valuable clothing and jewellery removed; otherwise it is one of those places which would repay examination by an expert. According to current rumour it used to be one of the abodes of the aborigines; certainly its position would make it an ideal stronghold. It was used as a retreat by the natives during the fighting that took place in the Gurkha period of a century ago, but at present it is only visited by Hindu devotees, and then very rarely, while the ordinary Bhotia regards it as a place full of demons and goblins, to be avoided at all costs. Many who had never previously entered it were very glad to take the opportunity of our going to accompany us, as they considered that spirits could do no harm in our presence.

From Garbyang the road passes over a plateau as far as Kalapani through some of the most beautiful scenery in the Himalayas. Kalapani is the supposed source of the Kali river, and therefore a very holy place, for there are some half a dozen springs here which fall into the main river, the actual source, however, being a few miles higher up. The Hindu servants threw a little rice into the stream, and at early dawn in the bitter cold bathed as a meritorious act. Hindu customs are excellent for the warm plains, but to bathe at 12,000 ft. at daybreak, and to eat food practically naked as a general rule, with the thermometer uncomfortably low, in driving rain and searching wind, are most unwise proceedings, and all earnest Hindus had to be gently but firmly dissuaded by me from working out their own dissolution. Throughout our tour in Tibet it was very difficult to keep the camp followers from bathing in icy cold water, which chanced to be particularly sacred, or from eating almost naked in bitter winds because their Hindu religion was supposed to enjoin the custom. As a matter of fact, all orthodox Hindus admit that in extremes of climate the ordinary rules should be invariably relaxed.

We saw a great deal of traffic during our march towards the Lipu Lekh Pass, as we were travelling at just that time of the year which is the best for trade. This pass accounts for over £26,000 worth of trade annually, and, considering what the road is, it is simply marvellous that the ordinary trader is willing to risk even five shillings, to say nothing of thousands of pounds. The Untadhura Pass is responsible for over £23,000 annually, and the whole of Kumaon, including all the passes, for £67,000 annually. The figures are not large, but let us remember that sixty years ago £2300 represented the entire trade over our easiest pass, viz., the Lipu Lekh, and that the

BLIND MAN WHO WAS CARRIED ACROSS THE LIPU LEKH PASS (16,780 FT.) ON A COOLIE'S SHOULDERS FOR HALF A CROWN

increase since then has been more than elevenfold. There is every reason to hope that there is plenty of scope for the future extension of trade, as Tibet is rich in gold (which has been hitherto very little worked), wool from innumerable goats and sheep, borax and salt, whereas we can supply tea, grain, manufactured goods, sugar and solid cash, the last of which is much appreciated. So easy is the Lipu Lekh Pass that it will be ideal for pilgrims. I even photographed a blind man last year who had made so little of the pass that he had been carried over on a coolie's shoulders from his village to Taklakot, a distance of about twenty miles, and who had paid the munificent sum of half a crown for the treat. It is quite easy to ride from Garbyang to Taklakot in one day, the distance being about twenty-six miles.

CHAPTER X

TIBETAN ADMINISTRATION IN WESTERN TIBET, OR NARI

UP to the time when the recent Mission was launched on its eventful advance into Tibet, there was the very greatest ignorance amongst even the well educated as to the country which that expedition was setting out to visit. To the man in the street, Tibet was a vast and dreary plateau, fenced about with the loftiest mountains, and the only place of which he had heard was Lhasa, 390 miles from Darjeeling. Since then we have become quite familiar with many names, such as Gyantse, Shigatse, the Karola and scores of others, but the whole of the knowledge that has been reaped has been confined, speaking broadly, to Central Tibet; Gartok and Western Tibet are to many still a sealed book. Lhasa is situated in Central Tibet, and the country further east is known as Eastern Tibet, while Nari, or Western Tibet, is the territory west of the Mariam or Mayum Pass, 16,900 ft. high, where the Sanpoor Brahmaputra river rises. Yet the concessions that have been obtained by means of the treaty at Lhasa in regard to Gartok are of greater importance to the native subjects of His Majesty than the whole of the concessions in Eastern Tibet. By far the larger part of the population of India is composed of Hindus, who are not traders or miners, to whom wool and borax do not appeal,

Pass

APPROACHING THE LIPU LEKH PASS (16,780 FT.)

NOTE THE EASE OF THE ASCENT

and who turn a deaf ear to the charmer that holds out hopes of fortunes to be found in the ground, for, in words familiar to us, they "care for none of these things." But the Hindu is first and foremost a devotee, and to him the claims of his religion incomparably outweigh all else that is secular.

We find him ready to appreciate to the full all those considerations which appeal to the religious side of his nature. It is impossible to go to Gartok by the best and shortest routes without passing by places which are viewed by the Hindu as exceedingly holy. Kailas, "the heaven of Shiva," and the Mansarowar Lake appeal to him as Mecca does to the Moslem. A pilgrimage to these most holy places has been, up to the present time, a practical impossibility for the ordinary Hindu. Fakirs up to the number of a hundred and fifty, or so, annually face the rigours of the passes and the inhospitality of the Tibetans, and when the "Kumb" Mela takes place once in every twelve years this number swells to four hundred; but the ordinary pilgrim, who will willingly venture to the Badrinath and Kedarnath temples, finds his heart sink within him, when he contemplates the inclemency of the country and the people where are situated those places which to him are objects of the greatest veneration. Whatever else has been accomplished by the Treaty of Lhasa, free ingress into Tibet is vouchsafed to every Hindu and a reasonable prospect of safety to his person and property, for up till now there has been a death penalty on the headman of any village who allows an European or native of India to enter Tibet. A concession of this nature should appeal very strongly to every Hindu in the country, and, as soon as the facts become generally known through the length and breadth of India, we shall probably find an enormous number of pilgrims wending their ways to these sacred places. While, then, it is impossible to prophesy as to the future increase in our trade with Tibet and the development of the mineral wealth of that country, both of which depend upon capital and the character of future relations between ourselves and the Tibetans, we may assert, without misgiving, that a very extensive pilgrim traffic is certain to spring up as soon as the Hindus of India realise that the way to Kailas and the Mansarowar Lake is no more difficult than the road to Badrinath. Further, this pilgrim traffic will be practically independent of the Tibetans, and it will be immaterial to the ordinary Hindu pilgrim whether the Tibetans regard us with affection or hostility. The holy places to be visited are only a short way across the border—in fact, so short that food can be carried on the person sufficient for the journey—and no doubt in process of time rest-houses, so common in our own hills, will spring up to shelter the traveller from the weather.

The administration of this western portion of Tibet is carried on by the Garphans, or Viceroys, whose headquarters are at Gartok, and by Jongpens and Tarjums, who are in charge of the outlying districts and are subordinate to the Garphans. A Tarjum is an official of lower status than a Jongpen, but they are not subordinate to one another, and the extent of their powers is in some cases practically the same, although the principal duty of the Tarjum is the forwarding of the imperial post, and often he has little territorial authority. These powers are very great, and include the right to order imprisonment for long terms, or the removal of an eye, hand or foot, and the infliction of almost unlimited castigation. All these officials, including the Garphans, are men appointed from Lhasa, where there is a school for the training and education of young gentlemen desiring government service, and hold their posts for a term of years, such as three or five years, and as they buy their posts by payment to the supreme authority, and in return are entitled to put all revenue, fines and other State income into their own private purses, it is not difficult to imagine that during the term of his office the first concern of each official is to recoup the original payment for his post and to have a substantial balance on the right side. When we understand this system of government we can at once appreciate why the old adage "e nihilo nihil fit" is so very applicable to Tibet. In that country nobody will do anything for nothing, and whatever the terms of the Treaty of Lhasa with regard to tolls, dues and fees, we shall always find that the local magnate has to be reckoned with, and that, unless he is carefully watched, he will evade every obligation of the Treaty, perhaps not in the letter, but in the spirit. We cannot, therefore, too warmly congratulate the Government on their far-sighted policy, when they have made arrangements by which they will ensure that obligations are carried out. The appointment of an European of established position, such as Captain O'Connor, at Gyantse, and of a native gentleman of good family, as Thakur Jai Chand, at Gartok, to safeguard British interests, is a step in the right direction. Gartok is situated at a height of 15,100 ft. and is a very cold place in the winter. For this reason it is only the summer headquarters of the Garphans, and in the winter is absolutely deserted. In fact, there are only a few substantially built houses there, by far the greater portion of the inhabitants living in tents. The total population would be about fifty families,

A VALLEY LEADING TO NAMPA (23,350 FT.) IN NEPAL: MORAINE OF THE NAMPA GLACIER

using the term "family" in the Tibetan sense, which includes every living unit of a family, as the members always dwell together and never separate. By the middle of November, as a rule, the seasonal exodus from Gartok has taken place. There is an annual gathering of all officials, Jongpens, Tarjums, and nobility at Gartok at the end of August or beginning of September, coincidently with the great fair, which has been held there from time immemorial. Eighty years ago Mr. Traill, Commissioner of Kumaon, wrote of this fair as follows :

" A periodical fair takes place annually in September

THE FINAL APPROACH TO THE LIPU LEKH PASS (16,780 FT.)

at Gartok the residence of the Lhasan Viceroys, which is principally attended by traders from Hindustan, Ladakh, Cashmere, Tartary, Yarkhand, Lhasa, and Liling, or China proper; under the first description are included Bhotias of this Province." At this annual gathering business, both official and mercantile, is transacted, and is blended with pleasure in the shape of horse-racing, the mounts being owned by the aristocracy and ridden by boy jockeys.

There are three principal approaches from the United Provinces into Western Tibet, viz., the eastern from Tanakpur, forty miles from the railway at Pilibhit, which crosses the Lipu Lekh Pass (16,780 ft.) and leads directly to the Holy Lakes and Kailas; the central from the railway terminus at Katgodam over the Untadhura Pass and two other passes, the highest being nearly 18,000 ft. and the lowest 17,000 ft.; and the western from Kotdwara on the railway through British Garhwal and over the Niti Pass (16,750 ft.). Of these the central approach is by far the most difficult; however, it is a very popular route with the pilgrim notwithstanding its difficulty. But the route which is the easiest of all the others, and which combines directness with comfort for the traveller to Mansarowar and Kailas, is the eastern, which passes over the Lipu Lekh Pass close to the spot where Nepal, British territory and Tibet meet. This pass is within our frontier, and although 16,780 ft. high is so easy that for the last twenty miles of the approach on our side and over the descent on the Tibetan side a cart road could be made without difficulty. Not that it is desirable to make a cart road at this stage of proceedings, but the fact shows how small are the obstacles to be encountered. Further, this pass can be negotiated at any time of the year, although in the winter a certain amount of trouble is experienced. With these advantages there can be little doubt that in the future it will become very popular with the Hindu pilgrim to Mansarowar and Kailas, though the central route will always claim a certain number of pilgrims, because by this means they can go by one route and return by another, thereby going from left to right, a consideration of great importance with the devotee. Nor is it to be forgotten that many a pilgrim who has visited Badrinath will be tempted to continue his way over the western approach by the Niti Pass, and will thence go the round of the sacred places in Tibet, eventually returning by the Lipu Lekh Pass and the eastern route to Tanakpur.

The public is now becoming familiar with the fact that Gartok is the seat of a Viceroyalty, but it has scarcely realised that there are two Viceroys or Garphans there, and that the system of Government is a dual control. Mr. Traill, the distinguished Commissioner of Kumaon, writing in the year 1825 in connection with Gartok, says: "The chief government is entrusted to two officers conjointly, who are called Garphans, with the additional title of Urgu Ma and Urgu Ya; they reside at Gartok, and are relieved after three years. Natives of Lhasa and of that neighbourhood are invariably nominated to these situations. The Urga Ma appears to enjoy superior consequence and consideration, but to give effect to his acts the concurrence of his colleague is indispensable." This state of things has continued ever since the days of Mr. Traill, and is in actual existence now, the only difference being that the titles have been changed, for the Garphans are now commonly known as Urgu Gong and Urgu Hog, the respective meanings of these euphonious titles being senior and junior, indicating that the former official enjoys the greater consideration and respect of the two. It has occasionally happened that the Garphans nominated from Lhasa have not themselves come to administer the offices with which they have been entrusted, but have sent confidential servants or relations to carry out their duties for them, a system which has only to be extended to India and our colonies to result in a great and immediate increase in the popularity of the Indian and Colonial services among Englishmen.

THE ACTUAL CREST OF THE LIPU LEKH PASS: PONIES RESTING: A BITTER WIND BLOWING

Mr. Traill makes another interesting statement with respect to Western Tibet. He says: "The only regular military force in the province is said to consist of two hundred horse, stationed at Gartok. This body must have been originally recruited from Tartary, as the men of which it is composed are described by the Bhotias as a horse-eating race. Each town and village has its enrolled militia, liable to be called upon whenever their services are required." There is now no regular military force at Gartok, and apparently there has not been for some years, but the system of an enrolled militia still continues, and men are liable to service at a moment's notice and, when called, are bound to appear mounted with gun and spear. The militia is not infrequently called out for the suppression of dacoity, or for the pursuit of dacoits and recapture of stolen property. The danger from dacoits is a real one in Tibet. These dacoits or Jykpas are a lawless body of men, with their hand against every man and every man's hand against them; but so great is the power they have, and so great is the terror that their name inspires, that there appears to be no systematic attempt made to put them down. They rob Tibetan officials, Bhotia or Lhasan merchants, and pilgrims of every country, and have no respect for the person or the property of any. They come to the trading-posts and engage in trade, they enter the holiest shrines and offer prayer, and give the richest gifts to the monasteries, and yet no hand is put forth to arrest them or bring them to justice. Occasionally, after some more than ordinarily brutal act of violence, the militia is called out to inflict some form of summary punishment; but apart from this no organised attempt is made to suppress them, and unquestionably, as the country is opened up to trade and pilgrimage, this special evil will have to be dealt with in a firm manner. The winter quarters of the Garphans are at a place called Gargunsa, situated two to three days journey from Gartok in a northerly direction on the Gartung-Chu, a main branch of the Indus. The whole population of Gartok migrates to this spot in the winter months, and there are to be found here many substantially built houses, a contrast to the few that exist at Gartok.

Just as the Viceroys of Gartok are supreme in civil affairs, so the Khanpo at Totling, also called Toling, which lies south-west of Gartok, is the Archbishop in all spiritual matters for the entire province. He ranks in honour officially with the Urgu Gong, or

YAKS: LEFT HAND ONE IS SADDLED PREPARATORY TO BEING LOADED: RIGHT HAND ONE HAS BEEN LOADED

Supreme Viceroy, and in universal respect he takes even a higher place. When he visits Gartok, as he did in 1904 by special request to offer prayers and work enchantments for the confusion of our expedition to Lhasa, the Garphans rise at his approach. The Khanpo, like the civil governors, occupies his post for a term of three years and is a native of Lhasa, or the neighbourhood, but, unlike the Garphans, he is never permitted to send a subordinate to represent him; he must be present in Totling in person. He further has a certain territory over which he exercises absolute authority, and he is in no case subject to the

Garphans: the only authority which he acknowledges is the supreme power at Lhasa. Toling was the capital of the ancient kings of Western Tibet and formerly a place of great political importance, while close to this spot is an iron chain suspension bridge, of cantilever design, said by some to have been built by Alexander the Great, and by others ascribed to the last king of Western Tibet. But its temporal glory has departed, and the ruins that are visible on all sides speak of a splendour that is no more. The city must have been abandoned four hundred years ago, and only a hamlet remains to mark what has been in the past. However, the monastery is one of the largest in this part of Tibet, having a population of three hundred Lamas; and, further, the estimation in which it is held has until recent years exceeded that which is shown for the monastery at Taklakot, although this latter place has lately become so rich from endowments of property, while the number of its monks has increased so greatly (they number 350), that it rivals the former now in importance, and desires to consider itself the Head of the Church in Western Tibet. The political advantage, therefore, which has been gained by throwing Gartok open is very considerably enhanced by the fact that adjacent to this centre of the civil authority are the headquarters of the supreme spiritual authority, and when the one place feels the effects of the outside influences which must shortly be brought to bear upon it the other place cannot fail to be similarly affected.

The province of Nari, or Western Tibet, is subdivided into districts, which are governed by officials who bear the title of Jongpen. Of these there are four, and a fifth who, although he does not bear the designation, still exercises the authority and enjoys the respect connected with that title. They are the

Nampa

A BEAUTIFUL VIEW: NAMPA (23,350 FT.) IN NEPAL: MORAINE-COVERED GLACIERS

Jongpens of Rudok, Chaprang, Daba, Taklakot, and the Tarjum of Barkha. Rudok lying as it does at the western extremity of Nari is brought into contact with some of the wildest and most dreary landscape in the world, and with geological phenomena of a weirdly interesting nature. The mean altitude of Siberia is little above sea-level, and of the plateau of Chinese Turkistan 2000 ft., while rising sheer above the plain to the south is the massive range of the Kuen Lun mountains with an average height of 20,000 ft. Nor is this imposing wall without support, for the plateau behind it, *i.e.*, to the south, is 17,000 ft. in height, extending with a gradually diminishing elevation, which is never less than 13,000 ft., up to the Himalayas themselves, whose line of water-parting is 18,000 ft., and whose snow-peaks stand out 10,000 ft. clear above the summits of the lower hills, which act as a buffer between them and the Gangetic plain which is but little above the level of the sea.

Rudok lies near the most elevated portion of this magnificent table-land, resting on Ladakh and the Karakoram range on the west, a giant chain commanded by Mount Godwin Austin, 28,250 ft., second alone in height to Mount Everest throughout the whole world, and touching on the north the bleak and dreary desert of Chang with the Kuen Luns in the background. Passes there are in the mighty Kuen Luns, but ever covered with snow, and impracticable to the trader as they lead from Chinese Turkistan into a country that is bleak and inhospitable beyond words, where immense herds of wild yaks, wild asses and antelopes roam, finding but slender sustenance; where, too, there is great scarcity of good water, for although the slope of the land is such that rivers can find no outlet and lakes are innumerable, yet the water is generally too salt to drink. Soda, salt and saltpetre are found everywhere, trees do not exist, and population there is none. A few hardy miners toil to wrest from the inclement soil its precious treasure of gold, which abounds on all sides, but the country invites none to visit it. Traders from Kashgar and the north prefer to face the Karakoram Pass, 18,550 ft. high, which yearly levies a heavy toll on the lives of beasts of burden, than the difficult passes of the Kuen Luns, which are almost impracticable. Central Asian caravans, after visiting Leh, pass near the Mo Gnalari Lake, on whose northern and southern banks are respectively the towns of Noh and Rudok, and thence continue their way to Lhasa through the goldfields north of Thok Jalung, which spot (16,200 ft.) is the highest inhabited all the year round in the world; or south through Gartok along the most frequented trade route in Tibet, which also leads to the Tibetan capital, past Kailas and the Mansarowar Lake. The distance from Gartok to Rudok is only a matter of some eight to ten days: there is a large population there, barley is cultivated and there is an abundance of salt, while the surrounding country is famous for its horses, which always acquit themselves well at the annual horse-races at Gartok, and invariably fetch a high price in the market.

The headquarters of Government are always at Rudok. Again the wisdom of throwing open Gartok by the Lhasa Treaty becomes apparent, for although Indian traders may not for some time visit Rudok itself, yet the mere fact that all the Jongpens and other officials assemble annually at Gartok for the fair ensures that the influence of the Indian Government will be felt as far north as this remote place. The road from Gartok to Leh, a distance of 200 miles, passes through the district of the Rudok Jongpen, going *viâ* Tashigong and Demchok on the Indus river, and does not present any very great difficulties. The Tibetans do a considerable trade with the inhabitants of Leh, with whom they are on excellent terms. The exports to Cashmere from this quarter of Tibet amount to £8000 annually, and are principally composed of wool, pashm, musk, salt, precious stones and tea, while the imports, valued at £5000 annually, are dried apricots (for which Cashmere is famous), European woollen and silk piece-goods, grain, sugar, tea and precious stones. A large quantity of solid cash finds its way also across the border. Pashm is obtained from the combings of the underhair of a breed of small goats, which are only found in the more elevated portions of the high table-land of Tibet. It is always much appreciated and fetches a high price in the market. A yearly caravan comes to Leh from Lhasa, apart from the trade of ordinary individuals, and every third year an official caravan visits Lhasa from Leh, bearing letters from the Maharaja of Cashmere for the Dalai Lama.

Although we may not in the near future hear so much of the Jongpen of Rudok, yet there is little doubt that we shall hear much of the other Jongpens and the Barkha Tarjum, for our relations with Tibet will throw us into intimate contact with them. Their charges are described in the following chapters.

When the expedition under Captain Rawling visited Gartok in 1904 it continued its journey through Shipki to Simla, a distance of 350 miles, which is generally covered in thirty-five stages, and the road is described as comparatively an easy one even during the winter months. It passes through a country rich in wool and pashm. To connect by means of a good road Gartok with Simla, the Tibetan Viceroyalty with the Indian Viceroyalty, will be only a question of time, and the fact that the mountains do not, comparatively speaking, present any very great difficulties, will assist in this work of speedy linking up, which should ensure the very best political results. At the same time we must remember that, to act effectually, we must utilise the natural routes and the easiest passes first. To spend large sums of money in opening up routes which will never be greatly used, and to starve others which are the natural means of communication, would be unwise. To connect Gartok with Simla is most expedient politically, and the sooner the link is riveted the better, while for the Hindu pilgrim wishing to visit Kailas and Mansarowar the natural route is *viâ* Pilibhit, Tanakpur, and due north over the Lipu Lekh Pass. These two routes excel all others and should be speedily put into good order. Further, it may be remembered that trade takes time to develop, but for the pilgrim the only requisite is a good road, and when expenditure is being incurred, let us not forget that the devotee is sure to be the pioneer of trade.

The Jongpens have divided the Customs derived from the different trade routes amongst themselves, and the arrangement has held good for years. The dues of the Nilang (or Lilang) Pass which leads through Tehri Garhwal to Mussoorie, together with those of the Mana Pass in British Garhwal, go to the Chaprang Jongpen; while those of the Niti and Untadhura Passes belong to the Daba Jongpen; and to the Taklakot Jongpen fall those of the Lipu Lekh Pass and the Customs paid by the Nepalese Humlis. Meanwhile the Barkha Tarjum, to whom fall the dues of the Darma and Lankpiya Passes, has found it worth his while to buy over from the Daba Jongpen certain rights to collect dues in his territory, and the result is that part of the profits from the large mart at Gyanema now go into his pocket. The largest markets at which trade is done, and which are only eight and twenty-five miles from our border, are Taklakot and Gyanema, and out of the whole trade of the United

THE DESCENT ON THE TIBETAN SIDE IMMEDIATELY AFTER CROSSING THE LIPU LEKH PASS. GURLA MANDHATA (25,350 FT.) IN THE DISTANCE

Provinces about nine-tenths are at present done at these two places. The actual trade with Gartok is very small, the reason being that traders are afraid of the ubiquitous dacoits or Jykpas, and they further find that the roads to Gartok are so rough that the wear and tear on their beasts of burden are very great.

Animals accustomed to the lower altitudes and easier roads of India find the rarefied air and rough tracks of Tibet very trying. Our traders, therefore, frequent these two places far more than any other. The total trade of Western Tibet with all parts of India, including Nepal and the native States, amounts to about £90,000 annually, and of this the United Provinces and Tehri Garhwal get £70,000.

The Tarjums are twenty-two in number, and their special duty is to be responsible for the postal arrangements between Gartok and Lhasa, a distance of 800 miles. They are posted, roughly, at a day's journey apart down the main trunk road to Lhasa (this road is a mere track), and each has a certain number of horses. As soon as the horseman arrives with the mail, it is their express duty to immediately arrange for the despatch of the letters to the next stage. And in cases of great urgency the rider is sealed on to his saddle to make sure that he will not dismount on the way to rest or smoke. Most of the Tarjums have a small tract of country over which they exercise authority, but not one in this western part of Tibet compares with the Barkha Tarjum, who rules over a territory which includes Rakas Tal and Mansarowar Lake and reaches to the British border.

CHAPTER XI

TAKLAKOT, OR PURANG: ITS OFFICIALS AND PRIESTS

THE extreme good-will of the Tibetans throughout the whole of this expedition is one of the things that must receive the importance that rightly attaches to it. Taklakot is many hundreds of miles from Lhasa, the post taking from three weeks to a month to cover the distance, and it was quite reasonable to suppose that the results of our expedition of 1904 would not be fully realised in such a distant portion of the Tibetan kingdom. However, our actual experiences were of the pleasantest, and the officials made it abundantly clear that, although they might not be in close touch with the counsels prevailing at their capital, still their desire was to treat us with friendship and cordiality, and that the Treaty of Lhasa marked a new era in their political relations with the Indian Empire. The first evidence of this good feeling was made apparent to us at Kalapani, which is eight miles from the pass on our side, for a messenger, a headman of a Tibetan village, saluted us there, and informed us that he had been sent to tell us that the Jongpen of Taklakot had heard we were coming (I had sent him the news) and had despatched his Nirba with a small party to escort us into his territory, and that this party was awaiting us at our next camp,

Sangcham. As we neared this place we were met by the Jongpen's Nirba and a party of five horsemen, one of whom represented the Taklakot Grand Lama (who

Nirba

JONGPEN'S NIRBA WITH ESCORT

The Tibetan saddle rises to a great height off the back of the pony, and the feet of the rider are placed in stirrups which come only a short way down, the object being to wrap the covering cloak well down the legs and so protect them from the high winds. Cloaks are frequently fur-lined on the inside

sits with the Jongpen in the administration of the district), and the others were leading gentlemen of the villages on the border. The greatest cordiality was shown on their side, and we were not slow to respond, with the result that from the very beginning a most satisfactory state of affairs was established. The Nirba made a small present of a rug and a few dried fruits, &c., saying that this was only a preliminary to further presents, which the Jongpen hoped to present personally on our arrival at Taklakot. On our side the Nirba and his party were entertained with food that evening, and next morning the Political Peshkar went to Taklakot to announce the time of our arrival, and took with him as a complimentary return present a table-cover and a silk handkerchief, both of which, we ascertained later, were much appreciated.

Sangcham camp was a cold, bleak spot, where fuel was not to be obtained, and where we had every possible discomfort. There was a bitter keen wind that numbed the fingers, a driving rain that penetrated everything, and, the altitude being 14,620 ft., every one's respiration was affected. Some men said they would die, others lay down like logs and never moved again till we started in the morning on our next march. Longstaff was kept very busy persuading unbelievers that death was not so imminent as it seemed, and that all should be stout-hearted and fill their bodies with vast stores of food so as to keep off mountain-sickness. But he was like a preacher of salvation by the eating of bacon to the sea-sick voyager in the Bay: men heard him not, and so next day on the pass some suffered untold agonies.

There is a very gradual ascent to the Lipu Lekh Pass all the way from Garbyang, the distance being seventeen miles, and ponies can be ridden up at a great pace. The height of the pass is 16,780 ft., and its position is such that very little snow, comparatively

THE VIEW OF TIBET FROM THE LIPU LEKH PASS (16,780 FT.). GURLA MANDHATA (25,350 FT.) IN THE DISTANCE

speaking, falls on it, with the result that it is open all the year round, and for eight months can be very easily negotiated. On the Nepal side there is the Tinkar Pass, quite close to the Lipu Lekh, which is of about the same altitude and is approached by just as easy a route. However, the Tinkar Pass is of little use to Nepal, as this portion of that country is cut off from the rest of Nepal by impassable glaciers and mountains; it simply affords an alternative route to traders from Garbyang.

Longstaff with his two guides made a short excursion into this district, ascending the great Nampa glacier lying in the valley to the north of the mountain of that name, and previously visited by Mr. A. Henry Savage Landor. Nampa is 23,350 ft. high, and as seen from Tibet is a grand pile dominating the entire neighbouring ranges.

The first view of Tibet from the Lipu Lekh Pass is magnificent, as, amidst all the other beauties of the landscape, the centre of the picture is occupied by four peaks, all over 22,000 ft., which are quite close together, the highest being Gurla Mandhata, 25,350 ft. This solid mass lends a grandeur to the whole which is quite awe-inspiring, and on all sides the most beautiful coloured rocks heighten the effect, so that the impression on the beholder is that the scene before him is truly one of nature's grandest handiworks. There are no trees or verdure to relieve the severity of what he sees, and the almost total absence of animal life adds to the feeling of intense desolation prevalent everywhere.

These divers colours among the rocks are quite a feature of the country all the way to Taklakot, and of the landscape round that fortress. There are sepia, burnt sienna, raw sienna, violet, all shades of yellow and many lovely shades of red. The brilliancy of the sunshine and the intense sharpness of all lines, added to the clearness of the air, which makes the most distant objects appear close, while all around is a penetrating glare, make one liken the landscape to

OUR FIRST CAMP IN TIBET AT PALA

nothing so much as that part of Arabia which one sees near Suez.

A descent of four miles brought us to Pala, which is a Tibetan outpost, the garrison being composed of one watchman, who is more frequently conspicuous by his absence than his presence. There is accommodation for travellers in the shape of two rest-houses, built to face north as a protection from the prevailing south wind. We camped in the lee of a knoll, and lazed the whole afternoon with our eyes riveted on the beauties of nature around us, and as moonlight softened the hardness of the lines and drew a veil over the severity of the picture, we found that evening hours had glided into night, and it was late before we could tear ourselves from things so beautiful, and even then the quiet scene, entering through the open tent, stole something from our sleep. The moonlight

SENTRY OVER LONGSTAFF'S TENT AT TAKLAKOT

Photo taken by moonlight in Tibet: Kodak film, five minutes' exposure, Voightländer lens. Note the sharpness of the shadows and of the detail. The sentry unfortunately moved

in Tibet is one of the most beautiful things in that country, and how often the words of Wordsworth came into our minds:

> "The moon doth with delight
> Look round her when the heavens are bare."

About one and a half miles from Pala cultivation begins with the village of Tashigong, and extends for miles. The fertility of the country round Taklakot is simply marvellous, and one sees fields of green crops

TAKLAKOT ON THE KARNALI RIVER, TRIBUTARY OF THE GANGES

reaching away into the far distance. Streams are diverted into well-made channels, and the water flowing from hamlet to hamlet irrigates the crops. All the fields are solely dependent upon this source of supply for moisture, and it is only where these channels are found that there are cultivation and verdure standing out in marked contrast to the barrenness of the surrounding country. The rainfall is obviously very small, and owing to the total absence of trees and vegetation on the mountains the water after a storm of rain must run off immediately in cataracts into the valleys, with the result that there is no moisture left in the soil. Nor is the falling of rain regarded as in any way a blessing; in fact, we were asked again and again to be most careful not to fire our guns anywhere near cultivation for fear that the concussion would bring on a storm of rain or hail, which might injure the crops. This was the one favour the Jongpen asked of us, and we, of course, readily agreed to it.

Purang, or Taklakot, is at the immediate foot of Gurla Mandhata and stands at the junction of three rivers, at the end of a high ridge which forms the apex of a V between the Karnali river and a stream flowing into it from the south. The position is a commanding one, and the fact that the cliffs descend sheer on three sides for 500 ft. must have made it difficult of assault in the past. On the fourth side is the ridge running at a uniform level for miles to the west. The residence of the Jongpen is a large white building to the east of the block of houses on the top, while the Gompa or monastery, rivalling in importance the Tolingmath sanctuary, is on the west, and forms the residence of a number of monks and the Grand Lama. These are the only buildings here, for although there is a small village of Taklakot, yet that name is generally applied to a tract of country where there are many villages, all at various distances from the fort itself. On this ridge there is no water, and, therefore, it would be impossible for the fort to become the

Orderly Syce

Nirba (Jongpen's envoy) Author Lama's envoy

OUR ESCORT INTO TIBET

nucleus of any considerable number of houses. All the inhabitants of the surrounding hamlets take it in turn to supply labour for the carriage of water daily from the spring below to the crest of the ridge, and as our camp was on one of the main routes used by the women who fetched the water, we saw them all day long passing up and down the hill, and heard their singing, which was very euphonious in the distance, resembling in some degree the yodelling of the Swiss peasants.

The Jongpen's Nirba is a petty official, who corresponds to the Kanungo of our hills in importance. This particular one was invariably associated in our minds with low comedy. He wore clothes and boots of the Chinese pattern, with a pigtail to make things complete, but his round Chinese cap had a peak to it which he kept over his right eye, like an eye-shade, and which looked so incongruous that, when further adorned by his beaming smile and plebeian countenance, and set off by his rolling walk, it made one immediately think of the stage in England. He certainly looked after us very well, and saw that all arrangements for us were perfect, and he did much to smooth down the petty inconveniences connected with an arrival in a foreign country. For instance, he had seen to the repairing of the bridge across the river, and conducting us through the village of Magram opposite the fort stood with us in the river bed and shouted directions with the best of us to the yak-drivers as our transport waded across the stream, and whenever we caught his eye he was immediately one broad beaming smile. He placed our camp on the bank of the southernmost river, next to the Bhotia bazaar and immediately under the fort, where we were quite close to the spring and were very comfortable. The Bhotias live in stone and mud huts, which are an admirable protection from the severe winds. For the roof they use cotton sheets, which admit the light and exclude the dust, and, as there is little fear of rain, they are the most suitable covering. On leaving Taklakot they remove these roofs and the huts remain empty and deserted till the following season.

The real Jongpen was at Lhasa, but was expected

at Taklakot after some little time; in the meanwhile, with the delightful simplicity characteristic of Tibetan government, his second son officiated for him. The eldest son would naturally have filled the post, were it not

Monastery and Fort

CROSSING THE RIVER TO TAKLAKOT

for the fact that he had been nominated as the junior Garphan, or Viceroy, at Gartok, apparently for services rendered to the State during the war of 1904, when he was wounded. By this promotion the eldest son ranks superior to his father.

The affairs of Taklakot were a little involved at the time of our arrival, for, shortly before, the Barkha Tarjum had been engaged in a quarrel with the Taklakot hierarchy, and had shot at, and killed, a servant of the Lama. The result was a summons to Gartok by the Viceroys of all the parties concerned, and the Tarjum of Barkha was absent as an accused person, while the Lama of Taklakot went as principal witness, and the real Jongpen's third son was called to explain any difficulties that might arise in the hearing of the case. So we found the Head Lama in charge of the monastery away, while a subordinate Lama performed his duties, and also the civil administration in the hands of a young man of twenty-eight years of age. It is then easy to understand how, in the absence of the heads of departments, these juniors were considerably perturbed at our visit, especially as they had no precedents to go upon. However, they played their parts with the greatest tact and cordiality, while we did our utmost to make their task an easy one.

In the afternoon of the day of our arrival the Jongpen and Lama in charge came to pay us a formal call, preceded by the Nirba at full gallop. The Nirba invariably rode a mare, which was accompanied by a very young foal. The mare was always full of spirits and it was generally as much as he could do to hold her at all, but, whatever the confusion due to mare, foal, and comedian, he never relaxed his all-embracing smile. The Jongpen's son was a very tall man of about six feet three inches in height, his dress was altogether Chinese in pattern, and although not in the least shortsighted he wore as an ornament enormous spectacles with glasses two and a half inches in diameter, a fashion common among high officials, while the Lama was a short man of very benevolent appearance, clothed in the universal monk's costume, and so painfully shortsighted that he needed glasses, which he did not have. Nothing could have been more friendly than the interview which followed, and which lasted about two hours. After the formal presentation of rugs, boots, a cap, dried fruits, &c., the visitors gave themselves up to an absorbing inspection of European

Lama's Attendant — Author — Jongpen's Attendant — Orderly

Rai Sahib — Pundit Gobariya — Grand Lama — Lama's Attendant — Nirba — Acting Jongpen (note the enormous spectacles) — My Serishtadar

THE JONGPEN AND LAMA

articles which were lying about in the tent. Guns, field-glasses, and photographic cameras were all most carefully examined, and much appreciated, while the general good humour was increased by the passing round of port wine in a tiny glass carafe and liqueur glasses. The Lama was a total abstainer, but not so the Jongpen, and as for the Nirba he at once asked for the whole bottle, but was made to realise that only the great folks were partaking at that particular moment. However, a sigh was whispered up to me that the Nirba hoped that, after the interview was over, the proprieties would allow him to have the bottle. The Lama was proof against cigarettes, and the Jongpen said he had made a vow a year ago not to smoke; however, he took a gold-tipped cigarette just to show good feeling and put it behind his ear, as a clerk does a pen. The Nirba said nothing, but his eyes and hands spoke volumes, for he knew these cigarettes, Longstaff having shortly before offered him some, when he could scarcely be dissuaded from taking the whole box.

The interview closed with a firm friendship on both sides, and our visitors were bid farewell with handshaking and much formality, the Nirba on his bounding mare being the only discordant element, for he nearly swept the Jongpen away in one of his wild rushes.

When we returned the visit as a compliment to the authorities, we did so in state with all my officials attending and the escort to the fore. The Jongpen met us at the gate of the fort, and conducted us up almost perpendicular stairs and along the darkest of passages, while prayer-barrels and prayer-wheels were turned zealously on all sides. The presents to the Jongpen included a handsome rug, black on one side and a design of leopards on the other, a leather hand-bag, a strong steel trunk, a light-blue sunshade, and, above all, the coveted glass carafe and liqueur glasses. It was ordained that we should drink the Tibetan spirit Arak (made from rice) out of the newly-presented glasses. The Nirba was anxious to clean the packing sawdust from the glasses with his finger, but some brave man told him to desist, when he resolutely wiped them out with a scrap of dirty paper. We all drank with the Jongpen, and there was the greatest good humour, which was enormously increased when some toys were presented by us. Musical boxes and penny trumpets were in great demand, but nothing

THE "CHUM," OR RANI, WIFE OF THE THREE BROTHERS

The tiara is of turquoise and coral; ear-rings of silver and turquoise; a silver charm is suspended from the neck; beads are fastened to the waist; the long boots are Lhasa-made. She is wearing a shirt with an apron, and a long robe (like a dressing-gown) with full sleeves. Behind the shoulders the hair is plaited, and the two ends are connected by coloured cord 2 ft. long

equalled the hen that ran along and flapped its wings. She was greeted with loud guffaws of delight, and so great was the general good feeling that the lady of the house, the wife of the three brothers, called by the familiar English name "chum," sent word to say that she wished to see the Pombo and the Amji, referring to myself and Longstaff. The former word means a high official and the latter doctor; but the ordinary word for Europeans is Peling or Piling. This was indeed a surprise, for she had previously declared that nothing on earth would make her see us, as she knew that our evil eye would blast her for ever. It was also told me later that she had one child, but was very anxious for another, and that some one had assured her that, if she would only see us, she would certainly very soon be the happy mother of a boy.

Anyhow, after a very long wait she came dressed in the most splendid state, with her face washed white (she generally has it smeared as a protection from the wind and wears a black patch on the nose), her hair brushed over the shoulders, a tiara of red balls of coral and turquoise on her head, and a silk sash over her gorgeous costume. It was explained to us that she was very sorry she had no better present to give us (what she gave us was really very good), for she quite realised that great things were expected of her as one of her husbands was a Viceroy-elect, and she hoped we would forgive her. Having said this much, she said she must go at once and feed her baby, but she would return soon and would like to be photographed, but by herself and not with any one else; and so she left us inwardly thinking she was quite capable of looking after three or, in fact, any number of husbands. In a few minutes, after what must have been a record quick meal for the child, she returned and was photographed by us, but not without endless questions as to whether she should stand or sit, as she thought she would like her dress to show at its best, and whether her hair was quite right, and as to how she should put her hands for the rings to show, and finally, as the critical moment came, she said her feet were not showing and she would like them in the picture. We were told later that after our departure the whole place was sprinkled with

Prayer-pole and prayer-flags

THE JONGPEN AND LAMA IN FRONT OF THE TEMPLE

water and devoutest ceremonies were performed, for the exorcism of all unpleasant spirits we had introduced into the fort. I can only say that the need for fumigation of our tent after *their* visit to us was only equalled by the number and size of the beasts of prey captured.

These officials of the "Forbidden Land" were at first a little anxious to cast a veil of mystery over things generally, and especially over all matters religious, and it was not for us to intrude where we were not wanted, but when the Jongpen came to our camp another day I took Landon's "Lhasa" and Waddell's "Lhasa and its Mysteries" and systematically took him through all the photos, pictures of persons, officials, temples and all the most sacred spots, and the most private details of the highest functionaries that are so beautifully portrayed in those two books.

I began with the Potala, the palace of the Dalai Lama, and ended with the Jokang, the cathedral of Lhasa and the most holy place in Tibetan Buddhism. His breath was completely taken from him, and, being a resident of Lhasa, he kept on recognising every spot, and would ejaculate from time to time the following and similar remarks: "Yes, and so and so lives by that gate." He knew also many of the officials and would give their names, when not printed under the photo, or would say: "I do not know this man, but I know those attendant lamas." When he had seen pictures of all that used to be so secret and mysterious in Lhasa, there was, in the words of Holy Scripture, "no spirit left in him." The finishing touch was to show him, in Waddell's "Buddhism of Tibet," the pictures of his gods and demons, of the service of the Lamas of the so-called "Eucharist of Lamaism," of the "Wheel of Life," &c., and when he realised that all the mystery of his religion was gone he was a different man, and even nicer to us than before, if that were possible, and certainly he held the British in the very greatest respect and those particular books in absolute veneration. He was, too, very humble about himself, and pointed out that he was only officiating, that he did not even wear the crystal button in his cap, which all Jongpens and his father wore, but still, officiating as he was, he ranked higher than all Tarjums, even than the Barkha Tarjum, who wore no button at all, not even a brass one, which is the mark of the lowest order of officials. He told us that the Daba Jongpen alone ranked with his father, and was entitled to the crystal button, whereas the Jongpens of Rudok and Chaprang wore the mother-of-pearl button, and came in the next order below. Of course his brother, the Viceroy-designate, would be able to wear the opaque blue button, which ranks next below the clear blue of the Council Ministers. The wearing of buttons as badges of office is also a Chinese custom.

He went home and told the Lama of the Gompa all that he had seen with his own eyes, about which there could be no deception, and the result was an invitation to see over the monastery, which was very readily accepted. His belief in his religion and the power of the Lamas was very strong, for when I had shown him in Waddell's book a printed charm of the Lamas specially guaranteed to protect from the death-dealing bullets of our guns, and some one in the crowd of listeners casually remarked that there were many Tibetans who had died from the bullets notwithstanding, he at once took up the matter in earnest, and pointed out that these charms by themselves were useless, but very effectual if the conditions attached to them were observed, such, for instance, as keeping from intoxicating drink, abstaining from women, &c. To break the conditions was to render the charm useless.

The Lama took me by the hand and led me from room to room, and up and down passages, some of them pitch dark, with low roofs and steps always in the most extraordinary places, trying in every possible way to show the greatest cordiality, while all the time he twirled the prayer-wheels which we passed fixed in the walls, and everybody before us and behind us did the same, until there was a whirr of revolving cylinders. The monastery at Taklakot thinks a great

THE GREAT BUDDHA IN THE TAKLAKOT SHIVLING (TEMPLE)

The altar is terraced, and on the terraces are images of the Saints, bowls for lights which burn in butter, and stands for lights. The whole is covered with precious stones. I think the feathers are peacocks' plumes

deal of itself, and, owing to increase of wealth, has begun to look upon itself as even superior to the Gompa at Toling, and as the head of the church in Western Tibet. To be, then, literally, conducted by the hand by the Lama in charge was a great honour, and this elderly gentleman even went so far as to say that he hoped I would give him a photo of the great brass Buddha inside, but as the idol was in a peculiar light it was not at all such an easy matter to take a photo. Still, he had windows opened and shut, kept the people back, and showed the greatest interest in all the preparations. At the entrance to the shrine there are pictures of demons and of the Wheel of Life, *i.e.*, of the phases of life in the Buddhist world, while in the main room, where the monks have their meals,

Banging cymbals

Drum beaten by stick like a reaping hook.

TIBETAN DANCERS WEARING MASKS

one sees a row of Chortens or funeral memorials facing the main door and lights burning before each, and images between the Chortens. All round the room there were hanging representations of deities (some of them very indecent), but the Lama, when questioned about them, said they were all old, and nobody there knew the stories of the gods or even their names. Certainly he could not tell the name of any deity, and had it not been for the assistance of Waddell's "Buddhism of Tibet" the whole would have remained a mystery. The Lama apparently did not wish to conceal anything, as he always seemed to tell all he knew, but he appeared to be absolutely ignorant about his own religion, and also of the books that were in the library. Leading off the main room was the library, and in it a very fine brass image of Buddha, viz., the one I had just photographed, surrounded by idols and burning lamps with a Chorten, or death memorial, placed immediately in front. In a third room there was a monk beating a drum and cymbals and reading a service from a book, while a prayer-balloon turned round and round driven by the hot air of a lamp. The drum is like a gigantic battledore and is beaten by a padded stick like a reaping-hook. The drum and cymbal are very common everywhere, and are the special instruments of the wandering dancers and singers, among whom generally the wife of the party thumps the drum, and expectorates on it to improve the tune, while the daughter bangs the cymbals.

In this room was the figure of a fierce warrior armed cap-à-pie, with helmet, bows, arrows, spear, sword and armour, and with pennons marked with one large eye on each, exactly similar to the eyes one sees on Chinese boats at Canton.

The Lama explained that boys come to the monastery when eight years old (we saw many of this age there) and remain as novices, or Chung Chung, until sixteen, when they have an examination and are promoted. They then become Dabas, or ordinary monks, still keeping the head shaved, and can choose whether they will join the order of Sakyas, the members of which eat and drink freely whatever they please, and in case of impropriety with women are only lightly fined, or the stricter fraternity of Giloos, to whom all wine and intoxicating liquor are absolutely forbidden, who may not smoke and for whom celibacy is a reality, the penalty in case of lapse being very severe. The supreme authority in disciplinary matters lies in the hands of the Labrang, or Abbot, who invariably hails from Lhasa, while in things spiritual the Khanpo, always a Giloo, and generally known as Giloo Khanpo, is the appointed chief, and is also a resident of the

TIBETAN DANCERS

sacred city like the Abbot. He is a recluse, living the greater part of his life in some cave and rarely seen by the public. His chief duties are in connection with special religious rites, and should a public curse or particular charms be required, as in 1904 against the British expedition, he is summoned to appear formally and pronounce specific spells and incantations. The Tibetans take great credit to themselves and their Lamas for the earthquakes which devastated the Kangra district and parts of the Punjab at the beginning of the year 1905, and point to them as the direct result of the potent spells resorted to in 1904 when our troops went to Lhasa and were formally cursed by all the most powerful wizards. "And to whom did the earthquakes do most harm?" they ask. "Was it not to the soldiers, whom we specially cursed, and who suffered terrible losses at Dharmsala?"

The Taklakot monastery is known very generally by the Hindu word Shivling (the Ling of Shiva) even among the Tibetans, the reason being that the numerous

This leaf folds in

TABLE AS USED GENERALLY BY TIBETANS

It stands on three leaves, which fold in, and the whole becomes a flat parcel, easy to carry on a journey. The pot is used for pouring water into bowls placed before the idols and is entirely of brass. Chequered boots (Baukch) as worn by Tibetans and Bhotias: the soles are of plaited string and the legs of woollen cloth

Hindus who go there on pilgrimage have given it this name, and this word has now come to be applied to any large monastery. Although this part of Tibet as far as Kailas annually sees large numbers of Hindu pilgrims and the shrines have many Hindu deities, *e.g.*, Khojarnath, which has no others, yet there is no trace of phallic worship and the Ling is quite unknown, never appearing in any temple or by any roadside, while the term is never met with except in this specific word Shivling. This is all the more remarkable when one remembers that the Tibetans obtained their form of Buddhism from India, where phallic worship is so general. There are certain monasteries at Lhasa known as Lings, but this is an entirely different word, meaning originally "garden."

The Shivling is exceedingly wealthy, having inherited large sums of money and land from pious donors, one of the most considerable estates being that of Jidikot, which one passes on the way to Khojarnath, and which at one time occupied a certain position of importance as the capital of a petty raja. On the death of the chief, the rani, as there was no son to continue the line, thought it best to obtain religious merit for her husband and herself, and so bequeathed the valuable property to the Shivling. As a matter of fact, the monastery is now far richer than the Jongpen, and special officers are appointed for the due administration of this wealth, the principal of whom is the Dazang, in whose hands is all executive power. He is generally chosen from among the local lamas. Subordinate to him is the Nirchang, whose term of office is three years, and who is the "Minister for Agriculture," all matters concerning tenants and revenue passing through his office. All the monks wear claret-coloured robes, and the distinction between the "yellow caps" and "red caps" lies in the head-dress and in the girdle, which are yellow and red respectively, though monks often go bare-headed.

In Tibet the question of the relations between the sexes is an open sore running through the whole of the national life, and offending every sense of decency which might otherwise exist in the wonderfully sturdy and virile race that lives in that country. In its aspect towards the church we find that in every family one boy must be set apart invariably for the priesthood, and similarly of the daughters one or more are assigned to perpetual virginity, nor are the children in the least consulted as to their own particular wishes. The girl's head is shaved, and she remains with her family in her village as a nun (Jamoo), or she goes and lives in some monastery where there are monks, or she combines a little of both lives; but it is not to be forgotten that owing to the inferior status of women a nun is considered scarcely better than the ordinary layman. At the Shivling at Taklakot there are some three hundred and fifty monks, who are distributed from the headquarters among numerous petty shrines, while there are only sixty in actual residence in that place. There are also here forty nuns, whose quarters are separated from those of the men; but although some attempt is made at this the headquarters to keep the sexes apart, yet in the smaller monasteries their rooms are side by side. It is small wonder, then, that men and women, who have been set apart to a life of celibacy from early childhood without their own wishes having been in the least consulted, should live in an immorality which is universally known, and which casts round all things holy an association of degraded impropriety. Yearly monks and nuns are ejected from their holy office, and girls who have taken the vow and are living in their own villages are punished for wrong-doing (and in respect of penalty Taklakot is three times more severe than Khojarnath); however, it is not the individual but the system which is to blame. What else can be the result of a society which is fundamentally rotten at the core?

Convents for nuns are unknown in this part of Tibet, but are apparently common in the central portion.

The marriage relations are quite wrong, as the prevailing practice of polyandry, combined with the fact

A TIBETAN WEDDING: THE BRIDE

that families never split up, but always and invariably (speaking broadly) remain joint, that is, all the descendants of common ancestors dwell in the same family mansion, removes from the home circle that veil which consecrates the marital ties and drags into garish publicity what should ever remain impenetrable. Should family dissensions compel the members to part and start for themselves a separate *ménage*, the whole property is divided into shares according to the male descendants, and the Jongpen takes first and foremost one share for the State, that is, for himself. "L'état, c'est moi" is better applicable to the Tibetan official than to any crowned head in Europe, and the Jongpen, with great care and thoroughness, chooses the best of everything for himself. It is scarcely to be wondered at that families remain undivided when the penalty for partition is so great. Families number as many as twenty and thirty members and the ancestral home grows to a great size. One of the first things one notices in coming fresh to the country is the large dimensions of the houses. Each household contains for all practical purposes three or four families, and one can imagine the atmosphere in which the children are brought up with polyandry all round them, and when the time comes for a girl to enter another similar household, and be the bride of numerous brothers, it may truly be said that there is no modesty left in her. Merchants and officials from Lhasa can anywhere get women throughout Western Tibet to live with them temporarily for the mere asking, even of the best local families.

In the midst of so much laxity there are still some stringent rules, the principal being that no marriage is to be regarded as binding unless and until the girl has been asked for from her parents with due formality. Sometimes a bridegroom is demanded for a daughter. The asker goes to the house of the parent and stands opposite the door, across the road, and takes his hat off to every soul that comes out of that house, be it the fair young lady, or the forbidding mama, or the complacent papa, who has a terribly searching eye for business, or even the last-joined scullery-maid: they must, all and sundry, be politely saluted, and these salutations must continue without intermission for days until the matter has been properly concluded. After

A TIBETAN WEDDING: THE BRIDEGROOM

settlement severe punishment is meted out to any man who takes liberties with the *fiancée.* The girl is generally eight to ten years of age, sometimes older, and the marriage ceremony takes place a few months after the formal asking. This is always attended by plentiful and liberal hospitality on all sides, but the actual binding portion depends upon the payment of hard cash for the bride, and the placing of a cobweb scarf (Khada or Khatag) of silk or cloth on the necks of all the bride's relations, and her own, and this custom is one of the chief ex-

A TIBETAN WEDDING: THE FINAL CEREMONY

penses in the marriage. A principal member of the man's family officiates in the ceremony of the scarf. This scarf is quite a feature of Tibetan life, for letters are sent wrapped in it, and when a petitioner approaches an official he lays the scarf on the floor to show his respect for the great man, and also, such is the popular sentiment, his feeling that, when the scarf is displayed, the other is bound of necessity to listen. For instance, some strolling dancers had been duly rewarded by us, but one woman sought a further present from a subordinate. He declined, whereupon she immediately produced a scarf and laid it on the ground, implying that he

TIBETAN DANCERS
Note the drum and mask in foreground

must now give something of necessity; and so in the marriage ceremony it seems to mean that the girl must of necessity be now given.

The bride then joins all her husbands, but it sometimes happens that husbands are numerous, and all do not find domestic bliss at home. These leave the household to make a home for themselves elsewhere, and by so doing lose all share in the family property; or they enter our territory as Khampas, which means in Kamaon naturalised Tibetans, and set up house for themselves there; or they visit the many unasked-for girls that exist in every village. It is a recognised custom that the mother's family shall bring up all illegitimate children, although there has been a departure from the recognised law at Taklakot in late years, as the father has been made responsible for male children, but this is considered very unusual.

The result of domestic life as described above is that a most unsatisfactory state of things exists in the society of this part of Tibet, which leads to very general impropriety between the sexes, and which forms a curse to a nation boasting so many qualities of endurance and manliness which cannot but otherwise call forth our admiration. Among these excellent qualities that of mercy cannot at present be reckoned, although to appreciate their stand-point one should go back to our own history only a couple of hundred years ago. During our stay at Taklakot there was a quarrel among the Tibetans of a village in which a man stabbed a woman through her breast, and she was dangerously ill in consequence of the wound. We asked the kind of punishment that the man would get, and the reply was that he would anyhow be beaten well, and to secure his confession every form of torture would be applied, such as suspending with the feet off the ground and driving splinters or needles up the quick of his fingers. In their desire to extort a confession the Tibetans resemble the Chinese. It is worth noting the practice that, if an accused person, although terribly tortured, refuses to confess, the accuser is tortured for bringing a false charge. Supposing the woman died, there were many things that might happen to the prisoner, for instance, instruments might be pressed on the temples until the eye-balls protruded, when they would be removed; or the skin of a freshly-killed yak might be taken

TIBETAN DANCERS
This party had visited India during the previous cold weather

and soaked in water to make it expand, when the victim would be sown up inside and cast into the sun, the result being contraction of the leather and death by pressure within a fortnight. But every death penalty could be commuted by a payment of one thousand rupees. Supposing the woman lived, a wooden board might be fastened round his neck and fetters be placed on his feet and the prisoner kept in the Jongpen's jail (Heaven help him!), or his foot might be cut off. This latter is a common punishment for thieving, as also the dropping of a heavy rock on the bound legs so as to fracture them, or the amputation of a hand, or both hands in the case of an habitual criminal. Immediately after the operation the remaining portion of the limb is dipped into boiling oil, and we were assured the effect was to prevent bleeding to death. An incorrigible criminal, who has had parts of his body removed without causing repentance, is seated on a red bullock or cow and transported to the border, ours or that of Nepal, and is left at the head of the pass, where he must assuredly perish, being maimed, unless some kind soul relieves his necessity.

The Tibetans hacked to pieces prisoners taken in the expedition to Lhasa, and their treatment in 1841 of the Ladakh troops belonging to Raja Gulab Singh, under the Commander-in-Chief Zorawar Singh, is also a case in point showing their horrible cruelty. This General established his headquarters first at Tirthapuri, and with 1500 men fought a great battle near Barkha against the Tibetan force of 8000 men, in which he utterly routed them, and followed up his victory by plundering monasteries and advancing to Taklakot, where he set up a form of administration. He compelled the Bhotias to trade in ways contrary to established practice, and on their complaining to Mr. Traill, the Commissioner, the latter came up to Kalapani with a small force to remonstrate, and gained his point. Hearing that the Chinese were sending reinforcements, Zorawar Singh left his Lieutenant, Basti Ram, strongly entrenched near Taklakot (the ruins of his fort are still visible), and with a handful of men attempted to place his wife in safety in Ladakh by personally escorting her as far as to Gartok. On his return he found that the Tibetan troops were between him and Taklakot, and an engagement took place at Toyo two miles from Taklakot. He was wounded in the knee and fell from his horse, when his men, seeing themselves outnumbered, threw down their arms begging for mercy. The only reply was a deliberate decapitation of every man, as if they were so many sheep. The whole Sikh army of many thousands of soldiers lost all heart and surrendered, and the men were beheaded in the most brutal manner possible.

Basti Ram with a few followers fled from his stronghold to Pala, whence he fled over the Lipu Lekh Pass, leaving camp fires burning and horses tied as a ruse to deceive the enemy. The bitter cold of winter almost annihilated the few survivors, and soldiers sold their swords, helmets and armour for a handful of grain. Some of these are still in the possession of the Rajbar of Askot, who has collected them as curiosities, and I have seen them. Had it not been for his generous assistance not a man would have escaped, and for this Mr. Traill, on October 18, 1842, gave him the following letter: "I give you this certificate as an acknowledgement of thanks for the good work you did in liberally assisting the Singhs who entered our territory from Tibet." As for the fallen Commander-in-Chief, the story goes that the Tibetans rushed upon him and pulled out his hair, which was like "eagles' feathers" all over his body, as they wished to keep it for the sake of future good fortune. Further, his flesh was cut up into small portions, and every family in the district took a piece and suspended it from the roof in the house, the idea being that the mere presence of the flesh of so great a man must of necessity confer a brave heart on the possessor. Rumour also says that these pieces sweated fat for many a long day, a sign which the most sceptical regarded as connected with the dead chief's bravery. There

THE TOMB OF ZORAWAR SINGH, COMMANDER-IN-CHIEF OF THE CASHMERE ARMY, AT TOYO, TWO MILES FROM TAKLAKOT

is a very big Chorten erected to Zorawar Singh at Toyo over his bones, and the place is regarded with veneration.

Subsequently the Nepalese invaded Tibet and there was some promiscuous fighting, but nothing of any importance. In the treaty that was finally made between the two countries the Tibetans undertook to pay an annual sum of Rs. 10,000, and this payment has continued for half a century. Apart from these two recent campaigns Taklakot has

Taklakot Fort Gurla Mandhata in clouds

Tank

TAKLAKOT AND GURLA MANDHATA (25,350 FT.)

THE DARK PARTS OF THE FOREGROUND ARE CULTIVATION. NOTE THE LARGE IRRIGATION TANK IN FOREGROUND

been a most peaceful abode, with the result that it has grown enormously in importance. It is worth remembering that the Nepalese have been by no means uniformly victorious in their conflicts with Tibet in the past, for in 1793 a Chinese force of 70,000 men penetrated the Himalayas and severely defeated the Nepalese in their own country.

The district of Taklakot contains thirty-seven villages,* which are situated on the banks of the Karnali and other streams that flow through this country. The houses are built of stone and mud or sun-dried bricks, and are very substantial and comfortable in appearance. It is this fact of dwelling-houses that makes this district stand out from the rest of the surrounding country, for travel wheresoever one will, one sees elsewhere very few houses and no village whatever with masonry residences except in a small portion of the Barkha Tarjum's territory, which adjoins the Taklakot district, and, being situated on the Karnali river, is really geographically a part of that district. The land surrounding each village is very carefully irrigated by means of water channels from hill-streams, and the crops are very fine. Barley, peas and mustard are the only crops sown, the output being on an average six times the quantity of seed placed in the ground. The soil is excellent and, if it were only treated a little more scien-

* These villages are: 1. Ser; 2. Khojarnath; 3. Kangji; 4. Gejen; 5. Doja; 6. Thanger; 7. Suji; 8. Kirang; 9. Mabo; 10. Kungarto; 11. Darkechin; 12. Gutkung; 13. Low; 14. Lukpoo; 15. Darjigang; 16. Jidikot; 17. Daikang; 18. Chokrow; 19. Phulak; 20. Chimi...ng; 21. Rilaser; 22. Gunnam; 23. Namey; 24. Magram; 25. Chilchung; 26. Tashigong; 27. Dalam; 28. Billi; 29. Taklakot; 30. Chetanchemo; 31. Toyo; 32. Lagon; 33. Dalaling; 34. Garoo; 35. Lin; 36. Tashilung; 37. Khilay.

tifically as regards manuring, the output ought to be very much larger than it is, but the total absence of trees renders the question of fuel an acute one, while the dung of all animals is utilised solely to replace firewood. There is no reason

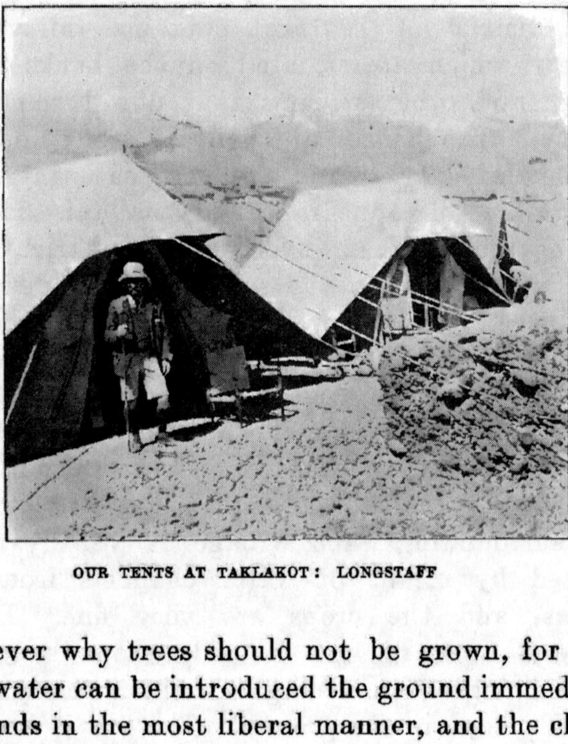

OUR TENTS AT TAKLAKOT: LONGSTAFF

whatever why trees should not be grown, for wherever water can be introduced the ground immediately responds in the most liberal manner, and the climate is such that snow does not lie on the ground for long even in the depths of winter. But mismanagement is written in large letters over the entire administration. The entire system of civil management is wrong. The Jongpen practically buys his office and then attempts to make as much out of it as possible, with the result that tenants are unduly squeezed and throw up their lands to emigrate into British territory. Men who have known the district for forty years say that the population has decreased in that period, and wherever we went it was only too plain that large tracts of land had gone out of cultivation which could easily and profitably have been growing fine crops. There must be a minimum cultivation in the district of 3000 acres at this present moment, possibly a good deal more, as it was difficult to see many hamlets which were snugly nestling in some of the valleys, but with a very little effort this could be doubled. The payment of land revenue takes the shape of cash (and it is to be noted that the land-tax has remained unchanged for centuries) and also of unpaid labour, the latter item being a very heavy tax. To start with, the Jongpen's fort and the monastery are on a waterless ridge, and every day the villagers take it in turns to supply water by personal transport to the fairly large population residing there. The villagers also cultivate the land of the lamas and the Jongpen without payment, and all land given up or relinguished is, so far as possible, added to the existing estates of these officials, the burden on the agriculturists thereby becoming heavier every year, as they have more and more free labour to supply. It is universally reported that the priests make the better landlords, though, of course, the Jongpen is the more feared. There are also pasture lands set apart for the horses of the officials, and the grass on these has to be cut, made into hay, and stored for the winter months, all of which duties the villagers perform without payment.

But the most trying of all exactions is the com-

VIEW OF THE HIMALAYAS LOOKING SOUTH FROM TAKLAKOT: THE DARK PARTS OF THE FOREGROUND ARE CULTIVATION

pulsory trade indulged in by all officials. The Jongpen and Tarjums make their fortunes out of tea, which is supplied from Lhasa. They buy at three rupees and compel the landholders to purchase from them at four, and if they cannot pay at once the debt is written down against them, to be collected later by seizure and sale of property. The result is general indebtedness, which is further increased by exactions on account of government transport and supplies. The official Government merchant, or Yungchong, comes from Lhasa with commodities of every kind, such as carpets, tea, cloth, &c., to be sold for the profit of the national exchequer. He travels free of charge; in other words, all villagers have to carry all his goods, including the government property and his own (for herein lies his profit), for nothing, and also to supply him with grass, fuel, fodder, tents and food without payment. He in turn sells to petty traders, who also receive duly signed warrants permitting them to receive supplies and transport free of charge, and these travel over the country as locusts devouring the people. If there is any deficiency in the local arrangements the Jongpen or Tarjum supplies from his own store and recovers the cost from the villagers, and it is a common trick to affect dissatisfaction with the supplies of humble landholders in order to exact further dues from them. The great annual fair at Gartok is principally composed of petty traders, who have gone there to meet the Yungchong, or official government merchant, and to pay up their accounts. Should the sheep or cattle of the Jongpen or Tarjum be stolen by dacoits, there is only one solution of the difficulty, and that is to recover the loss from the peasantry who ought to have prevented the robbery. It is owing to these endless exactions that the cultivators have fled from this district to our territory, and the history of the movement is written clearly enough in statistics, for the population of pargana Darma has almost doubled in the last thirty years, whereas in Taklakot there has been a decrease. Polyandry and celibacy have undoubtedly contributed their share to this result on the Tibetan side, while the more reasonable relations between the sexes amongst the Bhotias have also been an important item on ours.

Although the history of the agriculturist in the Taklakot district has been a chequered one, that of the trader has been the reverse, for during the last sixty years the trade has increased more than elevenfold. Nor is it possible to discover the exact dimensions of the present trade, as the old system of barter, although still continuing, is largely supplemented by the Indian rupee, and it is difficult to check the amount of solid cash and precious stones that cross the border. It is a patent fact, however, that the Indian rupee with all its fractions, and also the Indian copper coinage, are freely current in this part of Tibet, and I am informed, on good authority, that they are preferred in trade to the Tibetan coin and frequently to barter. Even the Nepalese coinage takes a prior rank to that of Lhasa in the popular estimation. Indian notes and British gold are still looked on with suspicion in this part of Tibet, which is in some ways a remarkable fact, as in the tracts of Nepal adjacent to these parts (and there is considerable communication between that country and Taklakot) Indian notes are at a heavy premium.

From the point of view of trade Taklakot is undoubtedly a rising centre, the principal reasons being that it is only 170 miles from the plains, the pass is easy, there are houses in which goods can be stored, when unsold, so as to be ready for the next season (this is a great consideration with traders, who at Gyanema,

KHOJARNATH MONASTERY ON THE KARNALI RIVER, TRIBUTARY OF THE GANGES

where there are no houses, and Gartok, where there is a dearth of houses, have to take back what is unsold or to sell at a loss); and lastly, the great wool country lying to the east of the Mansarowar Lake is most easily tapped from this place. As soon as the communications on our side are improved the effect should be rapidly apparent.

A visit to the monastery at Khojarnath gave us the opportunity of seeing the country with its picturesque hamlets and beautiful green fields along the banks of the Karnali river. The distance is about nine miles and the scene at the end of one's journey is quite fascinating. The monastery is on the banks of the river, which here makes a great bend, and the red colouring of the building set off by the paler hues of the village dwellings is charmingly reflected in the blue waters of the stream, while the great mountains in their many shades of sepia, red and yellow make an imposing background. There was a great fire at this monastery some five years ago and much of the interior, including books, fittings and ornaments, was destroyed. Since then the whole place has been redecorated in the most gaudy style and much of the interest attaching to the old surroundings has disappeared. We could not find one single Lamaist or Buddhist image, the principal idols being Hindu representations of Ram, Lachman and the goddess Sita (no one could tell us which was Sita as she was so like the male gods), and of the seven Rishis, or Sages, of Hinduism. There were also monster fiends acting as guardians of the entrance, a stuffed tiger, a stuffed yak and some fine antlers of the Sikkim stag, which resemble the horns of the wapiti of America. There was a service being held at the time of our visit, which consisted in the monotonous intonation of some liturgy by monks seated in two rows facing each other, while many wicks floating in butter cast a dim religious light, so dim, in fact, that it was impossible to see anything in the greater part of the building until a lantern was brought. There are sixty monks at this monastery and with them about a dozen nuns, all living in quarters adjoining each other.

As we returned to Taklakot we could not help being struck by the particularly commanding position occupied by the fort, and the extremely quaint dwellings built in the rocks and caves of the cliff, which, being painted white, are visible from a considerable distance. This is, so to speak, the "High Street" of Taklakot, connecting between the Bhotia Bazaar on one side of the river and the Humli and Nepalese encampment on the other. It is quite an ordinary occurrence to see members of the fair sex washing or combing their hair, and even bathing in the stream. Women wear knicker-bockers, the Baukch boots of many colours, a skirt and a dressing-gown, and sometimes a waistcoat without sleeves, and when they wish to perform their toilette or their ablutions they simply remove the dressing-gown, and stripped bare to the waist do all their desire in the utmost publicity, often holding a running fire of conversation with the passers-by. One could not help wondering what the public and the ever-observant policeman would say to such a state of things, say at the Serpentine or Richmond Bridge.

Frequent interviews with the Jongpen had produced the greatest friendliness and intimacy, and it was quite a pleasure to show him some of those things in which the West differs so conspicuously from the East. We explained the half-penny post of India and the penny post to England, both open to rich and poor alike, and he feigned to understand, but in a country where the only post is that of the officials it was impossible for him to realise the full meaning. He was immensely impressed with the fact that the *Pioneer* newspaper was published daily, and that in it there were telegrams from England only a few hours old, but he was much more impressed with the advertisements. He was ever anxious for medicine to make his hair grow (he had a beautiful head of hair) and to make his skin white, and could not grasp why such things were not in Longstaff, the Amji's, line. "The doctors of Lhasa have plenty of

THE "HIGH STREET" OF TAKLAKOT

NOTE THE CAVE-DWELLINGS AND HOUSES BUILT INTO THE ROCK: MANY PEOPLE BATHE IN THE RIVER HERE.

O

such medicines," he used to say, "and, therefore, why not those of Europe?" He revelled in the Hair Restorers, Skin Beautifiers and all the accompanying pretty pictures of the advertisements, and thought the paper wonderful. I had some copies of the Illustrated *Petit Journal*, which comes out weekly and always contains two full-page coloured cartoons, as well as two pages of photographs, the whole for five centimes. He thought the price absolutely extraordinary; in fact, he took some time to believe it. He was particularly interested in the sinking of ships in the Russo-Japanese War (about which he knew a good deal) and a picture of His Gracious Majesty in Paris. He could not understand how the Shah of Persia and the King of Spain (of whom he saw pictures) and our own King went visiting in each other's countries; "it is," he said, "so opposed to every thing in Tibet, where the Dalai Lama is rarely or never seen."

We parted on the very best of terms, and a bottle full of scent for his Rani (or rather Chum) seemed to cement what had already become quite a fast friendship.

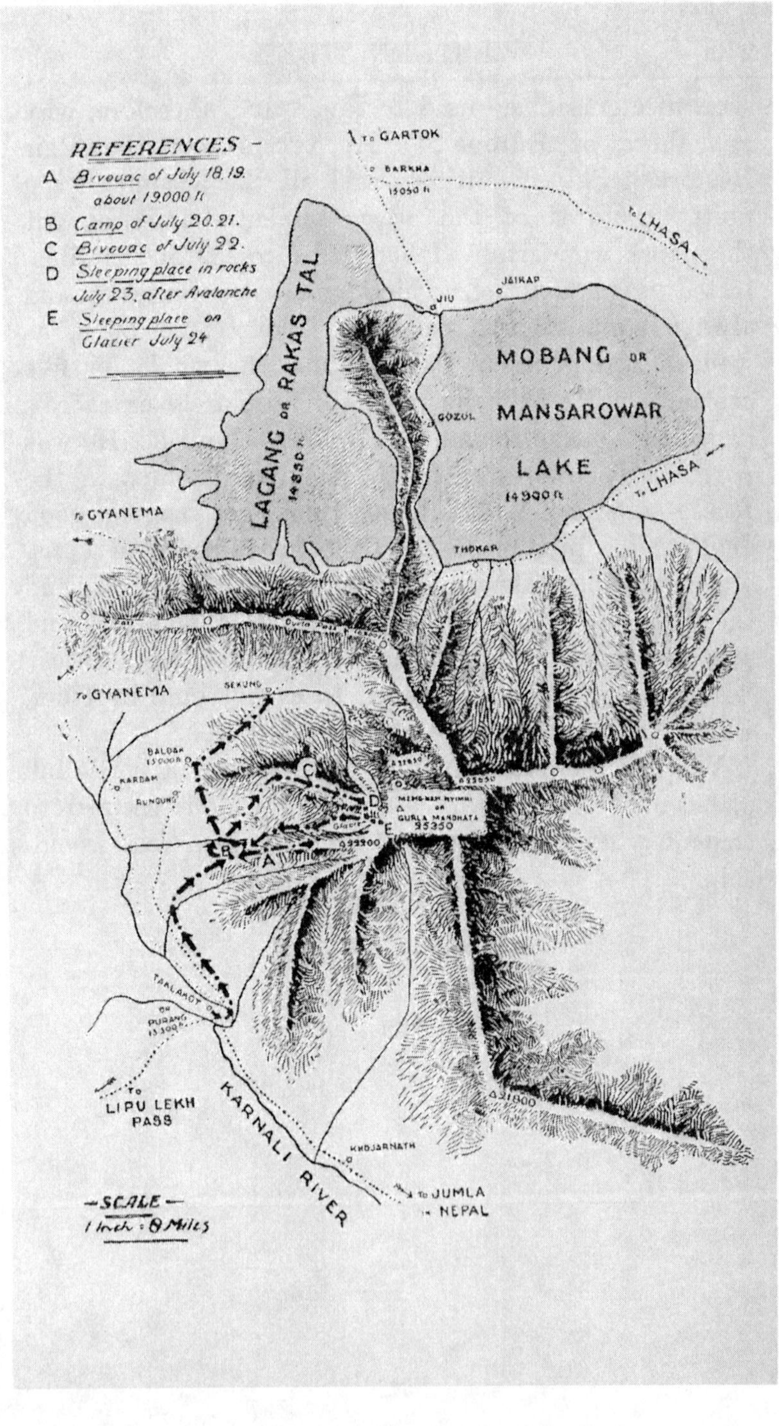

REFERENCES -
A Bivouac of July 18.19. about 19,000 ft
B Camp of July 20.21.
C Bivouac of July 22.
D Sleeping place in rocks July 23, after Avalanche
E Sleeping place on Glacier July 24
TO GARTOK
BARKHA
15050 ft
TO LHASA
JAIKAP
JIU
MOBANG OR
MANSAROWAR
LAKE
14900 ft
GOZUL
LAGANG OR RAKAS TAL
14850 ft
TO LHASA
TO GYANEMA
THOKAR
TO GYANEMA
SEKUNG
BALDAK
15000 ft
KARDAM
RUNGUNG
MEMO NAM NYIMRI OR GURLA MANDHATA 25350
22200
21900
TAKLAKOT OR PURANG
13,300 ft
TO LIPU LEKH PASS
KARNALI RIVER
KHOJARNATH
TO JUMLA IN NEPAL
-SCALE-
1 Inch = 8 Miles

CHAPTER XII

AN ATTEMPT TO CLIMB GURLA MANDHATA
BY T. G. LONGSTAFF

I HAVE to thank the author of this book for much official help and many private kindnesses during my mountaineering trip among the snows of Kumaon: further, it was he who obtained permission for me to accompany his party to Tibet. When, therefore, he asked me to write this chapter, I felt that it was not only a compliment but that compliance was a pleasant duty. I can only hope that the reader will not think this addition to the book is out of place.

Gurla Mandhata, or Memo-Nam-Nyimri, or Memo in brief, to give it its Tibetan name, is a group of snow-clad peaks, the highest of which attains an altitude of 25,350 ft.,* the others being 22,850, 22,650, and 22,200 ft., according to the latest sheets of the Survey of India. This massif lies close to the north-western corner of Nepal and the Kumaon frontier, but is situated wholly in Tibet, and is probably the highest mountain lying entirely within the limits of that country. So far as the writer is aware, no previous attempt has been made to ascend it, or even to explore its numerous glaciers, the reason being doubtless the political rather than the physical difficulties of access.

* On the map illustrating Captain Rawling's paper and published in the *Geographical Journal* for October 1905 (vol. xxvi. No. 4) the height of Gurla Mandhata is given as 25,850 ft.

LOOKING BACK TO THE HIMALAYAS FROM THE PLAIN BELOW GURLA MANDHATA. MORNING CLOUDS RISING

I started from Taklakot on July 18, 1905, with Alexis and Henri Brocherel of Courmayeur (with whom I had been climbing in Kumaon) and six Bhotia coolies

Lower spurs of Peak, 22,200 ft.

VALLEY TO THE SOUTH OF THE FIRST RIDGE A: VIEW LOOKING DUE EAST

who had come with us over the Lipu Lekh from Garbyang. We followed the track across the Karnali, which, after penetrating the Himalayas of Nepal, eventually flows into the Ganges, and past the tomb of Zorawar Singh to the foot of a great buttress on the western side of the mountain. As we had never yet had a clear view of the group, and had never seen its highest peak, the choice of this particular buttress was mere guess-work. I may remark that we found efficient reconnoitring one of our most difficult tasks in the Central Himalayas this summer, partly owing to persistent clouds and partly to the physical configuration of the ranges. Even more than in the Alps and the Caucasus does success depend on getting a good view from some moderately distant point before a new peak is actually attacked. Once upon the mountain itself, or even at its foot, it is frequently quite impossible for the climber to see what lies ahead of him. Had we had a clear view of Gurla Mandhata from the Lipu Lekh, we should have hit off the proper route much sooner, and thus having more strength, more time and more food at our disposal, I believe we should have succeeded in our last attempt, and so improved on the record of 24,000 ft. established by Mr. Graham on Kabru more than twenty years ago.

We began the ascent of the buttress (*vide* sketch map) at mid-day, and toiled up steep and apparently interminable stone slopes till six o'clock. By this time we had reached an altitude of about 19,000 ft., an ascent of some 6000 ft. from Taklakot.* It had been a perfectly easy walk, and I was not carrying a load; nevertheless I was suffering from severe headache. The guides did not appear to suffer any inconvenience from the altitude, but our six coolies straggled in all more or less affected with headache or breathlessness. They were immensely relieved when told they might leave us and spend the night and the next two days at the foot of the mountain.

* Taklakot is 13,300 ft. Plain of Baldak is 15,000 ft.

Our Mummery tent, 6 ft. long, 4 ft. wide and 3 ft. high, weighing about 4½ lbs., was quickly pitched, and in spite of the glorious sunset I at once crawled into my sleeping bag to rest without joining the guides at their supper. The night was fine and very cold, but in the morning the clouds were down on the ridge above us, so as I still felt unwell we decided that it was no good making an early start, and that I had better have a day's rest. And a glorious day it was. Clouds hid the snows above us and also the great peaks of Nepal and Kumaon, but 120 miles to the west Kamet (25,443 ft.) was visible from base to summit, a mighty cone keeping guard over the Niti Pass into Garhwal. Below, a great plateau extending westward as far as the eye could reach, bounded on the north by the Gangri peaks and in the far north-west by a range of mountains, partially snowclad, and probably that separating the sources of the Indus from the valley of the Sutlej.

I boiled a thermometer (Hicks') lent to Sherring by the Superintendent, Trigonometrical Surveys, and found that snow-water boiled at 169 degrees to 170 degrees F., indicating an altitude of 23,000 ft. But we were certainly not as high as this. Similarly at our bivouac of July 22 melted snow boiled at 165 degrees F., indicating an altitude of 25,400 ft.—a still more absurd result, for the summit of Gurla is only 25,350 ft. above sea-level by triangulation. The above calculation is based on the fact that 176 degrees gives 19,900 ft. and every degree decrease in boiling-point means a rise of 500 ft.

During the morning the two guides made a short reconnaisance up the first snow dome on our ridge, but the clouds prevented them from seeing where they were, and thus unwittingly we lost another day.

Next morning (July 20) we roused up soon after midnight; but making tea at this altitude is such slow work that we did not get off till two o'clock. Very slowly, in spite of the intense cold, we climbed the last stone slope; then the rope and crampous were put on and we began the ascent of a steep dome of snow. After turning a few crevasses we worked over towards the north, and suddenly we had a glimpse of Rakas Tal far below us, though Mansarowar itself was hidden by another great shoulder of the peak on which we stood. There was a grand moon to light us, and we had no need of our lanterns. Gradually, by almost imperceptible degrees, came the dawn, and the shadows melted from the valleys. Suddenly one of the great peaks of Nepal caught the first rays of the sun. It was far away to the south-east, seeming to over-top all its neighbours: it was perhaps Dhaolagiri (26,826 ft.), 180 miles away.

But a great disappointment awaited us on reaching the top of the ridge. We saw that the peak we were making for was not the highest one of the group, but evidently that marked 22,200 ft. on the map. Opposite to us, across a deep chasm down which flowed a beautifully white glacier,* was another great ridge leading up to the true summit. There were two possible routes to the top, one by the glacier below us and the other by the ridge just mentioned. I favoured the latter for several reasons. It would obviously be practicable to take coolies up to 20,000 ft. on it and make a bivouac on a patch of rocks amongst the lowest snow-fields. On the ridge there would be no danger of avalanches or falling stones; it looked fairly easy; and

* As this is one of the largest glaciers of the group, if not the largest, I propose to call it the Gurla Mandhata glacier.

lastly, I thought that we should find it less oppressive than toiling among the seracs and crevasses of the glacier below. However, in justice to Alexis it must be recorded that he favoured the other route.

RIDGE TO THE SOUTH TAKEN FROM ABOVE A
South-western gorge of Gurla Mandhata: mountains of Nepal beyond

There was nothing for it but to turn back, so we descended to our bivouac and had some food. Our camp and stores were packed up, and down we went, the guides very heavily loaded, to rejoin the coolies waiting for us below. On the way down I wounded a burhel (*Ovis nahura*) which, I regret to say, got away. Alexis put down his load and went after it, but without success. Meanwhile I tried to carry his pack, but it was with the greatest difficulty that I could get along with it at all, even down the easy slopes we were on at the time; it must have weighed very nearly 100 lbs.

Near the foot of the ridge we met the coolies and gave up our loads with no great regret. The two guides returned to Taklakot with three coolies for more petroleum and provisions, while I went on with the other three and made a camp at the foot of the next spur to the north of us by the side of the stream flowing down from the Gurla Mandhata glacier. On the way I managed to knock over a goa (*Gazella picticaudata*), the curious broad-muzzled gazelle of Tibet.

That night I had a grand twelve hours' sleep with the Mummery tent all to myself, and spent the next day very pleasantly in doing nothing. The guides got in about three o'clock after a very long tramp from Taklakot with supplies from Sherring, and almost immediately started off after a herd of burhel that were grazing on the slopes above us, bringing back a most acceptable store of fresh meat at nightfall.

At eight o'clock next morning, July 22, we started off with five coolies (they insisted that one must be left to guard their store of food) and tramped up a ridge very similar to the first one we had attacked, till half-past three in the afternoon, when we reached the first patch of snow from which we could get water. As before, I had a splitting headache, but the views on the way up almost reconciled me to it. Kamet and its attendant peaks were again magnificent, and we could distinctly make out the Sutlej, running westward through the Tibetan Highlands on its way to the plains of the Punjab through the Himalayas of Bashahr.

As before, we sent the coolies down, this time with orders not to expect us back for two or even three days: as a matter of fact, we were not to see them again for five days. This bivouac was a very high one: by comparison with the peak 22,200 ft. of the survey, I should estimate our altitude at about 20,000 ft. However, we did not feel the cold severely, at any rate not nearly so much as one night we spent at 19,000 ft. on

CREST OF GURLA MANDHATA FROM ABOVE C

The ridge along which we went on July 23; route indicated by dotted line

Nanda Devi in June. But I still felt unwell and consequently we did not get under way till nearly five o'clock on the morning of July 23.

The snow was in good condition, and the ridge quite easy at first, but proved to be much longer than we expected. We had left our tent and sleeping bags at the bivouac, carrying only two days' food, and thus lightly laden seemed to be making good progress. At two o'clock we reached a point at least 23,000 ft. above sea-level: from it we looked right over the top of the sharp peak marked 22,200 ft. on the map, which lay on the further side of the Gurla Mandhata glacier. In front of us a steep descent led down to a gap in the ridge, from which again rose the final arête leading to the

PEAK 22,200 FT. SOUTH-WEST OF GURLA MANDHATA FROM ABOVE C

summit, which still seemed a long way off. The usual afternoon clouds were already gathering in a threatening manner, and a lively discussion arose as to what we should do next. If we went on we should have to spend a night on the exposed ridge probably at an altitude of 24,000 ft., with no wraps except our gloves and jerseys. Henri suggested descending into the gap and passing the night in a hole in the snow. Alexis and

SUMMIT OF GURLA MANDHATA AND GURLA MANDHATA GLACIER FROM ABOVE A: BEFORE SUNRISE

Dotted line indicates route

I, however, thought it would be much wiser to descend the southern slope of our ridge and spend the night among some rocks which we could see standing up out of the snow slopes below us, finishing the ascent next day (as we fondly hoped) by the Gurla Mandhata glacier and the southern ridge of the peak.

We reached the gap about 3 P.M. and started to descend the slope. We moved down only one at a time, driving our axes deeply into the snow, for the slope was not quite to our liking. At first all went well, and we descended three or four hundred feet in this fashion. I had let down Alexis the full length of his rope while Henri steadied me from above. Just as I turned to take in the slack of Henri's rope I heard a curious hissing sound above me: the newer layer of snow, lying on an older and harder layer, had slipped from it; we had started an avalanche. Henri, lying flat, and trying hard to stop himself by driving the pick of his axe into the snow, came down on the top of me and swept me from my hold. As I shot down past Alexis I felt his hand close on the back of my coat, and we went down together. The sensation was a very curious one. The mind seemed quite clear, but curious as to the end rather than terrified. Time seemed annihilated, so slowly did thoughts seem to pass through the mind during the minute or so of our fall. The glacier below, with the rocks just above it, seemed to be rushing up towards us at an incredible pace, just as the engine of an on-coming train grows bigger and bigger each instant as it approaches. I distinctly remember throwing off my snow-spectacles for fear that I should damage my eyes when we reached the rocks below!

After what seemed an age I heard Alexis shouting "à droite, à droite!" I knew he was somewhere to the right of me and was trying to get us into safety. He had seen a gully filled with snow down which he hoped we might slide in safety past the first rocks to a large snow-bed far below. However I could do nothing but try and keep on the surface of the sliding snow. Presently I got turned round with my head downwards, and saw, a few yards off, a ledge of rocks with a drop on the far side. I seemed to rise on a wave of snow and dropped over a low cliff with Henri somehow or other mixed up in my part of the rope. We were, of course, *in* moving snow, and we fell *on to* moving snow, so our pace was only slightly checked and we hardly felt the shock of the fall. On we went, with the rope round my neck this time, but it was easy to untwist it. Then came a longer drop; surely this must be the last, I thought, when suddenly, to my intense surprise the rope tightened round my chest, stopping me with a jerk which squeezed all the breath out of my body. The avalanche had spread out and stopped of its own accord on a somewhat gentler slope of soft snow. Henri was half buried above me and Alexis was away to the right. I suppose that, being much lighter than either of them, I had been able to keep more on the surface of the avalanche. Both the guides lay quite still. The rope was so painfully tight that I cut it. I called to Alexis, who replied in an injured tone, "Why have you cut the rope?" It was a silk one—for lightness—and we had always been very careful with it. Then I started up towards Henri, who had not moved. However, he was merely more breathless than the rest of us.

By this time the reaction had set in and my knees were fairly knocking together. We crawled to the nearest rocks to take stock of the damage. Alexis was quite unhurt; Henri and I had only a few cuts and grazes. We had all three lost our topees and ice-axes, and the two men had each broken a crampon. We had fallen a thousand feet at least, and we fully realised what a miraculous escape we had had. I think we were to blame in having ventured to descend *any* steep Himalayan snow-slope after the sun had been on it all day, especially as most slopes in these mountains are really steeper than they look. In the Alps the reverse is usually the case, while the snows of the Caucasus take an intermediate position.

The men with great pluck at once started up again to recover the ice-axes, whilst I cautiously descended the rest of the slope towards the rocks where we intended to spend the night. On the way down I saw one of the topees; of the others there was no trace. After a little search I found a small platform of rocks, half overhung by a big boulder, and built a low stone-wall round one side to keep the wind off. The men came down about eight o'clock, having recovered all three ice-axes, a very fine performance on their part. Our dinner consisted of a box of sardines and a slab of chocolate, washed down with water. We put on what few spare clothes we had with us, and curled up for a cold night. However, sleep would not come to me, and, worse still, I had very little tobacco!

In the morning (July 24) we found that we had several rock gullies to descend before we could take to the glacier, and as we spent some time looking for our hats we did not start upwards again till half-past six, when we took to the upper part of the Gurla Mandhata glacier. Soon we began to feel the power of the sun, and Alexis most generously insisted on my wearing his topee, he and his brother wrapping jerseys and handkerchiefs round their heads. The glacier was much crevassed, but fairly easy when taken in big zig-zags, and the snow was hard. We toiled on as fast as we could and seemed to make height rapidly. But the heat in the hollow of the glacier was most oppressive,

BIVOUAC OF JULY 24–25 ON GURLA MANDHATA

and at two o'clock Alexis collapsed with a sun-headache. We put him into the shade of a small serac and told him to try and get some sleep. It was very hard luck on him and most unfortunate for our climb: we quite thought that we could get to the top of the peak and get down the short steep bit just below it before night-fall, finishing the descent with the help of our old tracks by lantern light. But Alexis was too ill to go back alone and we did not like to leave him to wait for us in such a condition. Henri immediately set about making a hole in the snow for us to sleep in. He is a great believer in this mode of spending the night; but then he never feels either cold or fatigue. I tried to help, but found the work was too heavy for me at that altitude, which in our opinion was over 23,000 ft. It is interesting to note that this is in any case the highest spot at which any one has ever attempted to pass the night, and that none of us suffered from the old orthodox symptoms of mountain sickness, such as bleeding from the nose and ears—or gums, as one ingenious writer has recently put it. In this respect our experiences entirely agree with those of W. W. Graham during his record ascent of Kabru.

Our food was nearly finished, so dinner had to be dispensed with. I wrapped my putties round my feet, coiled down the rope on the cold floor, and hoped that the roof would not fall in upon us. I dreamt that Sherring had sent a square khaki-coloured water-cart full of warm wraps up the glacier to us. However, when it arrived it contained only stockings, and the driver, in spite of my violent abuse, insisted that we were only entitled to one pair each. Hence I was so cold that I roused up the men about 2 A.M. on the 25th.

There was very little breakfast to have, so we started off by lantern-light in half an hour, threading our way up an icefall among big crevasses. After about an hour's climbing we were stopped by a crevasse with a veritable wall of ice on the far side. We tried to get across in two places, but it was soon evident that we must wait for daylight to find some way round it. I got colder and colder and indeed felt quite incapable of climbing another step. Want of sleep and food, I think, were more responsible for my condition than the altitude, which may have been over 24,000 ft; but as my barometer had been smashed a month earlier in

Nepal on the glaciers of Nampa I had no means of accurately estimating the height we had attained. The summit seemed to be within easy reach. The guides both insisted that we were only 300 metres from the summit. Personally I think that we were about 1500 ft.

SNOUT OF GURLA MANDHATA GLACIER: MAIN WESTERN GORGE OF GURLA MANDHATA, JULY 25, 1905

from the top, but as I have already mentioned, my barometer was broken and my attempts at boiling the thermometer were a fiasco, so that all we had to go upon was a comparison of the triangulated peaks around us. Henri urged me to persevere. "If you turn back now, and do not finish the ascent, you will regret it very much when you get down into the valley," said he. The natural retort was that, if I did not turn back at once, I never should get down into the valley.

And so at four o'clock we turned downwards. For men in good condition it would have been easy to complete the ascent, for the mountain is not really a difficult one by this route. But we had been climbing

GURLA MANDHATA FROM GURLA MANDHATA GLACIER

Note the fretted appearance of the seracs, probably due to excessive evaporation caused by the extreme dryness of the atmosphere

for two days on short commons, and had spent two nights without any proper covering. I was utterly exhausted and Alexis, not yet recovered from his headache, was in little better case. For Henri it must be said that he was not only willing to go on, but very much disappointed at my refusal to do so. I quite believe that he would have gone to the top alone.

In three hours we quitted the glacier and took to the moraine on its right bank. Here we finished our last scraps of food and had a couple of hours' sleep. Then down over endless moraine and still downwards beside the glacier stream till at four o'clock in the afternoon we reached our camping-place of the 21st. Here we expected to find our coolies, but they were nowhere to be seen, and as our camp, with food and rifles, was some four or five thousand feet above us on the great western spur, we pushed on to Baldak, and thence to Sekung, a camping-place, which we reached at half-past nine that night, thinking all the time what we would order for dinner when we got there.

We had spent a week on the mountain, and after a good deal of hardship had only succeeded in finding out the proper line of attack. People often ask what is the charm of mountaineering. Sir Martin Conway has endeavoured to answer the question,* and I have no desire to enter into competition with him. If mountaineering is such a poor game as many people make out, why is it that climbers are always looking forward to their next campaign instead of giving it up and taking to croquet?

* *Cf.* "The Alps," chap. i.

CHAPTER XIII

RELIGION AND GOVERNMENT IN TIBET

THE spiritual heads of the Tibetan Church are the Grand Lama of Tashilhumpo (Shigatse), aged twenty-four years, who has a great spiritual personality but little territorial power, and the Dalai Lama at Lhasa, whose authority is supreme in church and state. The latter has been hitherto ever a minor :—the ages of the last four incumbents being eleven years, eighteen years, eighteen years and eighteen years. A regent (Gyalpo) is consequently a perpetual necessity, and he makes it his business to see that his ward never attains majority. On the death of a Dalai Lama his soul reincarnates into a new-born infant, and curiously this infant generally belongs to a wealthy family: Tubdan Gyatso, the present Dalai Lama, took the precaution to poison his regent, and so has survived to the age of thirty years, the first to attain majority in the last one hundred years.

In Tibet the ordinary mortal transmigrates, while the Dalai and Tashi Lamas and many others reincarnate, and one must know the difference between transmigration and reincarnation, since half the pleasure of Tibet is lost unless one knows the rudiments of the Buddhist faith and a few of the more obvious teachings of the Lamas. The country is the most intensely religious of all the kingdoms on our earth, for the gods and demons of Tibet rival the two million deities of Hinduism in

TIBETAN CHARM, JUG, AND BELL

Silver casket with charm worn on the person

Jug for pouring water into the small bowls which are placed on altars in front of the idols

Bell with thunderbolt handle (dorje) commonly used by lamas in all temples. Note the face on the handle

their number and ferocity, while the government is in the hands of the priests and little or nothing can be done in Tibet without the interposition of the lamas.

Buddha, who died at least fifty years before Alexander the Great invaded India in 327 B.C., was born as Prince Gautama in India, and every spot in India connected with his life is still regarded as most sacred to Buddhists of every quarter of the globe. At Kapilavastu on the borders of Nepal and British territory he was born, and at Kassia not far from there in the Gorakhpore district of the United Provinces he died. The Tibetans curiously place Kassia in Assam and perform their pilgrimages accordingly, although there can be no possible doubt as to the incorrectness of their views. At Gaya he obtained Buddhahood, that is, he formulated his philosophy under the "sacred Bodhi tree of wisdom," which is the familiar pipal tree of India (*ficus religiosa*), and in commemoration of this fact the "yellow cap" lamas of Tibet always use rosaries of the yellow wood of that tree, in distinction to the brown rosaries of the "red caps," who are not of the established church. At the deer forest (Sarnath) of Benares the Buddha preached the law. The Tashi Lama, who has been visiting India during the cold weather of 1905-6, did not fail to visit the places so dear to the heart of every Buddhist, and his example will, no doubt, be followed by many Tibetan pilgrims in the near future. The more accessible the routes to India become, the more willingly will men from all parts of Central Asia visit the sacred spots so rich in past associations. Near the Bodhi tree of Gaya is the place where the daughters of Mara (Satan) tried to entice the Buddha with their allurements, but were changed into hags; and, again, another where Brahma asked the great Teacher to preach his doctrine to all mankind, while a tank still marks where he bathed after receiving

Silver charm-casket with turquoise centre, worn on person
Turquoise ear-rings worn by women
Silver chatelaine worn by women on the bosom: from left: ear-spoon, tooth-pick, brush for cleaning jewellery, flat instrument cleaner, thorn-extractor, useful for spreading medicine, etc, tweezers for pulling out hairs on the face. Turquoise is the lucky colour and keeps off the evil eye

enlightenment. Here also lotus flowers sprang up in his footsteps as he walked, and not far thence is the cave where the Buddha went in disappointment after six years' fruitless search for wisdom, and was told to return to Gaya, where his search would meet with final success.

Buddha was an idealist in his philosophy like almost every philosopher since the time that the science of philosophy sprang up: he preached that things were not real or substantial, but that they took the shape that man gave them when he perceived them, and that they existed only as perceived. Starting with this ground-work, we come to the "Three Holy Ones," who are Buddha, the Law and the Church. The Law is his doctrine of sorrow and human misery: look where one may, "man is born to sorrow as the sparks fly upward," and the Law is, therefore, comprehended in the "Four Noble Truths," which are (1) that there is no existence possible without sorrow; (2) that the cause of sorrow is Lust of Life; (3) that sorrow cannot end until the Lust of Life is completely overcome; (4) that the "Noble Eight-fold Path" can alone end sorrow.

This "Eight-fold Path" consists of:

(1) Belief.
(2) Aims.
(3) Speech.
(4) Actions.
(5) Right living.
(6) Proper endeavour.
(7) The right spirit within.
(8) Meditation.

And these are supported by the "Ten Commandments":

(1) Thou shalt not kill.
(2) Thou shalt not steal.
(3) Thou shalt not commit adultery.
(4) Thou shalt not bear false witness (*i.e.*, lie).
(5) Thou shalt not drink strong drink.
(6) Thou shalt not eat food except at the proper times.

(7) Thou shalt not use ornaments or scents.
(8) Thou shalt not use high seats.
(9) Thou shalt not enjoy worldly pleasures such as dancing, singing, &c.
(10) Thou shalt not possess gold or silver.

The teaching in the Law is that existence means sorrow, and that the existence of every living being is from everlasting to everlasting, and that he is born again as soon as he ends one life merely to live another life, the sphere of the new life simply depending upon the result of the good and bad deeds of the old life weighed in a balance as white and black counters (Karma). The law of Karma is an iron law; it leads every being from one rebirth to another as a driver leads some brute beast which knows nothing. From this it follows that the child which is born to happy parents is not theirs at all, it does not inherit their defects and virtues, it is merely the rebirth of another being who has nothing to do with them, who is utilising those parents to enter the world. This logical position is entirely opposed to all the European ideas of the Laws of Heredity.

There is a "twelve-linked chain" which describes the causes of the perpetual system of rebirths, or transmigration of souls, and these are rooted on the "Three Vices," of lust, anger and ignorance, which account for all the ills of this life. There are six spheres of existence into which a rebirth can take place, dependent ever on the result of our good and bad actions. They are:

(1) Gods.
(2) Titans.
(3) Man.
(4) Beasts.
(5) Ghouls (preta) with tiny throats and eyes.
(6) Hell.

The whole of the above is depicted in the "Wheel of Life" which one sees frequently in Tibet (we saw it at the Thokar monastery), which is held in the grip of a monster fiend.

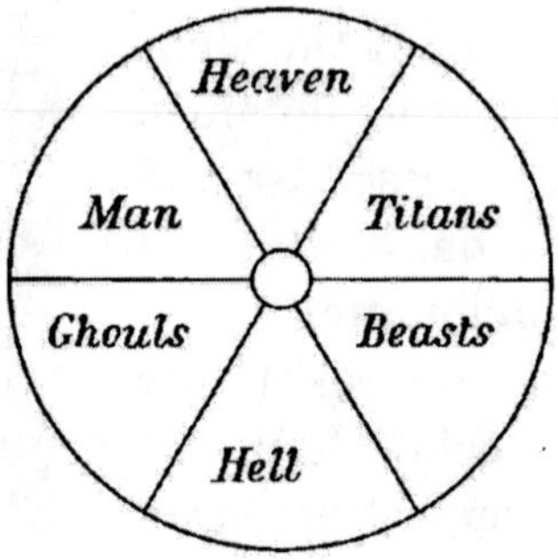

In the sub-divisions all forms of life are described, all revolving round the small ring inside, which holds a pig for ignorance, a dove for lust and a serpent for anger, while Yama (Tibetan, Shinje) stands in the top portion of Hell as Judge of the dead, weighing their actions and appointing the next rebirth.

It is ignorance that binds man to life and prevents him from escaping from the iron law of Karma, whereas wisdom and knowledge of the right path teach him to attain to that sinless state of Nirvana, when, having conquered all lust and desire of life, with every sin and wrongful thought subdued, he can obtain emancipation from rebirth, and, becoming an Arhat, passes into nothingness.

There are twenty-eight Heavens of the Gods and rebirth can take place into any one of those heavens; but if the god in question has not lived the life that he should have done, Karma drags him down to a lower grade such as that of Titans or men; in fact, Buddha himself was born twenty times as Indra or Jupiter and four times as Brahma, and Indra is generally depicted as Buddha's umbrella-carrier, while Brahma bears for him the cup of the elixir of life. Buddha, having obtained Nirvana, has finally passed beyond the regions of celestial bliss into a state of perfect annihilation.

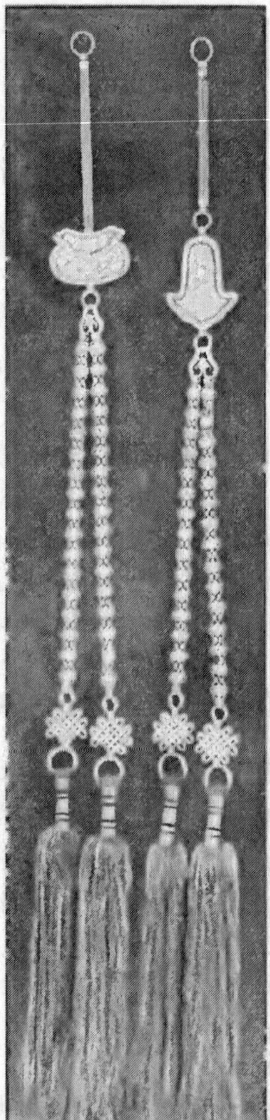

SILVER PENDANTS WITH SILK TASSELS WORN BY LADIES OF POSITION

Made in Lhasa. Charms are kept in the silver caskets

Similarly there are eight hot Hells and eight cold Hells, the latter appealing very strenuously to the residents of a country where the intense cold can be the most exquisite torture. The punishments suffered in these abodes of the wretched are portrayed with a realism of which the Lama priests gladly avail themselves to terrorise the minds of timid mortals, so that there may arise a horror in their hearts which will open the purse-strings of the most hardened for the benefit of the clergy, who alone can indicate the way of salvation from the most appalling future agonies.

> "I could a tale unfold whose lightest word
> Would harrow up thy soul, freeze thy young blood,
> Make thy two eyes, like stars, start from their spheres,
> Thy knotted and combined locks to part

> And each particular hair to stand an-end,
> Like quills upon the fretful porcupine."

There are two schools of Buddhism, viz., the Southern and the Northern: to the former belong Ceylon, Siam and Burma, while in the latter are included all the remaining countries which profess Buddhism, such as China, Japan, Tibet, &c. The Southern school admits that only a very small number of suffering humanity can attain to Nirvana, whereas the Northern throws the acquisition of this blessed state of salvation open to all mankind.

While renouncing the world as unreal and unsatisfying, men still made Buddha into a god, for did he not alone know the way of salvation, and had he not taught them by doctrine and example? So Buddha became a god all-powerful, all-good, all-knowing, possessed of every virtue, an essence permeating the whole universe, and every phase of his attributes was made into a separate godhead, not different from all the others, but simply calling attention to that particular quality in a marked way. Thus there is the Buddha of Boundless Light (Amitabha), of Eternal Life (Amitayus), the Everlasting, the Indestructible, the Great Physician, &c.; in fact, there are a thousand Buddhas. Thus was opened the gates of pantheism.

To these were added Bodhisats, or beings who are about to become Buddhas, *i.e.*, gods or human saints so good and holy that between them and Nirvana there lies only one step, one rebirth, and who were regarded finally as the Buddha himself, who having attained Nirvana is God omnipotent. These were sometimes regarded as emanations from the all-holy Buddha, *i.e.*, as his sons, and the next step, of course brought in by the Tantrik cult, introduced the female energy, and assigned wives to the gods.

Thus there are the "Three Lords" of Tibetan Buddhism, who are the "Defenders of the Faith," a triad

Jugs for filling water into bowls which stand on the altars in front of the idols
Bells with thunderbolt handles (dorje) used by lamas in the temples
Sauce-pan for pouring melted butter into bowls in which lights burn on the altars
Table with folding flaps
Trumpets made of human thigh-bones used by lamas in their rites: it has been said that those of criminals are preferred, but those in the picture belonged to holy men, and similarly the human skulls represented elsewhere

resembling Brahma, Shiva and Vishnu of Hinduism (Trimurti).*

(1) The God of Wisdom (Manjusri), a kind of Apollo, who sits with a sword in his right hand to cut all Gordian knots and the book of knowledge in his left. We found large numbers of clay images of this god in the caves, cast there by devotees, a fact clearly indicating his popularity.

* *Cf.* Waddell's "Buddhism of Tibet," p. 355.

(2) The God of the Thunderbolt (Vajrapani), similar to the Homeric Zeus: this name is given to him as he always holds in his hand the dorje, or thunderbolt, a weapon composed of a shaft joining together what are apparently two crowns. With this weapon all demons are scattered, and so holy is it that one of the most sacred relics in Tibet is the original dorje, from which all others are copied, which came flying through the air from India, and now reposes in the Sera monastery at Lhasa. This relic is annually carried to the Dalai Lama and the chief officers of state, who each place it on the head for a few moments.

(3) The God of Mercy (Avalokita). He is the son of Amitabha, the Buddha of Boundless Light, and is shown with four hands, or, again, with eleven heads and a thousand eyes—these emblems signifying that he is ever regarding the misery of men and that his hand is ever outstretched to save. To him is allotted as wife Tara, the Goddess of Mercy, and this pair has, therefore, very naturally become the most popular of all the deities in Tibet. It will be remembered that the King Sron Tsan Gampo, who introduced Buddhism into Tibet, had two wives, the one a daughter of the Chinese Emperor and the other of Nepalese royal stock. These are respectively the white and green Tara of modern worship.

When the gods of Tibet are so numerous it is useless for the ordinary traveller to overburden the mind with names; still, a description of the most important enables him to enjoy what would otherwise be a sealed book; and as the temples of Tibet are some of its most interesting features and are full of pictures on silk panels (tangka) and illustrations on walls giving representations of what one would suppose to be the common knowledge of the people and lamas, a certain familiarity with the subject is indispensable. An extraordinary thing, which we found to be the case, was that the priests and laity are, as a rule, hopelessly

MUD IMAGES OF THE GODS, FOUND IN THOUSANDS IN THE CAVES

Made by means of stamps: they each contain grains of corn (which sometimes sprout) to indicate the immortal hope

ignorant of their own mythology and divine representations, and few of them can give reliable details.

The coming Buddha, or Messiah, so to speak, is another most important Bodhisat. He is always represented in a sitting posture with legs hanging down as in the European fashion, and it must be remembered that it is to the West that Buddhists look for the next Buddha, who is to come from his seat in Paradise, where he now is, to reform the world. The antiquity of this idea and its representation is truly astonishing.

Palden Chamo, the Indian Devi or Kali, is a goddess of surpassing terror and ferocity. She has three eyes, drinks blood from a human skull, treads upon the mangled bodies of men, her crown is of skulls, her fangs are immense, the trappings of her steed are snakes, while the skin of a freshly-flayed man is cast round her. So greatly revered is this pleasant lady that the Tibetans, to show their mark of utmost respect to our good Queen Victoria, have uniformly stated that she was a reincarnation of this goddess: they could no more, they gave their best.

One more goddess, Marici, closes the list; she has a pig's face and is reincarnate in the Abbess of Yamdok, who holds in consequence such a position in popular estimation that she is entitled to ride in a sedan-chair, an honour conferred otherwise only upon the Dalai Lama, the Regent and the Chinese Ambans. She is the wife of Yama the God of the Dead, and also of the horse-necked Tamdin, a centaur god of great power.

The Lamaist scriptures which treat of all matters religious are called Kahgyur, and the commentaries on these the Tangyur. Writing is considered sacred in Tibet, and it has been said that no Tibetan will throw away or trample under foot any written paper: however, perhaps in Western Tibet the feeling is not so strict, for at the Khojarnath monastery we found piles and piles of sacred books cast upon the ground, and persons trod on them as a matter of course.

It will be remembered that Padma Sambhava was the founder of Lamaism, having been called from India by the Tibetan King, and that owing to his vast knowledge of witchcraft he exorcised all the demons of Tibet, who became subservient to him and were allowed by him to enter into the national faith so long as they behaved themselves, *i.e.*, were amenable to the spells of the Lamas, who undertook in turn to feed them and to help the laity to combat them. Hence arose the study of spells and incantations, and so far has the matter gone that there are now two state oracles at

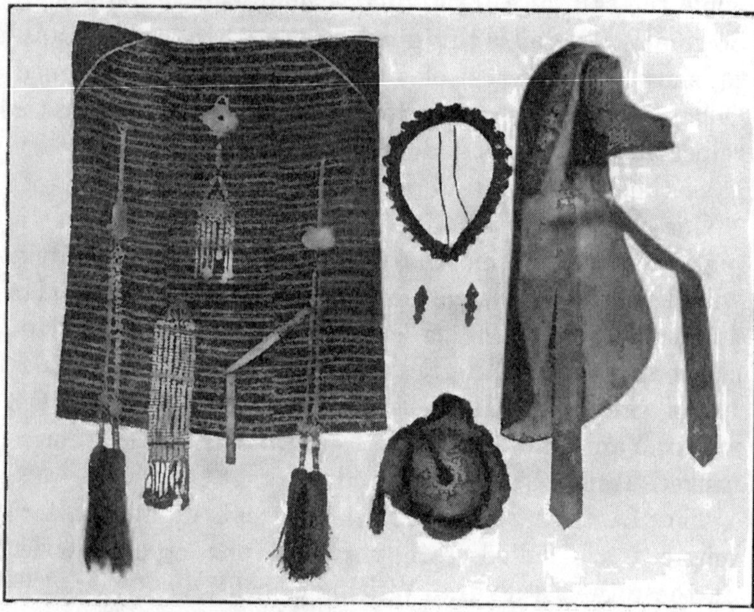

From the left: Apron with gold-thread corners worn by women: silver pendant and silk tassels worn by women: charms are kept in the caskets: chatelaine of white and blue beads and tiny brass bells, worn by women at the side: the tinkling of the bells as the women walk (all wear it) is very pleasing

Silver charm-casket

Silver chatelaine (described elsewhere)

Common knife and sheath worn by women

Woman's tiara made of red cloth mounted with coral and turquoise, both of which are considered lucky

Turquoise ear-rings: turquoise fends off the evil eye

Fur cap with ear-flaps worn by men of position

Scarlet hood with light blue silk lining, gold-thread embrodiery and blue silk ribbons, worn by high officials when travelling: red and blue are lucky colours

Lhasa, to which political matters are regularly referred and to which the laity repair as well as lamas to obtain forecasts as to the future. It is extraordinary that one of these oracles prophesied the expedition of 1903-4 to Lhasa a very considerable time before it took place. The Mongolian deity Pe is supposed to be incarnated in the head wizards of these oracles. Padma Sambhava has been deified, and is reverenced frequently with greater honour than is given even to Buddha himself.

The subject of reincarnation is closely connected with the history and politics of Tibet. We are familiar with the names of Timour, Tamerlane and Genghiz Khan, who are associated with the invasion of India from the north at the head of Mongolian hordes of Moslems and for the setting up in India of the throne of the Great Moguls, who ruled with an autocratic power and a magnificence that have become the wonder of all ages. The son of Genghiz Khan was Kublai Khan, the most powerful ruler that Central and Eastern Asia have ever seen, whose throne was set in that most wealthy of all countries, China. Kublai Khan made the head of the red cap priests, viz., the Abbot of Sakya, King of Tibet, and in return the red cap Chief Priest, or Grand Lama, consecrated the coronation of the Emperors of China. When this Mongol dynasty of Kublai Khan was ousted from China it fled to Mongolia, and having already turned Buddhist set up a Grand Lama for itself at Urga, where the present Dalai Lama has gone for refuge in consequence of our expedition to Lhasa. The Urga Grand Lama, it must be remembered, reincarnates always by the Dalai Lama's order in Tibet for political reasons and not elsewhere.

Next in the course of events we find that the yellow caps snatched the reins of government from the red caps, and were assisted in their enterprise by a Tartar prince Gushi Khan. This military commander, in putting the yellow caps on the throne at Lhasa, reserved for himself the post of commander-in-chief. The first yellow cap ruler was given the title of Dalai by the Tartar prince, and by this name, meaning "Vast as the Ocean," he has been ever since known to Europeans, though Tibetans give him another name. However, the name Dalai Lama is well known and thoroughly understood on the British Borderland of Kamaon. Lozang, the first Dalai Lama, instituted the doctrine of reincarnation. He set forth that the Bodhisats, who sit in celestial bliss, have no time to come personally to earth, but that, owing to their great desire for the salvation of all men, emanations from them are allowed to appear in human beings, who will assist poor humanity to find the path of right knowledge, which alone leads to the supreme happiness of emancipation from rebirth. He declared that in this manner Avalokita was incarnated in himself, and had been incarnated also in that most popular King Sron Tsan Gampo, who had brought Buddhism to Tibet. He further declared Avalokita to be the supreme arbiter as to the result of men's good and bad actions (Karma), and to be responsible for the phase of rebirth into which men were born again after death, *i.e.*, he pronounced himself to be the arbiter of transmigration.

The prayer found on the lips of every Tibetan—Om Mani Padme Hung, *i.e.*, "Hail! Jewel of the Lotus Flower (the Dalai Lama), Hail!"—can therefore readily be understood. The entire future happiness of every Tibetan and of every believer in Lamaism hangs upon the Dalai Lama, who can deal with him as he pleases. Again, as Avalokita is also the God of Infinite Mercy and the Dalai Lama is his incarnation, every Tibetan believes that according to his favour, or disfavour, the whole future will be bright or clouded. It is impossible to imagine a more powerful position than this one, which makes the Grand Lama of Lhasa the "Deathless" Buddha.

On the death of a Dalai Lama his successor is found in the person of some newly-born infant who came into the world shortly after the death of his predecessor. As the Tashi Lama was said to be the incarnation of Amitabha, the Buddha of Boundless Light, the father of Avalokita, he, therefore, occupies in one sense a more spiritually holy position than the Dalai Lama. In the old days these two Grand Lamas performed for each other the function of choosing the exact babe which had received the deathless spirit of the Buddha.

In the beginning of the eighteenth century a horde of Tartars from the north of Turkestan came across the intervening deserts of Central Asia on camels and actually sacked the sacred city of Lhasa, in consequence of which the help of the Chinese Emperor was asked for and obtained. When the Tartars had been cast forth from Lhasa the Chinese Emperor set up his claim to suzerainty, appointed a regent, and further posted two Ambans at Lhasa to assist in the government. In fact, the Ambans at times chose the Dalai Lama and sometimes acted as his regents, and effectually prevented the boy from attaining his majority by always murdering him in his early years. So absolute was the power of China that one Dalai Lama was formally deposed, exiled and finally murdered by the orders of the Chinese Emperor.

Against the Chinese suzerainty there has sprung up a national party which has supported the Dalai Lama, and since the defeat of China by Japan that suzerainty has been thrown off. It has been prophesied that the Dalai Lama will only reincarnate thirteen times and it is very noteworthy that the present Dalai is the thirteenth reincarnation.

The choosing of the babe is a ceremony that requires

From the left: Bowl used for drinking tea
Pipe with jade mouthpiece for smoking tobacco: the Tibetan tobacco is exactly like chopped chaff
Purse
Bowl for drinking: in it are Tibetan coins
Table for domestic use
Purse
Bag
Pipe with onyx mouthpiece
Purse: in the centre hangs a needle-case
Purse with flint, steel and tinder (matches are not common, though known and immensely appreciated)
Bag
Churn and piston-rod for making tea and mixing in it butter, salt and flour

great care, and there are two parts of it which are particularly important. The first is that, when all the infants have been gathered together who have been born under miraculous circumstances, they are severally shown the relics of the deceased Dalai, so as to see whether or no they can identify the property of the deceased. The new babe is presumed to be able to recognise instinctively its own property. Having passed this ordeal the names of all the infants are put on paper and placed in a golden vase given for this purpose by the Chinese Emperor, and the name of the next Dalai is found by drawing from the vase. The infant that has been chosen is then placed in a monastery and his mother is allowed for a certain number of years, generally two, to visit him for a few hours daily and suckle him, but as Buddhism places women in a very inferior grade she must live in a separate house to him otherwise she would defile him. The father is, however, immediately created a "Kung," a title which is one of the very highest in the land.

There are four "lings," or royal monasteries, in Lhasa from which the Regent is supposed to be always chosen, and there are three other monasteries, Depung, Sera and Gaden, which have great power in the administration of the state. The Dalai Lama is assisted by four ministers called Shapes, who are an executive committee, while the deliberative assembly, which also entirely controls foreign affairs, is the Tsong Du or national council, to which laity and churchmen of position belong, but which is free from the control of the Shapes, who are not allowed to attend its meetings, though they can overhear what is said while they sit on the further side of a curtain. It is in the Tsong Du that the three ruling monasteries of Depung, Sera and Gaden have such power. As the Manchu conquered China in 1651 A.D., the Amban is always a Manchu of the ruling Manchu family of China, and has been in the past the head of the army and principal instructor in the tactics of war. The Government as a whole is known universally as the Deba Jung.

From the above it is clear that the status and power of the Dalai Lama are absolutely extraordinary. He is revered with a reverence that is almost incredible, and any relic or article connected with his sacred person can always be disposed of at a high price in the market as a talisman against various ills: this extends to his cast-off clothing, hair, parings of his finger- and toe-nails, and even to his urine and excreta, which are considered potent cures in certain ailments.

The prayer Om Mani Padme Hung, "Hail! Jewel of the Lotus Flower, Hail!" is addressed to him and is a request that he give the suppliant assistance in the present life to reach the goal of salvation and look leniently upon the soul after death and apportionate it to a favourable region after rebirth. There are six syllables in the prayer and they correspond to the six phases of life, and each has a colour appointed to it which is typical of the peculiar phases. Thus:

Om is the gods and is white.
Ma, the Titans and is blue.
Ni, men and is yellow.
Pad, the beasts and is green.
Me, the ghouls and is red.
Hung, hell and is black.

These are known as the sacred colours, and in Central Tibet it is common to see lines of flags of these colours and the holy prayer painted with every syllable in its proper blue. But in Western Tibet we hardly ever saw these colours; in fact, we can only recollect one instance of stones coloured and inscribed with "Om Mani Padme

Hung," which was at Gyanema, and another of a string of flags on a bridge at Taklakot. In the latter case the colours were quite in the wrong order, viz., blue, red, white, green and yellow, and only five in number. These colours are found on the different "Wheels of Life" in the monasteries, but I doubt if they are as accurate in any way as those in Central Tibet.

Other peculiar emblems of the Tibetan faith are the "Three Precious Gems," in the shape of eggs, representing Buddha, the Law and the Church. It is not to be forgotten that the lamas are first and the laity nowhere. There are a few lay families of position who are a close and exclusive aristocracy and whose members fill important offices of state; but the posts so filled are a mere nothing to the power that the priests keep in their own hands. To start with, a layman has no hope of ever being a Bodhisat, while the lamas calmly arrogate to themselves a certain future prospect of attaining that blessed state, and the abbots of the different monasteries are always incarnations of some Bodhisat.

The lotus flower, as in India, is a common symbol of divine origin and purity, for the flower in its natural state floats on the surface of water and thus apparently is not attached to the earth, and its beautiful colour does not seem to be affected by its surrounding impurities. The garuda bird, a phœnix or stork, is also symbolic of enmity to dragons and is found in pictures near the Buddha. Tigers are frequently represented on walls, and bats are considered lucky, while charms against every conceivable form of misfortune, prayer-flags, prayer-poles and prayer-wheels are amongst the objects most typical of Tibet. Chortens are common in all temples: they are death memorials and symbolise the five elements—earth (base), water, fire, air and ether (tongue on summit), and sometimes the

Thunderbolts (dorje) used to expel demons by all lamas in temples, &c. The dorje is gripped with finger and thumb in the centre and turned backwards and forwards, while a bell is rung with the other hand
Stone engraved with "Om Mani Padme Hung"
Spoons and ladles used in domestic life, the right one is of brass and the left of silver, with a turquoise in the centre: the lower ones are of brass and copper

tapering upper shaft indicates the numerous heavens. Mendons or walls built of stones inscribed with the words "Om Mani Padme Hung" are found everywhere and mark the correct road from place to place. In Central

Tibet they must be passed on the left, but in Western Tibet this is optional.

The temples are pitch dark and slimy inside with the reek of burning candles, while the stench and the dirt must be experienced to be adequately realised. The principal of the arch is unknown and timber is very scarce, being obtained in Western Tibet invariably from the forests south of the Tibetan border, *e.g.*, Nepal, British Territory, Bashahr, &c. The result is that the architecture is deficient. There are tiny windows stuffed up with mud, rags and grass, or covered over with thin cloth. The cold and wind are kept out and so is the light, but in the absence of glass it is difficult to suggest what improvement can be made. The Holy of Holies, or Cathedral of Lhasa, is the Jokang, known as the Lha—sa, "place of the gods (Lha)," whence the name has been extended to the whole city, which, although situated in a marsh, has come to be regarded as the Sacred Heart of Buddhism. The "Jo" is an idol of the Buddha covered with the most sumptuous jewels and is said to have been brought from China as the dower of Sron Tsan Gampo's Chinese bride. So holy is the sacred city of Lhasa that no life can be taken within its precincts: the shambles of the butchers are situated outside the city limits.

The ritual and services in the temples do undoubtedly bear a resemblance to the observances of Roman Catholicism, for the priests are celibate, and shaved, while incense, rosaries, bell-ringing, terraced altar, images, pictures and vestments complete the comparison. We were particularly and most punctiliously asked not to tread upon the carpets on which the monks sit in church, and of course we were most careful in this respect, otherwise we were able to walk everywhere and see everything. The ordinary worshipper circumambulates the interior with his left arm towards the wall, but we were not expected to do this. All our Hindu servants were most careful to worship in every Tibetan temple and identified almost every image,

Velvet boots worn by ladies of position, made in Lhasa
Ordinary table used in domestic life
Swans' eggs from the Mansarowar Lake: these are sacred: it is forbidden to take these eggs from the sacred lakes
Wooden bowl made by the Rajis or wild men of Askot (Kumaon)

rightly or wrongly, as some Hindu deity. The most striking feature of the service of the priests is that they sit in two rows facing each other and intone the liturgy first from one side and then the other, and the most remarkable rite is the dispensation of consecrated bread and wine to those desirous of obtaining long earthly life, but after all said and done there is a difference as wide as the poles between the Tibetan worship and that of any European nation. The element of barbarity is so marked that one is apt to forget the first resemblances to European religions. Priests blow long horns and conch shells, play flutes, thump drums and cymbals, and in this babel the liturgy is intoned by men who drink tea and look about them and talk; there is no congregation that takes part in the service, though the laity come and look on, and women bring their babies for a blessing (we saw them at Khojarnath). Above all, the hideous and obscene representations of the deities and monster fiends, combined with the black gloom which makes the recesses invisible and the reek and stench which render the beholder faint, make the shrine rather a temple of Satan and the Powers of Darkness than of any deity of Light and Goodness: a strange commentary on the religion of Buddha, which one has been taught to admire for its beauty of conception and chaste precepts of life.

The religion of Tibet is found in Manchuria, Mongolia, Central Asia, Ladak, Nepal, Bhotan and Sikkim, and even in China there are one million adherents and a Lamaist shrine at Pekin, while there are Lamaist colonies in Russia on the Volga and elsewhere. To all these countries the Dalai Lama is a very sacred person and his favour is a matter of great consideration. The Bonpas, who are pre-Buddhist, are found in numbers east of Lhasa, but also exist throughout the whole country of Tibet: in the west they are called Dubas and are much feared by the people. They do everything in the reverse way to the orthodox: they go round Lake Mansarowar and Mount Kailas opposite to the "way of the wine" with us, and they even repeat "Om Mani Padme Hung" beginning from the end. They are famous in Western Tibet as exorcists and wizards, and are supposed, with many more orthodox lamas, to possess supernatural powers of invisibility and flying through the air.

No account of Tibet would be complete without a reference to the world-famous devil-dancing of that country, which is practised by the lamas before a large concourse of spectators with a view to impress upon them the importance of a thorough familiarity in this

Stone engraved with "Om mani padme hung": such stones are thrown in thousands on to heaps
Prayer-wheels with chain and knob to assist the revolutions
Thunderbolts (dorje) for expelling demons
Ling-shaped mud image with Shiva's trident (trisul) and streamer
Table for domestic use
Bowls made of human skulls in which water or blood is offered and sometimes drunk

life with the dread monsters that will be met with by the soul after it quits its earthly tenement. These devil-dancers are a great feature of the monastery at Takla-kot; in fact, that institution prides itself upon the magnificence and the realism of the allegorical dances that take place there. The shapes assumed are those of the most terrifying monsters, such as indescribably grotesque dragons, hideously malformed beasts of the brute creation such as only the most diseased imagination can conjure up, skeletons, devils, imps, &c., and the principle underlying the dance is that these evil spirits should attack and perplex the departed soul and should reduce it to a state of prostrate fear, when the *deus ex machina*, in the form of the lama, or some saint, interferes to protect the haunted wretch. The unvarying moral is to make friends by means of the mammon of unrighteousness with the priests, who alone can guide the poor voyager in the future world and guide him in safely to the desired haven.

CHAPTER XIV

MANSAROWAR AND KAILAS, THE ABODE OF THE GODS

In this western portion of Tibet there is a very clearly defined plateau of 15,000 ft. in height, which embraces the holy lakes of Mansarowar and Rakas, and extends towards Gartok and Daba and which is reached very soon after leaving Taklakot. The valley of the Karnali river, in which Taklakot and Khojarnath are situated, is considerably below this plateau, the former place being 13,300 ft. high and, speaking broadly, this rich and irrigated tract of country should be considered by itself distinct from the main plateau which adjoins it, as the action of the rivers and other causes have tended to lower the elevation. Journeying from Taklakot in the direction of the Mansarowar Lake there is a steady rise in altitude until a plain of vast dimensions is reached, which is about 15,000 ft. in elevation and which extends for miles. First one passes the village of Toyo, in which is the tomb of the hero Zorawar Sing, and then the monastery of Rungung, whence one can look down into the valley of the Karnali studded with green fields of waving corn and can detect Kardam in the distance, where in former times there used to be the seat of a Jongpen. When this appointment was abolished all this territory came into the hands of the Barkha Tarjum, who, already administering the holy lakes, strengthened his position by acquiring from the

Daba Jongpen rights in the large market of Gyanema, and by these means has now become one of the most influential officials in this part of Tibet. His border commences near Rungung, which is by far the most favourable spot to break the journey, as there is protection from the bitter wind and ample supply of grass for fodder, and includes Kardam and all the small hamlets situated on the upper course of the Karnali. Baldak, 15,000 ft., is in the centre of this plateau, a very cheerless place, to be avoided at all costs as a camping-ground on account of the night wind and the want of fuel. From this spot there are two tracks, the western going to Rakas Tal, the favourite with Bhotia traders, while the eastern traverses the Gurla Pass, 16,200 ft. high, and leads to the Mansarowar Lake (14,900 ft.).

The view as one surveys this holy place, venerated alike by Buddhists and Hindus, is one of the most beautiful throughout the whole of this part of the country. The Mansarowar Lake, forty-five miles in circumference, on the right, and Rakas Tal, of equal size and more varied contour, on the left, make with their lovely dark blue a magnificent foreground to the range of the Kailas mountains at the back, while the holy Kailas Peak, Tise of the Tibetans, the Heaven of Hindus and Buddhists, fills the centre of the picture, full of majesty, a king of mountains, dominating the entire chain by 2000 ft. The colouring of the rocks and the hue of the water, softened by the green of thousands and thousands of acres of verdant pasture-land, form a setting to the landscape which is indescribably charming, and although one misses the foliage of the forests, the colours are so exquisite in their brilliancy that they clothe the austerity of the mountains with a mantle that veils all their harshness. As one reaches the heaps of stones

RAKAS TAL (LEFT) AND MANSAROWAR LAKE (14,900 FT.) (RIGHT) WITH KAILAS (21,850 FT.) AND THE KAILAS RANGE IN THE BACKGROUND: TAKEN FROM THE SOUTH, NEAR THE GURLA PASS

(each traveller should cast a stone on the crest according to universal custom) and sees the monuments (Chortens) erected by pious hands which mark the top of the pass, and the view bursts upon the sight, prayers and ejaculations break forth on all sides from the weary travellers, giving place later to a feeling of absolute contentment that they have now been blessed to see "what kings and many mighty men have desired to see and not seen." Our camp was pitched by the very edge of the water, and thus we were able to enjoy to the full the delightful romance and poetry of the scene.

The first feeling is that the deserts of Tibet have given place to most luxuriant pasture-lands, which for richness and extent are a perpetual marvel in this barren wilderness. These lands stretch for miles and miles, as far as the eye can see, round the lakes and into the far beyond, and thousands of sheep and cattle can be seen grazing on all sides and continuing into the dim distance. The air is so clear that one scarcely realises the enormous distances, and it is only when one attempts to reach some neighbouring hillock for a more extensive view, or when the glasses are used to watch some apparently near object, that one discovers the immensity of the distances and the deceptiveness of the atmosphere. These grazing-grounds extend for untold miles to the east of the Mansarowar Lake and along the Sanpo, or Brahmaputra river, and also to the north of the Kailas mountains, and to a certain extent, with diminished fertility, to the west of the holy lakes; but there is no question that Mansarowar is the spot round which the whole of the wool trade of Western Tibet centres. Whether the wool goes to Ladakh or Nepal, to Simla or to Kumaon, the whole practically comes from this part and the country to the east, and in every question relating to the further extension of this trade this principal fact must not be forgotten. Salt also and borax come from the north of the Kailas Range from mines a few days journey in the same latitude as the holy lakes, and, as the cost of carriage on all these articles is the principle item for consideration, there can be little doubt

THE GURLA PASS (16,200 FT) FROM WHICH THE HOLY LAKES ARE FIRST SEEN

Note the large pile of stones and the small piles of stones (chortens), also the prayer-flags.

that, with the improvement of communications, Taklakot, which is only 170 miles from the plains, 210 miles from a railway, and two days from Mansarowar, will outdistance all its rivals which are not so favourably situated.

The first Europeans to explore the holy lakes were William Moorcroft, whose name will ever be remembered in connection with the tragic fate of the Mission to Bokhara in 1825, and Hyder Hearsey, whose wife was a daughter of the Mogul Emperor Akbar II.

Hearsey was originally in the Mahratta service, but subsequently joined the adventurer George Thomas, Raja of Hansi, and when the latter was crushed by General Perron, commanding the Mahratta forces, he set himself up as an independent chief in Mewat. When Lord Wellesley made war on the Mahratta Confederation in 1803 Hearsey joined the British with a cavalry regiment, and did good service as commandant of this corps, while later he took part in the contests with the Gurkhas, which terminated in 1815, when Kumaon was wrested from the Nepalese Government. In 1812 Moorcroft and Hearsey, disguised as ascetics making a pilgrimage, entered Tibet by the Niti Pass in Garhwal, visited Gartok, which had then, as now, only a few houses, traders living in tents during the fair season, explored Rakas and Mansarowar Lakes and saw the source of the Sutlej river. Hearsey surveyed and a pundit paced the distances. They found that even at that early period the Russians had been in the habit of trading with Ladakh and Cashmere by means of agents, but had visited Gartok in person to the number of five or six hundred men on horseback. It was in 1824 that the first Russian caravan visited Bokhara. On their return to the Almora district the two explorers were arrested by the Nepalese soldiers, but subsequently after some trouble were released (*vide* "Journal Royal Geog. Soc.," xxvi. 2).

Although there are many tribes in Western Tibet, the members all freely intermingle with each other in matters of food, marriage and customs, caste being wholly unknown. There is one exception to this rule, in that blacksmiths are popularly considered to be inferior, and they are left alone by other Tibetans in all matters of eating and social intercourse. The herdsmen of Mansarowar Lake are the Dokpas, or nomads, who wander with their flocks over the extensive plains to the east and north and, to some extent, the west. Men and women wear alike a long dressing-gown of leather, lined on the inside with thick fur and girt round the waist, and little babies and children wear diminutive garments of the same pattern and material. In

Mount Kailas Our tents

ORDINARY TENT USED BY BHOTIAS AND TIBETANS
The Dokpa shepherd nomads have similar tents, but made of yak's_hair for warmth and invariably black in colour

the heat of the day it is the ordinary practice for all men and women to slip the right arm out of this coat and expose half the chest, which is devoid of any other covering. Men frequently in working strip bare to the waist by removing the other arm also from the sleeve. These people are inured to the bitterest cold, and tend their flocks on these same plains even when Mansarowar and Rakas Lakes are frozen over with many feet of ice, and they have daily to dig with an iron crowbar to reach the springs from which they drink. These lakes do not freeze till late in the winter owing to warm springs. Their tents are made of yak's hair woven into a cloth, and are in two sections, the space between, along the roof, being left open for the passage of smoke from the interior. They are said to be extremely warm and excellent protection from the terrible winds. A Dokpa encampment can always be known from afar by the shape of the tents and by their invariable black colour.

A DOKPA WOMAN

She is wearing a robe lined with fur inside and covered with leather outside: her charge for being photographed was fourpence

The Dokpas to the west of the holy lakes are poor and unenterprising, and consequently resort to theft to obtain what they fail to get from thrift and capital; whereas their brethren of the east are immensely wealthy and their herds are numbered by thousands, and to be "as rich as a Dokpa" has become a household word among the Bhotias. They have, too, a regular organisation amongst themselves for self-protection against the raids of dacoits and robbers. They have men well-mounted on fast ponies and armed with the best weapons Tibet can supply (some have Russian guns), who always escort the flocks that go to the borax and salt mines to remove the merchandise, and are ready at a moment's notice to follow up and engage any band of villains which has driven off their property. That dacoity by armed scoundrels is more than a name in these parts cannot be too frequently urged upon the attention, and we were continually during our tour hearing of lawless deeds, which went unheeded and unpunished by officials and against which there was only the redress of private enterprise. A Tibetan traveller had his head cut open quite near our camp and his clothes searched for valuables; and more than that, we had twenty-one yaks and jibboos stolen from our own camp. We were in a position to effect our own redress, and, of course, there was a hot pursuit, and after a bloodless battle (the dacoits fled) our property was recovered at a distance of seven miles from where we were camped. Even the Dokpas near us had been, a month before, the victim of a daring raid in which 3500 sheep and goats had been looted, and so good was the capture, and so effectual the retreat, that they had not yet been recovered when our camp was in their vicinity. These are only a few among innumerable instances of violent acts and flagrant crimes of which we heard. The officials of Tibet are as much victims as the commonalty and the person of none is sacred, and yet no organised official attempt is made to put down this lawlessness. It goes without saying that in Tibet every man goes armed with a sword or a gun, and if he can afford neither he fits up a stick to look like a gun.

There are many monasteries situated on the lakes, which are visited by pilgrims, who make the round from left to right of the holy water. Some of these pilgrims wander about absolutely naked except for a loin cloth, and it is marvellous how they manage to exist in the midst of so much cold and, living as they do from hand to mouth, with so much uncertainty of food. We met many fairly well-clothed pilgrims who were suffering terribly from the inclemency of the climate, who could scarcely hobble as their feet were numbed or frost-bitten, whose faces were pinched from hunger and their fingers shrivelled with cold, who had lost their way hopelessly in these grim mountains, where the country is unknown, the objective unrecognisable, and the barren, stony wastes show no trace of road or track. But yet they had clothes to cover them, while these naked devotees expose their ash-begrimed bodies in all their nudity to the cruel cold and the pitiless blast, and ever there hangs over them the certainty of hunger if compassionate charity does not pity their estate. The monasteries round these lakes are under the government of different ecclesiastical chiefs; for instance, Gozul is under the Taklakot Shivling, Jaikep (Jenkhab of the maps) under the Ruler of Bhutan, Jiu is a Dokpa Gompa, and the head lama comes from Lhasa, &c. The word Gompa literally means a "solitary place" and hence came to mean a monastery.

The Dokpas are quite the dirtiest of all the dirty tribes who live in Tibet, and their Gompa at Jiu, which we visited, built by excavating the rocks, was the filthiest place conceivable, while the attendants were begrimed with a coating of black that plainly showed they had never in their lives come into contact with soap or water. At the doorway of many of these monasteries there is a little soap-powder placed in a box for the use of the inmates, which is really a very humorous custom, for in theory it is excellent, but in practice ablutions are more honoured in the breach than the observance. Although there is a great sameness in these shrines yet it is always interesting to visit each one, for many of them undoubtedly go back to a great antiquity, and there is generally some incident about each which one carries away in the mind; for instance, at Thokar (Thui of the maps) there was quite a good antler of the Sikkim stag lying outside, and we were told that the leading dacoit of the whole country with his gang of forty men was going to arrive

Bags full of borax ready for transport by sheep and goats — Doorway of the Thokap monastery — Dokpa man

Dokpa men selling borax — Monks

DOKPA WOMEN AND MEN

The hair of the women is plaited into strings, which are fastened on to long ribbons of cloth ornamented with white beads and reaching to the ground

there the next day to levy blackmail, and we were particularly asked to interview this chief and persuade him of the error of his ways. At Gozul there is a beautiful view of the lake of Mansarowar, as the Gompa is on a fine eminence; at Jiu is the famous channel connecting the two sacred lakes.

There has been much discussion at times as to whether

there is any connecting-link between the two stretches of water, but the remarks of Captain H. Strachey (J. A. S.

THE MONASTERY AT JIU

Our camp being pitched on the shore of the Mansarowar Lake

RUINS OF THE SHRINE BUILT OVER A NUGGET OF GOLD SAID EUPHEMISTICALLY TO BE "AS LARGE AS A DOG"

Rai Sahib Pundit Gobaria standing to show the height

Ben. xvii (2) 5 7), who visited the spot in 1846, would seem to have finally disposed of the question. He writes:

THE CONNECTING CHANNEL BETWEEN MANSAROWAR LAKE (14,900 FT.) ON RIGHT AND RAKAS TAL (14,850 FT.) ON LEFT WITH THE JIU MONASTERY ON THE HILL IN FOREGROUND: TAKEN FROM THE SOUTH

THE WHITE DEPOSITS IN THE CHANNEL ARE SALINE AND ALSO DUE TO HOT SULPHUR SPRINGS IN THE BED

"A large stream one 100 ft. wide and 3 ft. deep, running rapidly from east to west by a well-defined channel, is crossed; this is the outlet of Mansarowar, which emerges from the northern part of its western margin and falls after a course of, perhaps, four miles into Rakas Tal. . . . Cho Mapan, or Mansarowar Lake, is bounded thus: westward by the hilly ground that separates it from Cho Lagan, or Rakas Tal, of no great height, averaging 200 ft. perhaps." This statement is undoubtedly quite accurate, for we saw the channel which answered the above description. It is a fact that at this present moment no water is actually flowing between the two lakes, the reason being that storms blowing from the east have thrown up sand at the mouth of the passage to a height of about 4 ft., but the best native information on the spot gives it as a fact that after heavy rains the water traverses the channel. The last occasion was eleven years ago, when exceptional rain fell and there were floods accompanied by great loss of life to cattle. The exact year is remembered as it was the year of the Kumb Fair at Kailas. At present the bed is full of stagnant water (saline) and there are many hot sulphur springs, the water in some instances being too hot to touch with comfort.

The only boat that has ever been launched upon the Mansarowar Lake was one belonging to Mr. Drummond, at one time Commissioner of Bareilly. The incident is quite fresh in the minds of the people although it took place in 1855, and the course followed by the little craft was pointed out to us as remembered by tradition. It has been said that the Tibetan official in charge of this part of the country was decapitated by order of the Lhasan Government for permitting such terrible sacrilege, but our inquiries could find no corroboration of this detail, so possibly it never occurred, or it may have been forgotten.

So great is the sanctity attaching to these waters that fishing is forbidden, and whatever fish are cast up by the violence of the waves are considered peculiarly efficacious for the exorcism of evil spirits and the cure of all kinds of cattle disease. The fish, after being cleaned, should be carefully dried in the sun and kept until the time that a cure has to be wrought. A portion should then be cut off and allowed to burn on hot coals, and the noisome smoke and odour emitted should be conveyed into the nose of the patient by close application, when the resultant effects are wonderful, a fact which is easily credible. Some fish were cast up and duly appropriated during our stay at the lake, and we made earnest inquiries as to whether there was any person afflicted with a devil in our company, on whom the cure might be advantageously applied; but there was no response. The taking of the eggs of water-birds is also forbidden, and this is a good order as there has been a regular trade lately in swans' eggs. The Barkha Tarjum is the principal breaker of the rule, as he is partial to these eggs, but he enforces it strictly against others. Amongst their other duties the Tarjums are expected to wall up the streams entering the lakes so as to prevent the fish from going out of these waters on the occasion of bad weather, but as a matter of fact they pocket the sum allowed in the Budget and do nothing. At the time of our visit we noticed young broods of grey geese, Brahmani ducks and other birds. There are many gulls and terns on these lakes.

The Barkha Tarjum's headquarters are at the place

of that name, and as he is an influential official administering the country of the two lakes, as well as Kardam, the rich valley of the upper Karnali river, and the market of Gyanema, in addition to his regular duties of despatching the imperial post between Gartok and Lhasa, we naturally expected to find a little of that style and dignity, possibly barbaric, which ordinarily surround the representative of law and order in most parts of the world. Away from the valley of the Karnali river houses are exceedingly few, and, omitting gompas and residences of officials, the total number of houses between the eastern border of Mansarowar Lake and Gartok could be easily reckoned on the fingers of both hands; therefore, we did not expect to find many residences of private individuals, but our actual experience was peculiar. The king's highway, so to speak, passes through Barkha, and search where one might one could not find it, and if it was not for the fact that the infallible map traced it quite clearly one would not even know of its existence. Barkha is on an enormous plain, viz., the plateau of 15,000 ft., which extends for very many miles, and until one actually reaches it it is very difficult to see, being concealed on the east by a bank. The approach is over hummocks of sand and juniper bushes, and it is impossible to travel fast. The traveller who did not know the exact spot on the horizon where this place lay would certainly fail to find it at all, and this description applies to all travelling in this part of the country. There is no apparent track anywhere, and the only course possible is to fix the eye on the desired goal and to wander across country, fording streams and avoiding bogs, until in the fulness of time the spot is reached, and woe betide the wretched traveller or pilgrim who does not know the country or confounds one range of hills with another exactly similar. A weary, weary march and much fruitless wandering will be his reward, as so many pilgrims testified to us.

BARKHA TARJUM'S HOUSE

Prayer-pole in front and prayer-sticks with connecting lines of prayer-flags on the top of the building, which is made of sun-dried bricks, some of which are lying in the foreground. The roof, as usual, is made of mud and a little thatching

At Barkha there are two houses: one for the Tarjum, a kind of glorified hut, in which ordinary peasants of our territory would scarcely deign to live; and the other, quarters for official travellers posting on the high road. This latter was composed of pitch-dark rooms, the only windows being tiny apertures bare to the outside air (glass being unknown), and full of every sort of filth. In most houses elsewhere thin cloth gauze usually takes the place of window-panes, the object being to admit light but exclude dust. Glass is quite unknown in Western Tibet. From years of exposure to the smoke of cow-dung and sheep-dung fires (for chimneys are unknown) the roof was covered with a black enamel, which is wonderfully durable and a great preservative. This peculiar effect of the smoke of the above fuel was also noticeable in caves in the cliffs, where the black enamel had become a thick cake on all the walls and roof, and this incrustation, being highly polished, was quite an ornament to the place. There were a few Dokpa tents, by one of which was stored the tea which the official government trader (Yungchong) had left to be sold, and there were groups of women milking ewes and goats. These latter are tied neck to neck in a long line, so closely together that movement is impossible, alternate animals looking in opposite directions, and the women go up and down the lines with great rapidity. The milk is made into butter, being much too valuable to drink plain, and is then sewn up in skin coverings, the natural fur remaining outside. The smell and taste are appalling. Throughout our trip we used tinned milk, as it was quite impossible to obtain any other, and in consequence it was particularly difficult to diet any members of our party who fell ill.

The Tarjum was away at Gartok undergoing his trial for the murder of the servant of the Taklakot Shivling, and his brother, who was in charge during his absence, was at Gyanema managing the fair that was at its height. The only representative of authority was the Goba. This official is of the nature of a rural magistrate, and is to be found everywhere in Western

Tibet. He is in charge of a certain number of village headmen (Makpan) and (for the latter are empowered to settle simple village quarrels and can inflict light whipping and fine) hears all those disputes which are too complicated for the headmen. From the Goba appeal lies to the Jongpen or Tarjum, and in parts where these do not exist to the Chikep, or District Magistrate, whose appointment emanates from Lhasa.

Black tent of Dokpas

MILKING SHEEP AND GOATS AT BARKHA.

The Goba supplied us with wood and changed some of our baggage animals, and, in fact, did generally all that could be reasonably expected of him. It cannot be too frequently noted that throughout our travels the Tibetans showed the greatest friendliness towards us, and were always pleased to converse with us in front of their tents, and to show their little knick-knacks and engage in amicable barter. The next march was to Darchan, at the very foot of Kailas, where all pilgrims first assemble before circumambulating the mountain, the journey being across the wilderness of bog, morass and sand hummocks, while we seemed to be perpetually fording streams. The fact is that the whole of this land as far as the foot of the Kangri or Kailas range of mountains must at one time have been a lake and part of the Rakas Tal, for the ground is very little higher than the level of that lake, and in times of much rain becomes absolutely waterlogged and very difficult to traverse. There are also other marks to lead to this conclusion.

Here in the very midst of Tibetan territory we found an administration ruled by the Ruler of Bhutan, independent of the Gartok viceroys and of Lhasa itself. Apparently the whole is in the nature of a religious endowment, in which the Bhutan representatives will not now tolerate any interference, and so far have matters gone in the past that the retainers of the Darchan ruler have met those of the Garphans and blows have been exchanged, even fire-arms being brought into use. During the last three years the appointed officer, who bears the title of Dashok, has been absent from Darchan without intermission, and his faithful servant has done the work in the ordinary course of events as prevailing in Tibet, until now, finally, his master has been reported to be dead, and as no one has come to replace him he has become the virtual ruler. When we reached Darchan the whole establishment, great and small, was drunk; but by the evening we were able to effect communications with a few of the less inebriated, and in the morning we were on the best of terms with the master, who was extremely grieved that owing to severe indisposition he had been unable to see us on the preceding evening. His post is an important one, as he is the head administrator of Darchan;

of two monasteries, Nendiphu and Zutulphu (Jamdulphu of the maps), which are situated on the holy way round Kailas; of the Jaikep (Jenkhab) gompa on Lake Mansarowar; of the very important place Khojarnath; of Rungung and Do on the upper Karnali river; of Gazon near Gartok; and four monasteries Iti,

Mount Kailas

This woman's hair goes down to her feet

MILKING SHEEP AND GOATS AT BARKHA

Gonphu, Gesur and Samur in the Daba Jongpen's territory.

The actual circuit round the holy mountain of Kailas, the Heaven of Shiva, and one of the most sacred places in the Hindu religion, occupies on an average three days, the distance being about twenty-five miles. The path is not good, walking is absolutely obligatory, and the track rises in one place to a very great height, namely, to the Gauri-Kund, which is a lake that remains frozen at all times of the year, even in the hottest weather. As some persons measure their length on the ground for the entire distance, and others are aged or accompanied by women, and others again linger on the road, either for contemplation or to bathe in the icy waters of the Gauri-Kund (though the ordinary pilgrim merely breaks the ice and puts a little of the water on his head), it is easy to see that the time occupied by the journey varies very greatly. One and all condemn the record-breaker, who hurries round in as short a time as possible, and they apply to him the opprobrious epithet of "Khi-kor," the man who runs round like a dog.

Buddhists as well as Hindus do the pilgrimage, for the former place Kailas, which they call Gangri and Tise, in the same same category of holy mountains as Mount Everest and Mount Chari in Assam, and a pilgrimage to these three holy mountains in their opinion confers on the devotee a virtue which cannot be excelled. The ordinary pilgrim of means takes with him a tent and, stopping wherever his inclination dictates, accomplishes the journey with dignity and comfort, and a deliberation which betokens reverence. The man of humbler status takes refuge at the different gompas (or monasteries) and is thankful for the charity which has erected these places of rest. Ordinarily the first monastery visited is the one at Nendiphu, where there is a quaint offering to be found among the many matchlocks, swords and shields which have been given by the devotees of past generations, in the form of a pair of elephant tusks. These tusks are a curiosity in this part of the world, as elephants are very rare in Tibet. They have been found in Lhasa, but, speaking broadly, they are practically unknown in Tibet, and it is, therefore, startling to find these tusks at Kailas. The next monastery is at Dediphu, and thence the road goes *viâ* the Gauri-Kund frozen lake to Zutulphu (or Jamdulphu). About this latter place there is an interesting legend to the effect that in times gone by two lamas

SHEEP CARRYING LOADS: ONE DRIVER IS IN FRONT

met here, the one journeying round Kailas from left to right and the other from right to left, and they argued long as to who was in the right. Finding argument unavailing, the one heaved an enormous boulder at the other, who nimbly caught the missile in his hand and supported it like the strong man at the Aquarium, but, unlike the latter, to remove the doubts of all unbelievers he left the imprint of his fingers on the rock, visible to this day. It is needless to say that there are devotees who still think that from right to left is the proper method for the pilgrimage, and perform the journey accordingly. Perhaps the monastery that will be one of the most interesting in the future is the one at Gangta, where there is a library of books on religious subjects. Darchan is the spot where the circuit usually begins and ends.

The element of humour is rarely wanting in Tibet, a country in which prayers to the Divine Being are put in a barrel, or a wheel, and turned, and thereby are just as efficacious as if they had been reverently repeated on bended knee; where, for a consideration, a proxy can be found to undergo the punishment of the culprit; and where Viceroys and Jongpens can send their servants or relations to perform their duties while they themselves are absent from their charges. In the same way proxies can be found (they are at Darchan in numbers) who are quite ready to go round the holy mountain, either in the ordinary manner by walking or by measuring their lengths on the ground. The wages to be paid for this meritorious labour are one rupee and five rupees respectively, though by introducing a healthy amount of competition they can be lowered to half a rupee and three rupees. However, strange to say, there is a feeling prevalent that in things sacred it is not quite fair to exploit the market, and the purest minded devotees do not haggle over the higher prices. There is a stream at Darchan which descends direct from the holy mountain and the faithful bathe in its cold water. Carrying the argument of proxy to its logical conclusion, we asked whether bathing could also be done by proxy. The astonishment of the listeners was quite unaffected: the mere idea of a bath-proxy in Tibet was fantastic, where nobody ever bathes if he can help it, and where, should any one desire to acquire untold merit by doing such a rash and dangerous act, he might possibly perform the ablutions for his own personal salvation once in a life-time, but never would he trifle with his health to such a degree as to do them for another.

Tibetan pilgrims are very numerous and come from the most distant parts of Central Asia ; representatives of almost every nation and tribe throughout this vast area can be found, and every twelfth year, when there is a "Kumb Mela," or twelve-yearly fair, the numbers of the pilgrims are increased almost tenfold during favourable seasons. The next Kumb fair will take place in 1906 from the middle of May to the end of September. Pilgrims start for their homes with a herd of yaks, sheep and goats, on whose flesh and milk they live, and which they use as beasts of burden to carry a little merchandise for purposes of barter. Some devout men improve upon this prosaic system of honesty and start destitute of everything, but by intelligent diplomacy and prudent circumspection find themselves in possession of the herds and flocks of their neighbours, who chase them as dacoits. It is these hungry-eyed pilgrims who are the menace of the country, for they wander from place to place and, being sturdy and well armed, think nothing of driving off any cattle that are not carefully guarded, and as they are absolutely nomadic it is very difficult to get a clue in these desert wastes as to where the thieves have gone to. We met pilgrims from Kham (east of Lhasa), Mongolia, Lhasa, Ladakh and, in fact, from all the most distant places. Many of them paint their sheep red as a certain safeguard from every disease and all misfortune, and it was quite picturesque seeing these coloured animals on the barren plains. The whole country is full of sacred associations, and wherever one goes one meets devotees who generally manage to combine religion with

Our men crossing the ford

THE VALLEY OF THE SUTLEJ RIVER AT TIRTHAPURI

a little business: the markets of Gyanema and Taklakot are full of them and their numbers influence the trade.

On the western edge of the holy country of the lakes and Mount Kailas is Tirthapuri, a great centre for pilgrims, three days' march from Darchan, on the river Sutlej. The actual source of this river is at the monastery of Dalju, where there is a large spring, though a dry channel is continued up to the Rakas Tal, and in places in this channel water is found.

The local statements all agree in asserting that there is an underground flow of water throughout the entire length of this dry channel, which occasionally comes to the surface only to disappear later on. There can be no doubt that during a season of very heavy rain and floods this dry channel would connect the source at Dalju with the Rakas Tal. At Tirthapuri there is a strong flow of water in the river, and the presence of hot sulphur springs, combined with the old time traditions of the place, renders the locality peculiarly interesting to the devotee and the traveller.

When the world was young, so goes the tale, a demon by constant service and whole-hearted devotion made himself the favourite of the great god Shiva, who, pleased with his attentions, asked what favour he could show in return. The demon asked for the power of instantly turning to ashes any one on whose head he placed his hand. Shiva handed him his bracelet and conferred that power. Then evil thoughts filled the mind of the other, and he sought opportunity to destroy great Shiva himself by means of this bracelet and seize the reins of omnipotence, and snatch for himself fair Parbati the goddess-mate of the great deity. At this Shiva fled and concealed himself in the earth, and a shrine faithfully indicates the exact spot of this rapid retreat, while the demon went to dally with his beautiful consort. But Parbati, alone, was not without resource, and she insisted, as a preliminary to any advances, that the demon should dance the great and famous *pas seul* of Shiva, or for ever withdraw his attentions. In this dance the arms are alternately thrown over the head, and while the demon was executing this movement the dreaded bracelet struck him on the head and instantly reduced him to ashes, which are still visible as an object of religious enthusiasm on the banks of the river. At this spot there is a very hot sulphur spring, so hot that it is impossible to touch the water with the hand, and one might well be forgiven for thinking that the demon had been boiled and not blasted. The gompa rivals the one at Jiu for filth and stench, but its picturesque situation at the junction of three valleys, with the river winding through acres and acres of green grass, redeems what otherwise would be intolerable. A sacred circuit has been marked by Chortens and piles of stones, and here Hindus and Buddhists pace the holy way amidst some of the most beautiful surroundings of this part of Tibet. The gompa is under the direct management of the large monastery at Toling, but Ladakh has also a certain minor concern in the general administration, though owing to distance that concern has dwindled to insignificance.

The valley leading to Missar, euphemistically described as two miles from Tirthapuri, is full of excellent grazing grass for cattle, and opens out into a wide plain at Missar itself, which is sheltered on all sides by mountains from the prevailing winds. This is a post-station of a Tarjum, and owing to its being on the Lhasa, Daba and Gyanema cross-roads is a very busy place. The jurisdiction is really that of the Jongpen of Daba, but, according to Tibetan ways, the Chaprang Jongpen has leased the whole countryside from him on an annual rent of a thousaud rupees, and thereby has acquired the executive authority in this part. The duties of the Tarjum here consist simply in the forwarding of the imperial post and the providing of transport to travellers. He was away and his trusty servant was doing his work, and very well he performed it. He met us some way out on our road, and, conducting us to the camping-ground, supplied us with fuel and milk and next day with transport for our further journey. Nothing could have exceeded the affability and attention which he showed us. It appears that Tarjums, like most other officials in this world, have an inspecting

CHORTENS AND PILES OF STONES

officer called Sipchu, who occasionally visits them (generally when there has been some complaint of irregularity) and examines their books minutely as to the times of arrival and departure of the imperial post. The post in Tibet answers to the French description of goods traffic on the railways: there is *grande vitesse* and also *petite vitesse.* The former takes twenty-two days between Gartok and Lhasa, and the latter has been known to take four or even more months, and nobody to be one penny the worse. There is a third class of Specially Urgent, and this is always regarded with the greatest reverence, for the messenger is sealed in the saddle and rides day and night, the post thereby covering the distance from Gartok to Lhasa in eleven days, the least default or delay calling down heavy punishment on all concerned. There are always ponies in readiness owned by the Tarjum and the local residents, the latter paying part of their government dues by the supply of post-horses, and as nobody ever has the least idea when the next post will come or go, whether to-day or to-morrow or next month, every one is always on the *qui vive.* A regular log-book is kept at the post, and if on examination the inspecting Sipchu is dissatisfied—and it is always to his advantage to be dissatisfied—a fine is levied, which, of course, goes into the inspecting officer's private purse, as he purchases his post and makes what he can out of it.

While at Missar the assistant of the retiring official merchant (Yungchong) (the post is held for a year only), passed through on his way from Gartok, and his approach was heralded by riders carrying flags and much jingling of bells on the ponies' necks. We had a long interview with him, made all the more interesting from the fact that he knew all parts of Tibet, being a resident of Lhasa, and had also visited Calcutta. A singularly shrewd and intelligent man, he was much struck by the pictures of Lhasa and other places in Waddell's "Lhasa, and its Mysteries," and Landon's "Lhasa." The picture "The working of the heliograph being explained to the Chinese General Ma" especially appealed to him, and he readily grasped the system of long and short flashes, which is the basis of all telegraphy. European journals with pictures of royal visits, motor-cars, bicycles, and generally of a world totally different from his own, were the more appreciated as he had some knowledge of European life as seen in Calcutta and Darjeeling. It is impossible to imagine a more unpopular department than his, and, whether personally agreeable to him or not, there can be no question that habits of oppression had hardened the man and given a look of sternness to his otherwise pleasing appearance. The system of trade at fancy prices carried on by compulsion reminds one of charity bazaars, where one is forced to buy something one does not want at an exorbitant price. In the latter case one has the consolation of religious motives; but in the former the mere fact that each official is trying to make the most out of his post and advantages entirely overwhelms whatever feeling of patriotism may exist to persuade the victim that the impost is merely a lawful form of state taxation.

During our stay at Missar a Ladakh merchant was set upon by thieves and robbed of all he possessed quite close to our camp; he asked us to assist him in recovering his property, but no clue whatever was obtainable as to the route taken by the dacoits. Properly authenticated news also reached us of the seizure of two hundred goats and sheep and fifteen jibboos at Gyanema by dacoits, who, when pursued, made a fight of it and only yielded their booty when one of their number had been shot dead and four had been captured and bound. The captives were taken to the Daba Jongpen, and no doubt they will wish that they had died rather than been taken alive to be tortured. In this case the persons who had been robbed, finding that nothing but extreme measures were of the least avail, hired a professional Tibetan desperado who made it a practice to lend his services for a consideration to shoot dacoits. This man had shortly before shot three other dacoits, and was quite a well-known character. This picture of the state of things in Tibet illustrates the lawlessness that exists there, and the helplessness of officials to suppress the bad characters. Every man takes the remedy into his own hands.

Tibetan yaks differ from those of the Bhotias in that they never have the nose pierced for a ring and cord except in the case of those meant for riding, with the result that they are much more like wild animals than domesticated beasts of burden. At Missar we exchanged almost the whole of our transport-yaks and jibboos, hitherto supplied by the Bhotias, for Tibetan yaks, and the scene during lading on that eventful morning baffled description, while many of those actively engaged in the fight ran short in their vocabulary for expressions which adequately and faithfully portrayed their feelings. The yaks smelt our servants and bolted, while the Tibetan drivers knew no Hindustani and were indifferent. There was no way of catching and holding the yaks securely, as the rope round the necks was useless for purposes of control, and yak after yak, when half-loaded, would break across country and buck off all the half-adjusted baggage, while properly loaded yaks standing near by would follow suit to show their sympathy. Every body said all they thought, but the Tibetan drivers, in ignorance of what was said, only smiled, and, notwithstanding the breakage of many precious things, it was really impossible not to treat the whole affair as a huge joke. We said good-bye to the good people of Missar amidst beaming smiles and the best of good humour, while the yaks went bounding and bucking across the plain.

CHAPTER XV

GARTOK AND THE VICEROYS

THE plateau of 15,000 ft. in which the Holy Lakes are situated continues without interruption to the neighbourhood of Missar, where there is a gradual descent to an elevation of 14,300 ft., as this place is in a hollow, situated on one of the tributary sources of the river Sutlej. Travelling thence in the direction of Gartok, along wide stretches of green grass, the plateau of 15,000 ft. is rapidly regained, and is found to extend as far as Gartok (15,100 ft.), the only interruption being the Jerko La, 16,200 ft. high, a pass which is so gradually approached that the elevation is scarcely perceptible. Soon after crossing this pass one of the sources of the Indus, the Langboche, or Elephant's Trunk, is met with, and the meadows of verdant grazing-ground continue along the whole extent of this stream, which becomes the Gartang, past the summer seat of the vice-royalty, Gartok, and the winter quarters, Gargunsa, until the northern tributary of that mighty river is reached a little south of Demchok, an important centre of the trade to Leh and Ladakh.

Everywhere from Taklakot onwards we found tail-less rats ("mouse-hares," ochotona) and hares in myriads, but the flesh of the latter is not very sweet to eat, and their skins are so thin and fragile, and the fur so readily drops off, that they are of no commercial value. One cannot help feeling what a pity it is that this is the case, as were it otherwise there is an almost inexhaustible supply of the softest and most delicate fur that could be desired. Kyangs, or wild asses, are seen everywhere, and form the food of many Tibetans, especially those from Kham and Nakchiu near Lhasa, although there is a strong feeling amongst certain classes that they are not lawful for this purpose. Residents of Lhasa and the more self-respecting Tibetans of Western Tibet are against the practice of killing the kyang for food, and our Bhotias and Hindus go so far as to place the kyang in the same category as the cow, and refuse even to touch it. The Mania Tibetans, sometimes spoken of as wild men, are principally addicted to the chase of what is generally known among Tibetans as the wild horse (kyang), and make it a staple article of diet, and one finds portions of the carcase in out of the way spots marking the scene of a successful hunt. A very remarkable fact, which we found widely vouched for, is that so many of the wild asses hunted down and killed are geldings, the theory being that in early youth the mothers effect the rather delicate operation of castration. There can be no question that the fact is very generally stated on the authority of those who make the kyang an article of diet. Kyang foals if brought up by a domesticated mare can be broken to work. Pundit Gobaria, a Bhotia of Garbyang, had three large kyangs at one time in his own possession, which all worked. They are only fit for light riding as their hooves are too soft for the hard ground and their skins too tender for heavy loads.

Marmots are also eaten by certain Tibetans of the lower class, who are looked down upon for practising this custom, while the yak, domestic and wild, considered by Hindus in the light of a cow, is generally

GARTOK, ALSO KNOWN AS GARYERSA, OR GRERSA, ON A BRANCH OF THE INDUS RIVER

THE RIVER IS BETWEEN THE HOUSES AND THE MOUNTAINS: THE WHITE IN THE PICTURE ON THE PLAIN IS RUNNING WATER, NOT SNOW

eaten by all Tibetans in these parts and is much prized for food. Bhotias are in the stage of betwixt and between: those who are non-Hinduised eat it readily, while those who are taking to themselves the respectability of Hinduism consider it as sacred and to be avoided at all costs.

Fowls are not to be found anywhere and consequently eggs are unobtainable—not that the Tibetans of these parts have any religious or social scruples against the keeping of poultry, like many high caste Hindus, but apparently they find the climatic difficulties insuperable. The Jongpen of Taklakot started a poultry-farm which prospered during the warm weather, but in the winter the fowls' feet were frozen off and they became cripples. One cannot help feeling that with a little effort difficulties might be overcome, for the cold is not more severe than in Canada, where poultry-farming flourishes, but it is just in this quality of enterprise that the Tibetan of Western Tibet is lacking. He has the most perfect country for road-making, immense level plains, no gradients and a small rainfall, and practically all he has to do is to remove the stones on one side and a splendid road is made; but this small amount of energy he is unequal to. The greater part of Western Tibet is a country of stones: they may be small or large, great rocks or medium-sized boulders, but they cover the whole country far and wide and cut the feet of all baggage animals to pieces. It is impossible to take even the best beasts of burden along these tracks for many days continuously, as their hooves get so worn by the stones that they become quite lame. All that is required is to make a track clear of stones, a work which could easily be done by the local residents along the route and the expense

Rakas Lake

Gurla Mandhata (25,350 ft.), scarcely visible: it rises sheer 10,000 ft. from the plain.

A TYPICAL VIEW OF THE COUNTRY IN WESTERN TIBET

THIS GIVES A GOOD IDEA OF THE STONES WHICH LIE EVERYWHERE, AND OF THE DIFFICULTY OF SHELTER FROM THE CUTTING WIND

would be very small. Bridges for rivers and culverts for streams are at present out of the question, as there is no timber for the former, and the principle of the arch in architecture is absolutely unknown for the latter. Still, the rivers need not be as dangerous as some of them undoubtedly are, being full of stones, sharp, slippery and so situated that the feet of ponies and other animals frequently get caught between them as in a vice, and the driver has to remove the stones so as to free the imprisoned limb. As an instance, there is the stream at Nakiu, five miles from Gartok, where there is the seat of a Tarjum. This stream is practically unfordable for six miles at least above Nakiu, as no one will take the risk of laming his animals. The principal ford is opposite the Tarjum's house, where some attempt has been made to remove the boulders, but the work has been so badly done that the crossing is very dangerous, and one Bhotia, arriving after dark, preferred to spend the night 200 yards from the camp of his friends on the opposite side of the river rather than risk injury to his baggage animals by attempting the crossing in the dim light of the moon. A very little labour would remedy this defect: certainly in a couple of days the stones could easily be cleared and a first-class ford made. But it is in these and similar matters that there is no directing head. Each official buys his post and as the period of his appointment is limited his sole thought is to fill his own purse, and the wide interests of the public are entirely a secondary consideration.

The responsibility attaching to the Tarjum's work at Nakiu, the first post-station out of Gartok, falls on the Jongpen of Chaprang, and he has the whole executive administration of this part of the district. He appoints one of his own retainers as Tarjum, but does not thereby divest himself of any of the responsibility, and in consequence this official is in reality of very inferior status and lives in a small mud-hut. On our arrival we found that, like most officials in Tibet, he was elsewhere on some very important business, and that,

THE TARJUM'S HOUSE AT NAKIU

The first post-station out of Gartok on the way to Lhasa

according to the easy-going customs of the country, his wife was in charge of his duties. She certainly was quite capable of doing her husband's work, and the way she supervised her male subordinates was admirable. She presented herself with her child, five years old, at our camp and formally asked us about our wants. I showed her a photo of my own little daughter, and we compared the ages of the two children amidst the greatest good humour, and then, giving this five years old child the breast, she proceeded to discuss the business of a change of transport animals, fuel and all the minor necessaries relating to our comfort, while we and a dozen men sat round and entered into details. She was the only woman at this post-station and was not in the least abashed at her responsibilities. She and her little girl chased yaks, threw stones at wandering cattle, brought milk, sat at the cook's tent and examined our food, shouted directions to servants half a mile away, and finally, when we left, mother and child helped to load our yaks, and riding astride on a pony drove the baggage animals to Gartok.

Soon after leaving Nakiu one reaches the famous racecourse of Gartok on which is run the great annual pony race, in which the officials, nobility and landholders take part. The course extends about four miles along an ideal plain, which, an exception to the general rule, is almost devoid of stones and, for Tibet, affords very good going for horses, there being no natural obstacles throughout except one small stream. But we were told that the glory has departed from this sporting event, in that the competition has lost all its element of genuine rivalry owing to the grasping meanness of officials, who insist on winning by fair means or foul. Rudok is famous for its horse-flesh, and almost invariably a Rudok pony comes in first. A Rudok landholder, in years gone by, won the race three years running with the same mount, a series of successes which could not be tolerated by the Garphan, who compelled the sale of the famous winner and for some years won the event himself with the same pony. So far has this unfairness gone that nowadays mounted retainers are stationed near the winning-post to prevent any but the Garphan's ponies winning, and the result is that landholders have lost all interest in the race, entering ponies merely to fill up the list, and even Jongpens, *e.g.*, the Jongpen of Taklakot, find excuses for non-attendance at the races, and send hired ponies to represent them in the annual contest. The prizes are valuable as heretofore, namely, a first class pony, a good yak, and so on,

THE WIFE OF THE TARJUM

Officiating for her absent husband: her little girl is on her back, but penny trumpets could not persuade her to be photographed

while the last in, on the analogy of the wooden spoon, gets a basketful of dung. The jockeys are young boys of about twelve years of age, and generally come from Rudok, where they have been well grounded in the theory of race-riding. The saddles are of the lightest, and some of the ponies are most handsomely turned out as to their trappings; in fact, all is excellent except that the element of honest sport is gone. After the great race is over the Garphans sit on a raised platform under a large tent and watch feats of horsemanship executed by the local militia. Some 200 to 300 horsemen take part in these exercises, the principal being firing two shots at full gallop at different targets with a matchlock. To effect this the rider carries two guns slung round his shoulders, and uses first one and then the other, the pony travelling at full speed the whole time. Another exercise is firing under similar conditions, but in this instance with bow and arrows, which used in former times to be the Tibetan national weapons: their generals are still called Depung, or Lords of the Arrow. Besides these there are acrobatic feats on horseback, such as the rider standing on his head while the pony is at full gallop, and exhibitions of skill in horsemanship such as causing the pony to rear and remain in that position. The lack of enterprise which is noticeable everywhere is apparent here also, in that the state platform is in hopeless disrepair, the Rudok Jongpen's quarters occupied by him at the time of the races have tumbled into ruins, and the visitors' apartments in the village are falling into decay. All the houses in Gartok, fifteen to twenty in number, are built of sun-dried bricks, and are actually mud huts of the most inferior quality, the only two dwelling-houses having the least pretensions to comfort and magnificence being those of the two Garphans.

At the time of our visit the two viceroys were in the act of changing from their winter to their summer head-quarters and were daily expected to arrive in Gartok. In the meanwhile the official government trader (Yung-chong), who was on the point of retiring from his office, received us and did the honours. He was dressed

THE VICEROYS' HOUSES AT GARTOK

in Chinese costume, and in accordance with Chinese custom wore the nail of the little finger of an inordinate length, the object being to conclusively advertise the fact that manual labour was an impossibility. He informed us that he and his brother official, the Sarpen, usually started from Lhasa together, and while he took the southern route *viâ* the Holy Lakes, the other took the northerly one passing through Thok Jalung, and that after their annual tour they met at Gartok. He told us that he himself had only just returned from Ladakh and was now waiting for the Sarpen to arrive from the north. The word Sar means "gold," and this officer bears this name inasmuch as, in addition to his ordinary duties of selling government goods as an official government trader, he collects the taxes from the gold-diggers. The tax is from ten to twelve rupees per head annually and is a poll-tax on every digger. Considering the output, the tax is merely nominal. The gold-mining industry has declined of late years, the principal reason being the absolute want of enterprise characteristic of all things Tibetan. There is a perpetual haunting fear in the minds of the official class that any innovation may disturb the mahatmas, or spirits, of the earth, and hence the general policy of *laissez faire*; let the old order continue, but all things new are strictly taboo. Bhotias found, and worked, a borax mine a little to the north of Gartok, but the order peremptorily closing this industry was soon issued, for no apparent reason, and this field of enterprise is now shut off from the trader.

Gartok is also known as Garyersa, which is abbreviated into Grersa, and is situated at a height of 15,100 ft. in the middle of an enormous plain, where the wind can sweep over it from every side. It is the fact of this exposed position that makes it so unpopular with the Garphans, and which leads them to live at Gargunsa, four days' march further west, for the greater part of the

Viceroy's son

THE SENIOR VICEROY, OR URGU GONG

High officials wear a long ear-ring of turquoise, &c., in the left ear: the robes are of Chinese silk, and the boots Lhasa-made

year. The word Yersa means summer, or heat, while the term Gunsa means winter, or cold. There is a defect in part of the water-supply at Gartok, as at times of drought there is a white efflorescence exuding from the ground, which is so dangerous to animals that if eaten with grass or otherwise it causes the hair to fall off from the whole body, when the animal becomes unable to bear the great cold and dies. The Indus river is full of magnificent fish which are caught by our Bhotias with the hand by means of tickling (there are no nets or rods), while the Tibetans refuse to enjoy what nature has so lavishly bestowed on them. For some inex-

Viceroy's son

THE SENIOR VICEROY

plicable reason they consider fish and birds an improper diet, to be avoided as anathema, and thereby they make for themselves even greater difficulties than already exist in this very trying country, where vegetables are unobtainable, poultry does not exist, grain cannot be grown (this does not refer to the low valleys of Taklakot and Daba), and milk is so valuable for butter that it is scarcely ever drunk by itself.

Marital relations are a little confused in the case of the Garphans. The Senior Viceroy, or Urgu Gong, has a son, a nice boy of something over twenty, living with him, who in the usual course of events is married. When the father lost his own wife it was thought proper that he should become a joint husband of the

THE JUNIOR VICEROY, OR URGA HOG

Note the pendant ear-ring: the cloth on the right is the window-pane, removed to give light during our interview in the room which comes out black in the photo

son's wife, and this is the existing *ménage*, father and son owning the same wife. Nor is this state of things considered in the least disgraceful, for the father is a most respectable man of excellent family, and would scorn to do anything by which a slur might be cast on his name. Apparently it is an orthodox custom in Tibet for father and sons to share the same wife, the only condition laid down being that she shall not be the son's mother. As in polyandry, the eldest husband is called father, and the rest "little" father. This custom is analogous to the one by which a man, when he marries a widow, is allowed to marry at the same time all her daughters; for instance, a widow with daughters aged twenty, fifteen and ten would become his wife with her two elder daughters at once, and, when the youngest girl had grown up, she would also join the others in the conjugal life.

The Junior Viceroy, or Urgu Hog, on the other hand, is living a life which is universally condemned. In reality he is only the son of the Junior Viceroy, but his father owing to ill-health has not been at Gartok for the last six years, and throughout that time his son has done the work. This boy (he is only twenty-four years old) has also been in poor health, and is now on the point of being relieved of his duties by the son of the Taklakot Jongpen. Meanwhile he is, and has been, a man of great power, as the position of affairs is such that one viceroy cannot act by himself, for there is dual control, and the authority of both Garphans is necessary to ratify any matter. So far is this the case that the box with the joint seal remains in the custody of the one while the key remains with the other. This boy is in the hands of one of his retainers, who has so strong an influence over him, owing to the fact that his wife is the other's mistress, that he interferes publicly when the two Garphans sit in Court and goes unrebuked. It is a particularly trying state of things for the Senior Viceroy to find himself, although the elder man, continually baulked by a boy, who is only the son of the real incumbent, and is absolutely in the hands of an unscrupulous subordinate. The friction will soon come to an end, as the Taklakot Jongpen's eldest son is the new Viceroy-elect (we saw his wife at Taklakot) and will take over his duties very shortly. The out-going Viceroy will, however, (according to Tibetan custom) remain a year to collect all pending debts due from the peasantry.

The Senior Viceroy, or Urgu Gong, is very popular with all classes and enjoys a good reputation. It was his lot to succeed a most high-handed and arbitrary officer, the Garphan Chakta, who had oppressed the people to such an extent that finally there was open insubordination to his rule, and the whole matter was reported to Lhasa. His principal vice was to wring money out of the peasantry by all legal and illegal means. The annual revenue was collected with a rigour that was indefensible, and the sales of government property, such as tea, carpets, &c., to the people, always an authorised but unpopular form of revenue, were conducted with a harshness and cupidity that meant absolute ruin to all. Thus it came about that, although the peasants had accepted government property at the sales, they refused point blank to make the payments, and arranged to have their interests represented at Lhasa. When the present Urgu Gong succeeded Chakta he remitted all land-revenue for a term, and enormously reduced the fabulous payments due on the government property already bought. Some years of his term of office have now passed and he is in universal favour, while at the same time he is shrewd and thoroughly statesmanlike in his official dealings. Certainly in all our business with him he showed a courtesy and a grasp of detail which made him a very pleasant official with whom to have any transactions.

Gartok is the capital of Western Tibet, known as Nari, and the two Viceroys exercise almost unfettered power in the territory under their jurisdiction. Nari begins at the Mariam La, or Mayum La (16,900 ft.), a pass east of the Holy Lakes, and stretches to Ladakh on the west, while on the south is the Indian frontier. That part of Nari which is south of the Kangri, or Kailas, range of mountains is called Nari Khorsum, or Hundes, while the part to the north is known in our maps as Monyul; but the Garphans do not call it by this name and place Monyul farther to the east. They speak of Thok Jalung and the other goldfields as being in Northern Nari: the land itself is under the Rudok Jongpen, but in administrative matters the Sarpen, or gold officer, is supreme, though of course subordinate to the Garphans. Thok Jalung is 16,200 or 16,300 ft. high and is practically on the outskirts of the habitable world, being the highest spot in the world inhabited all the year round, for beyond is the great Chang Tang plateau averaging an altitude of 17,000 ft., where there are only wild yak, kyang and deer, and few men can live owing to the want of water and the bleakness of the climate. The Garphans did not know the northern limit of their own province of Nari, for, as they said, the matter was of no importance whatever, as no human being dwelt in the Chang Tang plateau. They had never heard of the Kuen Lun mountains, which our maps show as the northern border of Tibet. They also stated that they never toured through the territory subject to them, and in fact never left Gargunsa, or Gartok, without special and definite orders from Lhasa. We asked the Senior Viceroy, a stout gentleman of middle age, if he ever went out on foot or horseback for a constitutional, and he was simply aghast at the bare idea. He replied emphatically "No." The pale, pasty complexions of these high officials and of their families amply corroborate this statement. All the officials of considerable standing whom we met were effeminate in their physique, and their bodies lacked that firmness of muscle and vigour of bearing with which we are so familiar among our own race.

The post of Viceroy is nominally for a time of three years, but almost invariably the term is extended for another similar period, and thus becomes six years in all. The officials are appointed from Lhasa on condition of

OUR YAKS FORDING A STREAM, WHICH IS, AS USUAL, FULL OF STONES AND BOULDERS

paying to the Imperial Treasury a certain sum of money, which enables them to take the province on farm, that is, like the ancient Roman Proconsuls, they try and make as much profit out of the appointment as possible, and it is a recognised state custom that all revenue, fines, &c., go into their private pockets. They trade on their own account, and also are bound to dispose annually of a certain quantity of government goods, such as tea and carpets. The Garphans have not gone so far as the Daba Jongpen, who made it a practice to buy cheap Indian tea and label it "Chinese," and putting it in the regular Tibetan government skins to sell it to the peasantry as the best Tibetan article; but they rejoice almost openly when some *cause célèbre* brings parties of position before them. In the case of the Barkha Tarjum, who shot a servant of the Abbot of the Taklakot Shivling, the income they derived from the trial was very considerable. First of all, both parties bribed the court to view the case leniently, but from the beginning the Barkha Tarjum gave out that he would be the successful party, and unquestionably he was very free with the precious metal. The final judgment in the case is really more fitted for a Gilbert and Sullivan comic opera than for the prosaic facts of life. The Garphans with masterly insight fined both parties, the Grand Lama Rs 1800 and the Tarjum Rs 1100 and put the proceeds into their own pockets!

At Gartok there is now stationed a British Agent to protect trade interests, and his appointment is the direct outcome of the Treaty of Lhasa. Thakur Jai Chand is of excellent family, being the nephew of the Thakur of Lahaul, and while commanding the respect of the Tibetans is of material assistance from a political point of view. Lahaul is a portion of the British district Kangri in the Punjab, and as all its inhabitants are traders with Tibet from their earliest years they are all familiar with the Tibetan language. Lahaul does not itself border on Nari, being cut off by Spiti, which is another division of the Kangra district; but, curiously enough, although all the Lahaul residents are traders yet the inhabitants of Spiti, a cheerless country where there are no trees, are entirely agricultural and will have nothing to do with trade. Men from Lahaul are to be found at Rudok (they utilise a route between Demchok and Hanle) and at many other places in western Nari, and their principal trade lies in wool and pashm, *i.e.*, fine goat's hair, and they annually import about £3500 worth of these articles. In return, strange to say, they have practically nothing to give in the shape of goods, but pay for these imports in solid cash, and this fact further accounts for the popularity

THAKUR JAI CHAND, BRITISH TRADE AGENT AT GARTOK

and the wide circulation of Indian coinage noted in the previous pages. At present Ladakh and Lahaul take the greater part of the trade of western Nari, for there is very little trade with Simla direct, although when the new road has been opened there are hopes of a considerable increase. Further, the only other competitors, the Bashahris, come a long way behind these two.

Thakur Jai Chand is on intimate terms with the Garphans, and has frequently witnessed the administration of justice in the Tibetan Supreme Court. As soon as an offender is brought before the tribunal, before any inquiry or investigation of any sort, he is whipped. This is called the introductory whipping, as it introduces all parties to the justice of the courts. It is to be remembered that, in inflicting corporal punishment, the victim is tied face downwards on the ground, and two men sit on him with whips. When each man has given one stroke a third official counts one, in other words, a punishment of one hundred stripes is really one of two hundred stripes. This is the universal Tibetan practice: it is a humorous custom, of which the humour is scarcely appreciated by the victim. The blows are always delivered on the tendon above the knee, the object being to prevent the wretched man from walking for some considerable time afterwards.

The next event is the investigation, which takes place on some day fixed in the future. Proceedings open with whipping number two, to encourage the prisoner to be free in the disclosure of facts. Evidence is recorded on slats of wood by the Garphans, and is subsequently copied on to paper to make the record. The accused is never questioned, except for purposes of a confession, and his evidence in defence is never taken. He is almost invariably condemned practically unheard, and as a prelude to any other punishment is whipped for the third time. This is known as the final whipping, not that it is so really. One favourite sentence is to send the condemned to each of the four Jongpens, each of whom on his arrival immediately administers castigation, and after keeping him for a time sends him on to his next-door neighbour. The wife and children are handed over to the headman of some village, where they lead the lives of slaves for the rest of their natural term, doing all the unpaid labour that is so generally required by officials from villagers.

The Garphans always sit and act together, and although the Senior Viceroy enjoys a certain amount of extra consideration owing to his years, still no act is valid until ratified by both. This form of government

TIBETAN WOMEN

They are carrying baskets on the back: the woman on the left has hanging from her waist strings of beads and tinkling bells: this is a common practice and a woman walking can be heard a long way off

is very common in Central Tibet, where the Jongpens are always appointed two at a time and there is dual authority; but in Western Tibet it is unknown, except in the case of the Garphans. It is true that at Taklakot the Abbot sits with the Jongpen, but there can be no question that the civil officer far outweighs the priest in all civil administration. The houses in which the Viceroys live are of the poorest description and extremely uncomfortable. They are cramped, dark, dirty and by no means rain-proof, and must be dreadfully unpleasant to live in ; yet such is the lack of energy in all things official that no attempt is made to improve the accommodation.

It is impossible not to feel an admiration for the masses of the people of this portion of Tibet, who are ridden with no light hand by their two masters, the officials and the priests, and yet are able to mingle so much pleasure and happiness in their life. From early years the up-bringing of the youth of the nation is a hardy one ; notwithstanding the extremely trying climate, little children are seen running about naked, and there can be no question that only the sturdy ones are able to survive this treatment, the others dying in childhood. It is this early exposure to all the changes of the weather that renders men and women so indifferent to dress in their later years. Men were frequently seen on the coldest days of summer, when we were all glad of very warm clothing, working stripped bare to the waist, while it is a common practice for men and women to expose the right half of the body, the remainder being covered with a fur coat, and both sexes almost invariably have the neck and part of the chest uncovered. To such lengths do these people go that they cannot endure the warmth of our hills, even in the winter, and always complain of skin eruption when they visit our territory, due to the change in climate. This is analógous to what is a matter of common knowledge, viz., that yaks from Tibet cannot descend below 8000 ft. without succumbing to the change of air, and Dokpas never care to bring their sheep, goats and other beasts of burden below 10,000 ft.

The majority of the common people are intensely ignorant, and in the grasp of a debasing superstition that enters into the whole life. It is a common sight to see a man covered with charms, one for small-pox, one for accidents, one for disaster in business, and so on. The whole nation is devoted to wearing in ear-rings, finger-rings, amulets, &c., the blue turquoise, which is a specific against the evil eye (but the blue must not

A TIBETAN CHARM IN A SILVER CASE, AND TWO STONES INSCRIBED WITH THE WORDS "OM MANI PADME HUNG"

have lost its colour), and Bhotias do a large trade in this article. However, it is a cruel commentary on the efficacy of charms that the Dalai Lama has had small-pox. Wherever one goes one sees extracts from the Buddhist scriptures carved in Tibetan and Sanskrit, and the magic formula, "Om Mani Padme Hung," inscribed on stones round monasteries, by the road-side and on the tops of mountain passes, all offerings of the devoutly inclined, while the words of the sacred formula are on the lips of all who tell their beads or twirl their prayer-wheels, and yet the meaning of these sacred things is hidden from the masses. "Om Mani Padme Hung," "Hail! Jewel of the Lotus Flower, Hail!" (referring to the deified Dalai Lama) is generally regarded as a potent charm protecting from every evil and calamity that human nature is heir to, and the words have become a sort of talisman to be conjured with.

However, the people are thoroughly aware of the advantages of education, for although there are no state or private schools of any kind yet they make an effort to secure private tuition, either at the monasteries or at the Jongpen's fort, or from some illiterate person in the village, and it is quite wonderful how many of the men are literate. Female education in Western Tibet is much neglected; in this respect there being a marked contrast to the state of things at Lhasa, where it is not uncommon, so we were informed, for the wives of merchants and persons of position to be able to read and write.

Combination also for purposes of resisting the unlawful exactions of officials or the depredations of dacoits is not unknown; for example, it was the people of Rudok who led the great revolt against the exorbitant exactions of the unscrupulous Garphan Chakta, and the Horpas, east of the Holy Lakes, are as adamant in their dealings in the purchase of official goods with the Yungchong, or government merchant, for they are immensely wealthy and can represent their interests (by bribery) at Lhasa. There is always a cheeriness about the men that makes them the most pleasant companions on a march, or under adverse circumstances, and one cannot help regretting that they are under a government which shows no consideration for their interests, and subject to officials and priests who bleed them on every possible opportunity. The women are physically far inferior to the men, and their bodies lack that vigour and their faces that cheerfulness which are so marked a feature of the Bhotia women, the reason being undoubtedly in great measure due to the practice of polyandry. The European custom of hand-shaking is common everywhere, and it is

A caitya or death memorial

THESE ARE MUD IMAGES OF TIBETAN DEITIES, THE IMPRESS BEING MADE WITH A STAMP

They are placed in hundreds by devotees in caves and sacred spots. Each contains a few grains of corn, which have germinated in some of the above: this practice signifies the immortal hope after death

quite an ordinary thing to see friends, meeting after an interval of separation, use the form of salutation to which we are all accustomed. All officials in greeting us, or bidding us farewell, shook hands invariably, and we also saw Bhotias and Tibetans use the same salutation. The removal of the cap from the head with the hand is a common practice on the part of merchants and persons of position in the presence of the Jongpen, or when meeting that officer, while the lower classes put out the tongue, not a little way, but as far as it will go.

The drinking of tea is the usual accompaniment to a bargain at the shop of a merchant or when paying a call, and during our interviews with officials their servants would generally enter two or three times and offer their master tea in a cup, which would be sipped and returned. These cups are made of onyx and jade, and are sometimes very expensive, the one shown to us by the Yungchong being worth six guineas, and the more influential the visitor the more costly the cup set before him by the host. The Yungchong showed us cups of different grades suitable to callers of varying position. The tea in general use is the well-known brick-tea made of leaves compressed into a solid mass, but it must be carefully remembered that there is an admixture with the tea, which gives to the beverage its red colour and also a very stimulating effect. What that admixture is, is a secret very carefully treasured by the Chinese manufacturers, but it was accidentally discovered by one Kumaon firm, the Berenag Tea Company, as a cake of Chinese brick-tea opened by them was found to have a leaf of the herb utilised left in it by an oversight. This leaf was carefully examined and was traced to a wild plant which grows very generally in many localities in our hills, and as soon as experiments produced the red colour and the stimulating effect in the beverage it was known for certain that the whole secret was discovered. The tea of this company in consequence is very popular in Tibet, while the Daba Jongpen has been in the habit of passing it off as the Chinese article; and for all trade purposes in the future, the factor of this admixture being present or not will have a great influence in the sale of the commodity.

Nothing could have been more successful than our

visit to Gartok, and our relations with the Viceroys were all that could be desired. Their dress, like that of all officials, was in the Chinese style, while the hat of state was yellow, with a handle and tassel attached to it by means of the large opaque blue button indicating

OFFICIAL TIBETAN TEA PACKED IN LEATHER CASES LEFT BY THE YUNGCHONG FOR SALE

The men are Dokpas wearing fur-lined coats : the tent is black and made of woven yaks' hair

their office of Viceroy, the third rank in the state. Large spectacles, worn as a means of giving an appearance of intellectual proficiency, gave the finishing touch. These were removed during the course of our interviews, as they were only in the way for seeing and examining the various Western objects of interest which we showed them. There is a recognised custom among the gentlemen and nobility of India of handing round scent, cardamums and betel-nut at all friendly interviews, and I thought that possibly the Viceroys might be so well acquainted with Indian ways as to expect us to conform with the universal Indian practice. I, therefore, ordered some Parisian scent of a superior quality to be opened, but the effect was immediate and ludicrous. The Junior Garphan held his nose in a most ostentatious manner and begged to be spared. Tibetans detest scent of every description. Rifles and pictures supplied more food for conversation than anything else: the former as an indication of the power of a European nation, and the latter on account of the entirely new world which was laid before the eye. When we parted a firm friendship had sprung up between us, and the Viceroys did everything in their power to make our return journey as smooth as possible. Had it not been for this assistance we should have been delayed on our way, and we were extremely fortunate to have the Viceregal order with us compelling instant attendance to our needs. The fact is, that Tibet is marked out into stages and the yaks are carefully told off accordingly, and the practice of years has made every one fully acquainted with the rules. For instance, the Missar yaks go to Nakiu, to Barkha and to Gyanema, while those of Barkha go to Missar, to Thokchan and Taklakot, and those of Nakiu to Gartok and Missar, and so on. If the traveller arrives at the end of his stage and finds the yaks for the next stage gone away with some one else's belongings to some other place, he cannot proceed until they return, and this may mean almost a week's delay. However, the Viceregal order over-rode the demands of all others, and everywhere we found the transport animals ready for us. The Garphans could not have done more to show their friendliness, and we on our side were not slow to do all in our power to make our visit interesting as well as a means of cementing friendship.

X MOVING CAMP: THE YAKS ARE TIED IN A ROW ON A ROPE

The pitching of camp at the close of day bears with it many memories which bring before the mind much of that daily life in Tibet which is liable to be forgotten by reason of its sameness or its supposed lack of interest, though in reality nothing affects the health and happiness of a company so much as a pleasant situation and genial surroundings. Camps are sharply divided in the memory into three divisions: intolerable, tolerable and delightful. The first brings with it the most dreary associations. A long march in the face of biting winds; a particularly obstreperous herd of Tibetan yaks, which periodically buck off their loads; an arrival at sunset at a wind-swept plain where, look as one may, there is no particle of shelter from the freezing blast and no brushwood for fuel; where the yaks, seized by the horns, rush hither and thither refusing to be unloaded, and tent-poles and boxes are hurled helter-skelter in their headlong flight, while the drivers whistle and whirl their long slings and one hears the sharp thud of stones on the recalcitrant animals; the tent-peg mallet lost or half the tent-pole missing; the pitching of tents in a storm of rain and the piling of boulders on the tent-flaps to keep out all the wind that is possible; a dinner off cold leavings, such as they are, for ourselves, while the rest of the company, less fortunate, eat sugar and uncooked sweet flour, for no fire to cook the evening meal can burn in the driving blast; then the final quiet which marks deep slumber, while the weary sentry paces his rounds, envious of the warm beds of his comrades; such are the memories connected with encampments which can deservedly be called unpleasant. In contrast to this is the other extreme, and its delightful associations linger long in the mind. Picture a verdant meadow with a gently flowing stream, in which the camp-followers spend the day catching fish with their hands (they have no nets), a spot sheltered from winds, rich in fuel, where the tents form a picturesque setting to the beauty of the scene, and later cheerful camp-fires speak of the evening meal enjoyed in comfort, and cheery laughter, heard late into the night, is witness of general contentment, while the glorious moon sheds a dazzling radiance unequalled elsewhere in the whole of this fair world. Such scenes and such memories are not lightly forgotten, and, mingling with those that lie between the one extreme and the other, form some of the most lasting recollections of Tibet, for the simple reason that they were our daily experiences.

CHAPTER XVI

THE MARKET OF GYANEMA, THE SUTLEJ VALLEY AND THE KINGDOM OF THE AMAZONS

TRAVELLING from Tirthapuri towards Gyanema one rises twice to a height of some 16,500 ft., viz., first over the Chitumb Pass and next over an outlying spur of Chhujathol. There are only two spots where camping is possible, because of the water-supply: one is on the banks of a small stream and the other is by a puddle. There is absolutely no other water anywhere else, and yet in one map, which I will not specify, the country is cheerfully represented as full of rivers. It fell to our lot, of course, to pitch by the puddle, and we should all have fallen ill to a certainty had not a sentry continually watched the trickle of water and regulated the filling of vessels and the watering of all animals. The final approach to Gyanema is over a perfectly level plain, and one sees the fort named after that place from a great distance, as it is situated in a commanding position. All the buildings are now in ruins, but there is enough to show that in the past the place must have been quite formidable. This plain is a plateau of roughly the same elevation as the one further north, in which are the Holy Lakes, and which stretches to Gartok and the west. The Gyanema plateau runs westward past the market of Shibchilam and along the Sutlej valley, commencing at a height of about 15,000 ft. and gradually sloping

THE GYANEMA MARKET

down to 14,000 ft. Along the Sutlej there are the following villages: Khyunglung, 14,700 ft., Dongpu, 14,200 ft., Daba (the seat-of a Jongpen), 13,900 ft., while below the plateau in the valley of the river are Totling (or Toling), the monastery of the Archbishop of Western Tibet, 12,200 ft., and Chaprang, 12,400 ft., the summer residence of another Jongpen.

The Gyanema plain is wonderfully free of stones, which are such a sore trouble in the more northerly plateau, and it was quite a pleasure to be able to travel in comfort again and to know that the poor beasts of transport were not cutting their feet to pieces. A further feature is the intense cold of the ground during the night due to the close proximity of the snowy ranges of the Himalayas, the soil at a depth of some three feet remaining frozen for the greater part of the year. As we were warned of this fact at the very beginning the camp followers, who always slept on the ground, were able to put plenty of bedding between them and the earth and so escaped all illness from chills. There are two markets to which traders resort for two months during the year, distant four miles the one from the other: we call the one Gyanema and the other Chhakara, whereas the Tibetans call the former Kharko and the latter Gyanema, and this variation in the names is very confusing to those who are not well acquainted with the border. They are both in the jurisdiction of the Barkha Tarjum, who, as has been remarked in previous pages, is thrown more in contact with the residents of our territory than any other Tibetan official, with the exception of the Taklakot Jongpen. The traders coming to Gyanema do a trade of £26,500 annually, *i.e.*, during the two months when the markets are open. Notwithstanding the extent of this trade, and the fact of Gyanema being written very large on the maps, there are no houses at this place of any kind whatsoever, as the Tarjum will not permit building for fear of disturbing the spirit of the ground, The whole plain is covered with tents of every hue, size and

THE BARKHA TARJUM IN FRONT OF HIS OWN TENT
Note the pendant ear-ring: his robe is padded for warmth

description, and one sees the smart white tents of the Lhasan merchants side by side with the black ones belonging to the Dokpa nomads, while the Bhotias from the various passes and parts of Bhot, such as Niti, Johar, Darma and Byans, live in unostentatious but comfortable tents of a different colour and shape from those of the Tibetans. The traders are very anxious to build houses of some description for the storage of their goods, but up to the present the foolish and childish superstition of the Tibetan officials has prevented any attempts. Similarly in Taklakot the

Bhotias, who have already built walls and foundations for their houses by the consent of the Jongpen, are not allowed to roof them with slates, which are obtainable in the neighbourhood of a particularly good quality, because of fears regarding the sentiments of the spirit of the ground. They have instead to use cloth coverings, which are tightly stretched as awnings over the walls, and are sufficient to keep out dust but would be useless against rain.

During the year of our travels, 1905, the rainfall in Western Tibet was smaller than it had been for many previous years, with the result that the whole country was parched and there were general fears as to the failure of the grass on the pasture-lands, a state of things which spelt loss, perhaps ruin, to thousands of owners of cattle. Scarcity of fodder in the bitter cold of winter is an appalling calamity in this pastoral country. As an instance of this take both the Gyanema markets, which are situated close to what is usually marshy ground, extending for many hundreds of acres over the plain, where there is usually splendid grazing for thousands of sheep and jibboos; this year the moisture was entirely absent from the soil, and at the end of August, which is generally a rainy month, the traders were complaining bitterly of want of pasture, and the Tibetans had the most gloomy forebodings as to the future. The dry season was, of course, very pleasant for our expedition, as we enjoyed very much warmer weather than we otherwise should have done, and we received many congratulations on our good luck, as we were considered very fortunate, but we could not help being sorry when we saw the general depression prevalent everywhere and heard the complaints of the hardy shepherds, who freely told us of their troubles.

The climate of Western Tibet is at all times a trying one. The sun is so hot when one is sheltered from the wind that an Indian sun hat is most acceptable, while

A TIBETAN LAMA SPINNING

Tibetans and Bhotias, both men and women, do this all day long, while they are walking, sitting or carrying loads

the Bhotia traders state that cakes of sugar, which have stood the heat of the Indian plains in the cold-weather and of the valleys on the way to Tibet, are frequently melted by these powerful rays. Even in the wind, which blows strongly for the greater part of the day, one cannot forget the sun, but should clouds come up or a shower of rain take place the fall in the temperature is instantaneous, and a change from a sun hat to a Balaclava cap is often very welcome. It is these little details that make the matter of dress such a difficult one; at one moment one is almost frozen and the next almost baked. Again, tents must be such as to stand high winds, and be so constructed that stones can be piled on the flaps and the wind thereby more effectually kept out. A blanket-lined tent is a good protection from the wind and night cold, the little extra weight being amply compensated for by the untold comfort. So annoying is the wind that it becomes the principal bugbear; in whatever direction one places the doorway the wind will always manage so to veer round as to find an entrance. Often the guides and the camp-followers closed their tents altogether and lived inside in semi-darkness while it was broad day-light outside, and I have frequently been in my tent with every flap tightly fastened down, the only aperture being a minute hole meant for a stove-chimney. Stoves cannot be successfully used owing to the want of proper fuel, as juniper wood smells strongly and cow-dung is unpleasant. Another discomfort is the want of lights in the evenings: oil is unobtainable and candles (which we burnt) were too expensive for the camp-followers, who in consequence generally remained in the dark. The glare during the day is always trying to the eyes, and a plentiful supply of boracic acid powder is a necessity: we found that the camp-followers very quickly appreciated the simplicity of the cure and the benefit of continually washing the eyes with this medicine. Dysentery, due to bad and improperly cooked food, had to be continually guarded against. Bhotias live on tea, sweet flour and meat, and can go weeks on no other food, but the ordinary hillman is unaccustomed to this diet and simply cannot live on it. To him rice, unleavened cakes, called chupattis, and vegetables are a supreme necessity. Now the last-named are unobtainable anywhere, and rice requires much boiling at these altitudes before it is fit for consumption, so much so that all the men gave up rice as a diet owing to the illnesses which always came in its train. To cook unleavened cakes fuel is necessary, and kneading and baking take time. In camping-grounds where the wind was very strong and fuel scarce the men often found it impossible to cook and frequently went hungry, as they could not bring themselves to sweet flour, which is the constant food of the Tibetans and Bhotias, or to their tea, which is a concoction of flour, butter and salt boiled with tea-leaves for an hour or more and then churned in a cylinder. It is a stimulant and very supporting, being almost a food, but our men simply abhorred it (and so did we), preferring the ordinary tea, which was freely supplied to them, and which they much appreciated. Looking back at our trip and talking the matter over with the men, it is certain that all discomforts of cold, mountain sickness and exposure can be easily borne, whereas the problem of proper food is almost insuperable.

At Gyanema we found the Barkha Tarjum, who had been recently playing the part of the villain in the murder-trial before the Garphans, when he had been charged with killing the servant of the Taklakot Abbot. He seemed none the worse for his fine by the Garphans, and general report said that he considered he had won a great victory over the Church. His suavity and blandness made our interviews pass most pleasantly, and having lived in Lhasa for many years, and knowing every niche and corner of the place, he was more than ever interested in the photographs and pictures in Waddell's and Landon's books regarding that place, and gave most searching criticisms on what he saw. Every thing European, such as rifles, guns, cameras, binoculars, &c., and pictures of European state event sand the Russo-Japanese War were closely scrutinised. I had shown these pictures and photographs to so many officials that I had come to know them almost by heart, and I had shown our guns, rifles, cameras, &c., so often that the exhibition must have palled on the interpreters, but they were most faithful and invariably with every new official tried to rouse his interest to the utmost. It is to these untiring efforts of these excellent men that I attach no small part of the success which we achieved everywhere. The Tarjum was in these respects different to the new Yungchong, or official vendor, the successor of the retiring Yungchong (whom we had met at Gartok), whom we also found at Gyanema. This latter official, although a good listener and much interested in what he saw, seemed all the time to be calculating in his mind how much he was going to lose by the free importation of Indian tea. He told us that he had large quantities of Tibetan tea, which he had brought for sale to the inhabitants from Lhasa, and he was evidently much perturbed at the prospect of Indian tea flooding the market. Official Tibetan tea is sold at ridiculous rates to raise a state income, and so Indian tea has a splendid future before it, and being cheap and acceptable to the people ought soon to be largely sold.

Nothing could have exceeded the cordiality of our interviews with these two officials, and before we parted they asked for, and were promised, photographs of themselves. The Tibetans quite understand about photographs and ask for them freely, and always think that they should be developed, printed and supplied on the spot. The Yungchong we met at Gartok held these sentiments, and when I demurred,

THE BARKHA TARJUM AND HIS DAUGHTER

at once remarked: "Oh, but the Moravian Missionary in Ladakh gave me photos immediately," and to crown his argument produced some beautiful pictures. The Tarjum's daughter was also photographed: she was a little shy at first, but her father sternly called her from her tent, and, when she still delayed, a trusted male attendant, who looked is if he fully realised that the great man's orders could not be trifled with, produced her blushing. She was really charmed beyond measure to have her picture taken, but thought a little coyness proper for the occasion. So friendly were the Tarjum and his family that his wife actually sewed for me a Tibetan tiara, such as women wear, which I was taking with me as a curiosity. From Gyanema we said farewell to the fearsome yaks of the Tibetans and travelled with jibboos, a cross between a yak and a cow, belonging to the Johari Bhotias. These traders use jibboos in preference to yaks because they are more docile, and, therefore, better fitted for the very bad tracks which lead across the Untadhura Pass to Milam. So tractable are they that their noses are not even pierced for the nose-ring and cord. Although they carried smaller loads and travelled slower than the Tibetan yaks yet they were a great relief after the others, which had broken so much of our property and every day, by their unrestrained wickedness, had roused the evil passions of all our camp.

The plain to the west of Gyanema is infested with dacoits, who conceal themselves in the hills and watch from their point of vantage for small parties of traders, whom, if they think them defenceless, they attack with great brutality. A few miles west of Gyanema there is a walled enclosure, erected by the Bhotias as a place to which they can rally if suddenly attacked in this way. These lawless robbers manufacture their own ammunition; they get saltpetre from Rudok and also extract it from the manure of sheep and goats, by a process of burning, and make their own charcoal from thick stems of the larger juniper brushwood so common everywhere. Sulphur they obtain by means of barter from Bashahr and Ladakh traders, while they cut bullets out of yaks' horns, for lead is very scarce throughout the country. These bullets are frequently weighted with lead, as otherwise they are found not to travel to any great distance. During the expedition to Lhasa the enemy used red-gold copper bullets and stones covered with lead. Apart from these human beasts of prey, wolves are plentiful and do much harm to the herds of sheep and goats. An ordinary grey wolf will enter a flock and, for the mere lust of slaughter, will kill twenty-five

ROUGH-LOOKING TIBETANS

or thirty sheep and leave them lying dead without devouring one. The black wolf is common west of Shibchilam and is far more savage, being so powerful as to attack even the yaks of traders single-handed, and fastening on to the neck will retain its grip until the poor victim is finally pulled down and killed. The grey wolf is said to have been frequently tamed and kept by traders and Tibetans as a dog to be a companion in the house and to go on the march. A so-called tame wolf was brought to us and was said to be quite docile with its attendant, and we were urged to keep it, but as we saw it very nearly remove the fingers of that attendant in a fierce snap we did not feel equal to running the risk of losing portions of our bodies by retaining such a playfully disposed pet.

Along the valley of the Sutlej cultivation is to be found in many places, but apparently the only crop that will grow is barley, other crops, such as peas and mustard, which are found round Taklakot, not being sown here. Irrigation by means of channels from mountain streams is universal, and without constant watering the crops would be a failure. Rain is not depended upon for this purpose; in fact, the people dread that rain will mean hail, and are, therefore, most anxious to escape it, and even order that no guns be fired off anywhere by sportsmen or others lest the dragon in the sky growl in thunder, and hurling hail on the standing corn destroy the patient labour of many weeks. There are fields at the markets of Khyunglung (which place is also notable for an enormous piece of crystal), Dongu, Dongpu, Daba and elsewhere, but not Shibchilam. The inhabitants are very partial to living in caves, and although houses are to be found yet these caves are by far the most popular residences. Some of these cliff-dwellings are quite intricate, one set of caves connecting with the next in a wonderful way, one of the most interesting places being a village called Dam. On the other hand, much cultivation has been abandoned or allowed to remain fallow, and there are villages full of dwellings which are lying uninhabited, and the empty houses give a dreary and cheerless aspect to the scene. An instance of this is Hala, where it is said there used at one time to be a fairly large population, but for some reason the families all became extinct, and now no one cares to live there. Superstitious feelings always arise in these cases and they are very difficult to combat. There is one cave in this valley in which there is a stone,

THE GLACIER OF THE GORI RIVER
Our party crossing the Glacier which is near the Untadhura Pass (17,590 ft.)

and lamas say that whoever puts it on his head will, if he is a sinner, find it heavy in proportion to the greatness of his sin, and if he is a righteous man he will feel no weight at all. I asked the Bhotia, who told this anecdote and firmly believed the truth of the lama's stories, as to what he felt, and he was diffident as to the reply, but said it was not very light. The traders of the Native States of Bashahr and Tehri

Garhwal, and of that part of British Bhot called Mana, visit Chaprang, which is the summer residence of a Jongpen, while those of Niti in British Bhot visit Daba, the seat of another Jongpen, and also with the Joharis go to the markets of Shibchilam and Gyanema. The real Jongpen of Daba has not been seen there for the last three years and his trusty servant has been doing his work for him.

It is interesting to remember that an Amazonian kingdom existed in this trans-Himalayan valley of the Sutlej, which was visited by the great Chinese traveller Hwen Thsang, whose statements have been corroborated by the Chinese annals. Atkinson in his "Himalayan Districts" writes: "In the Chinese annals we have a record which corroborates the statement of Hwen Thsang, and proves that the Amazonian kingdom lay in Tibet and was a reality. From it we learn that there was a tribe in Eastern Tibet known as the Nu-Wang, from the fact of their being ruled by a woman. In the Sui history an account is given of an embassy from these Nu in 586 A.D., in which it is stated that the people in each successive reign make a woman their prince. They build cities in the mountains with houses of many stories, the sovereign's house having nine, in which there are several hundreds of female attendants and a court is held every five days. The men, having nothing to do with the government, only fight and cultivate the land. Both men and women paint their faces of many colours. They live principally by hunting. They have had frequent wars with India. When the queen dies they collect a large sum of gold money and select from her family two clever women, of which one is made the queen and the other the lesser sovereign. The title of the queen is Pinchiu.

At the burial of their sovereign several tens of the great ministers and relatives are buried at the same time. Since the year 742 A.D. they elected a man as ruler, and a few years afterwards the state was absorbed by Lhasa."

A GLACIER NEAR THE UNTADHURA PASS (17,590 FT.)

One can imagine the life in this state under the great sovereign Pinch You (such a characteristically feminine title) in which the mere man was utilised to fight the ladies' battles when scratching and hair-pulling did not suffice; where Courts were held by command every five days, and, of course, man had to attend otherwise there would be no fun, and had also to paint his face with the highest art, or he would realise the power of Pinch You.

CHAPTER XVII

THE PASSES TO WESTERN TIBET, AND CUSTOMS OF THE WESTERN BHOTIAS

THE different passes leading from India into Western Tibet are as follows:

(1) There is the route from Srinagar in Cashmere, which goes through Leh and up the valley of the Indus to Gartok, and is used by the traders of Cashmere and Chinese Turkistan.

(2) From Lahaul, in the Kangra district of the Punjab, traders visit Rudok by means of a pass between Hanle and Demchok.

(3) Kulu traders of the Kangra district pass through Spiti and use the Shangrang Pass by means of a bad coolie track.

(4) The Simla route follows the Sutlej river and goes over the Shipki and Sirang passes: this is the principal road for the traders of the Native State of Bashahr, and it is hoped that in the future there will be a great increase of other Indian trade also.

(5) For the Native State of Tehri Garhwal there is the Lilang Pass: this route connects with Chaprang in Tibet and Mussoorie in British territory.

(6) In British Garhwal there are two passes, the Mana, 17,890 ft., and the Niti, 16,750 ft., divided by the giant mountain Kamet, 25,445 ft.: the former, called by Tibetans Tunyila, leads from the country near the sacred temple of Kedarnath to Chaprang, and the latter from near the temple of Badrinath to Daba.

Lapthal in the hollow

LOOKING TOWARDS TIBET FROM THE ASCENT SOUTH OF LAPTHAL: A DREARY LANDSCAPE

NOTE THE EASY SLOPES

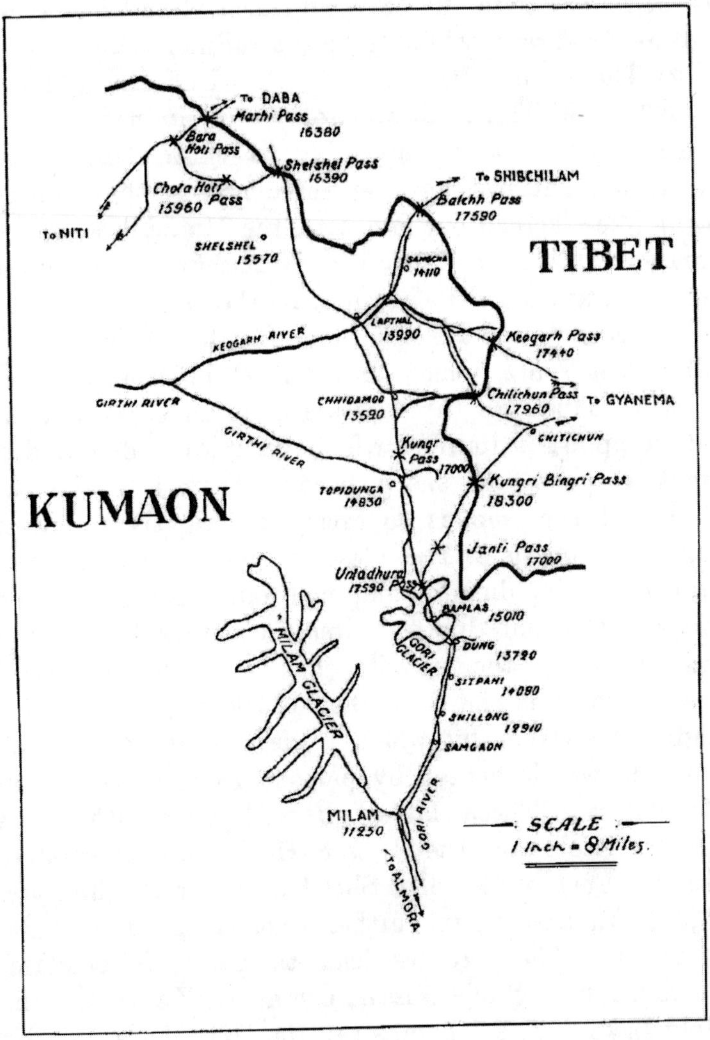
To DABA
Marhi Pass
16380
Bara Holi Pass
Shelshel Pass
16390
Chota Holi Pass
15960
To SHIBCHILAM
Balchh Pass
17590
To NITI
SHELSHEL
15570
TIBET
SAMGCHA
14110
LAPTHAL
13990
KEOGARH RIVER
Keogarh Pass
17440
GIRTHI RIVER
CHHIDAMOO
13520
Chilichun Pass
17960
To GYANEMA
GIRTHI RIVER
CHITICHUN
Kungr Pass
17000
Kungri Bingri Pass
18300
TOPIDUNGA
14830
KUMAON
Janti Pass
17000
Untadhura Pass
17590
BAMLAS
15010
MILAM GLACIER
GORI GLACIER
DUNG
13720
SITPANI
14080
SHILLONG
12910
SAMGAON
MILAM
11250
GORI RIVER
To ALMORA
SCALE
1 Inch = 8 Miles

These routes unite and traverse Garhwal and find their exit at Kotdwara, where there is a railway.

(7) The Johar Bhotias use the Untadhura Pass, 17,590 ft., which is, however, only a preliminary to two other passes. It is impossible to enter Tibet from Johar without passing over three passes, the country being like a spread-out fan, with the Untadhura as the handle. Having crossed the Untadhura two passes face the traveller, the eastern being the Janti, 17,000 ft., which leads to the Kungri Bingri, 18,300 ft. If traders adopt this route, which they almost invariably do in going to Tibet, all three passes must be crossed without stopping, a journey which occupies a day and a night for goats and sheep, because there is no fuel *en route* and the cold is so great as seriously to affect baggage animals. The western pass is the Kungr, 17,000 ft., Topidunga camping-ground lying between this and the Untadhura. After the Kungr Pass, going towards Tibet, the traveller has a choice of several passes: there is the Shel Shel, 16,390 ft., on the west leading to Daba, by which traders return from Gartok, and which is used by persons going to Niti from Shibchilam. These latter proceed over either the Greater Hoti or the Lesser Hoti, two alternative routes. East of the Shel Shel Pass is the Balchh Pass, 17,590 ft., and again further east is the Keo Pass, 17,440 ft. These routes lead to Daba, Shibchilam, Gartok, Khyunglung, Missar, Gyanema, Kailas and the Holy Lakes. The Tibetans call the Untadhura Pass by the name of Kyunam La.

(8) The Darma Bhotias use the Darma Pass, or Neo Dhura, called by the Tibetans Nooi La, or Shekhu La, 18,510 ft., which leads to Gyanema.

(9) The Byans Bhotias use the Lankpya Lekh Pass,

18,150 ft., and sometimes the Mangshan Pass, though the latter is very difficult. The former leads to Gyanema and the latter to Taklakot.

(10) The Byans and Chaudans Bhotias use the Lipu Lekh Pass, 16,780 ft., called by the Tibetans Jang Lhaula, and also the Tinkar Pass in Nepal of the same height. These lead to Taklakot.

(11) The Humlis use a pass in the extreme North-Western corner of Nepal when they visit Taklakot.

We crossed by the Balchh and Kungr passes, halting in the valleys at Sangcha, Chhidamoo and Topidunga. There is a very notable feature in the whole country which is worth noticing, viz., that, generally speaking, the sides of the mountains facing northwards in the direction of Tibet all have gentle slopes and easy gradients, whereas those looking to the Indian, or south, side are extremely precipitous. The ascent of the Balchh, Kungr and Untadhura passes from the north is gradual and causes little distress to men or animals, whereas the ascent of the same passes from the south is quite the reverse, being in places so steep and slippery, the wretched track passing over such dangerous spots, that it is a great strain on all, men and beast both suffering many hardships. In bad weather many hundreds of sheep and goats die on these mountains, and even jibboos and ponies are lost in numbers.

Travellers are often anxious to enter Garhwal from Milam by a quick route, and there is a track along the Girthi river through Topidunga to Niti in Garhwal which is very short, but it is only feasible for coolies and unladen animals. Transport animals with loads cannot go through, as the track is too difficult, the result being that this route is of little material use to anybody.

Far and wide over these mountains, *e.g.*, at Lapthal,

LOOKING TOWARDS THE TIBETAN BORDER FROM THE KUNGR PASS (17,000 FT.)

NOTE THE GRADUAL SLOPES

Chhidamoo, Topidunga, and at such heights as the Kungr Pass, 17,000 ft., marine fossils are found lying broadcast, and many are of the most beautiful shapes, all of which add an additional interest to the other wonders of nature.

There is a pretty story told of the first advent of the Shokas, or Sokpas, into Johar, where they followed a people who were covered with hair even to their tongues. In those early days there lived a great bird of prey on the Gori glacier, which daily fed on one of these hairy inhabitants, and by its ravages reduced their number to a mere handful. To free them from this curse a holy Lama, who with his magic powers of flight used to flit to Lapthal and other places, sent his servant with a bow and arrows to kill the evil bird, and gave him for a guide a man who ever changed his form. This guide took the form of a dog, hence the pass Kungri Bingri, the former word meaning a dog; then he became a stag, hence the name Dol-Dunga; then a bear, hence Topi-Dunga; then a camel, hence the pass of Unta Dhura; then a tiger, hence Dung-Udiyar; and finally a hare, at Samgaon. Thus the route from India to Tibet was first shown, for up till then there was no way known and there was no communication between the inhabitants of the two countries. The servant killed the bird of prey, but by this time all the hairy inhabitants were dead, and the servant, although wishing to make a colony there himself, demurred to do so owing to the want of salt. The holy Lama then took salt and sowed it over the land like grain, sufficient to provide to this day herbage so saturated with salt that there has never been any want for the Bhotia flocks. The Lama then flew away out of sight, but when Buddhist priests visit the valley they still ask for alms in the name of the Lama who gave the people salt.

As a matter of fact, at the present day Bhotias do not feed their flocks on the salted grass, as they have

The Pass

THE ASCENT TO THE KUNGR PASS (17,000 FT.) FROM THE NORTH
Note the easy slopes of the approach

become so rich as to use the ordinary salt of commerce, but the practice is still to be found among the Tibetans, who march large herds over the border for the sole purpose of feeding them on the salted grass in British territory.

On our return journey from Tibet after crossing the Untadhura Pass we entered Johar, the country of some of the Western Bhotias, who are obviously not pure

Mongolians. They live at the mouths of the Mana, Niti, and Untadhura passes, and are the most Hinduised of all Bhotias. The Niti valley is inhabited by Marchas and Tolchas and the Mana valley by Marchas only. The Marchas of Mana are divided into five clans which

THE CONTRAST ON THE SOUTHERN SIDE OF THE PASS
A steep place in the descent from the Kungr Pass: the path does not exist

all intermarry, and are connected with the famous Badrinath temple. As the Badrinath temple is on Bhotia land the Marchas of Mana receive an annual payment from the temple of fifty rupees in cash, forty pounds of grain and one puggaree. This is a fixed payment and is conditional on the fact that at the Janam Ashtami festival, when the idol is carried through Mana to be bathed at the waterfall and fed at the Mata Murati, the women of Mana, led by the Malpa women, clothed in festival attire, shall sing hymns in honour of the god.

The Bhotias living at the mouth of the Untadhura Pass in the Milam valley are known as Rawats, or

A VERY STEEP BIT ON THE BANKS OF THE GIRTHI RIVER NEAR TOPIDUNGA

On the way down south from the Kungr Pass : a great contrast to the northern side

Shokas, or Sokpas ; not that they admit any connection with Sok or Mongolia, although they cannot account for the name. The Rawat ancestor of the Milamwals obtained permission from the Gartok Garphan to establish himself in trade and built Milam and Burphu, and received a grant of Chunpal from the Huniyas. The connection with Tibet is still kept up, in that the headman of Milam has a so-called Jagir at Khyunglung in Tibet, which entitles him to receive annually as a gift five goats and two rupees' worth of butter, and as many beasts of burden or coolies as are necessary for the carriage of his effects, whenever he goes to, or returns from, Missar in Tibet.

The Rawats of Johar are earnestly striving to follow all the ordinances of the Hindu religion and invariably speak of themselves as Hindus; in fact, so far has their progress gone that some authorities have classified them as Hindus. There can be no question, however, that, whatever opinion these Rawats may hold concerning themselves as orthodox believers in the Hindu faith, the other Hindus do not consider them orthodox at all, and the lowest castes even will not eat with them, although all, except Brahmans and superior Hindus, will smoke with them.

There could be no greater mistake than to suppose that the Hindu Law applied to any of the Bhotias; in fact, excluding Johar, the Bhotias do not even know what the Vedas are, on which Hindu Law is based. It is in questions relating to property, the law of inheritance, adoption and woman's property that the difference between the Bhotias and other Hindus is most clearly seen. A Bhotia woman has no special property of her own, as in Hindu Law, although at the will of her husband or father she may be allowed to keep what she earns by spinning wool or making blankets, but this is entirely dependent on the pleasure of the man concerned. The Bhotia laws of inheritance are not those of Hindu Law, and the principles applicable to adoption, as found in Hindu Law, are unheard of. As a matter of fact, in cases of adoption among Bhotias the choice invariably falls upon the heir. Again, the Hindu idea of a joint-family is quite unfamiliar. The Bhotia father is the absolute owner of all family property including ancestral, and can mortgage on his own signature without reference to his sons, a state of things quite unknown to Hindu Law. Lastly, when the infirmities of age impair the father's business capacity,

River in this chasm

THE ROAD BY THE GIRTHI RIVER, NEAR TOPIDUNGA

The difficulties on the south far exceed those on the northern slopes of the different passes

the sons in a Bhotia family divide the property, and he is more or less entirely at their mercy. There is no fixed share, as in Hindu Law, apportioned to him, but custom generally insures that some extra portion is put aside for him, and he lives with the son who is his favourite. Frequently the Bhotia father is neglected, and cases of great hardship on parents who have been rich, but whose property has been taken by the sons, are often met with. A son can at any time insist on partition. Their domestic life is being brought more and more under the influence of Hinduism.

On the fifth day after childbirth Pancholi is performed, the woman and child being allowed to occupy a separate room or house, but no one is permitted to touch them. Should any one even by accident touch them the only purification is by sprinkling cow's urine on his own body and tasting the urine, a disgusting practice which is strictly in accordance with orthodox Hinduism. On the eleventh day Namkaran, or "name-giving," takes place. On this day Brahmans purify the woman and the child and they may then enter the house and touch water. A horoscope is prepared according to the rules of the Hindu horoscope scriptures. When the first two or three children in a family have died young the right nostril of the new-born child is pierced, or the child is given to a fakir, who shortly after returns it. When the first born has survived, but others have died in early youth, a large piece of sugar is broken upon the back of the first born, so that the newly born infant may start its young life with the bad luck of the past broken. A child born under certain signs of the Zodiac is handed over to some third person, with whom it remains up till its tenth or eleventh year, the parents not seeing its face till then.

The rite of the sacred thread takes place between the ages of eight and twelve years. However, the sacred thread is not as a rule put on at this ceremony; in fact, only a few Bhotias wear the thread, the reason being that the attendant obligation of bathing daily is so irksome in the cold journeys to Tibet that few care to incur the obligation. However, after the

THE UNTADHURA PASS (17,590 FT.) FROM THE KUNGR PASS (17,000 FT.)

NOTE THE GRADUAL APPROACH TO THE UNTADHURA PASS, A CONTRAST TO THE DESCENT INTO A SHEER ABYSS FROM THE KUNGR PASS

Z

ceremony they never eat without washing the hands and face, which is a distinct advance on the prevalent dirty habits of some of the other Bhotias.

A Bhotia explained to me that, as the Joharis bought their wives (often for £15 or £20), they were superior to the Eastern Bhotias, who did not do so. "Besides," he said, "having bought my wife I can order her about, and if she objects I can beat her!" Truly this is an advance in civilisation.

In regard to marriage the ordinary Hindu customs are followed. Some person, often the family priest, is sent in search of a bride. The formal asking takes place between the ages of nine and twenty-five years, and after the asking usually six months elapse before the formal marriage, while consummation takes place at the age of maturity. In all marriage arrangements the girl is never consulted; the parents on both sides usually make all their plans absolutely regardless of the children concerned. Every man and woman is married, and this is a notable difference between the Western and Eastern Bhotias, where in every village many unmarried persons are to be found, the reason being that there marriage depends upon the will of the parties, who are always of mature age at the time of the marriage contract, and instances are not uncommon of men and women who have remained unmarried all their lives because nobody would marry them.

Brahmans perform the ceremony according to the Hindu Scriptures. An altar is made and fire placed on the top, and at the four corners are little trees, and all round the altar are pine trees. The bride and bridegroom take seven turns round the fire and the altar, this being the binding part of the ceremony. The bride puts her foot on a Sil, or stone used for grinding, and as she goes round pretends to slip and is caught by the bridegroom each time, in this way signi-

THE MILAM VALLEY

Milam is 104 miles from Almora

fying that in future all lovers will be ground to powder.

Before marriage a girl wears a nose-ring called Bali, but

after marriage and until her husband's death she invariably wears the Nath nose-ring.

A man can, and often does, have two or three wives. A marriage is always accompanied by lavish expenditure.

The funeral ceremonies are on the analogy of the Hindu rites. If a boy dies before the sacred thread ceremony he is buried, and not burnt, and salt is put into the grave with him, otherwise the usual custom is cremation, and all sons and kinsmen shave the head, moustache and beard.

Gold, called Hiran, is put into a dying man's mouth, and after death the body is tied in a coarse white winding-sheet and fastened on to the bier, while over all is thrown a silk shroud. The funeral procession is composed of mourners who go bareheaded, preceded by three boys or men, holding a strip of white cloth one at each end and the third in the middle, a peculiar custom which is unknown in Kumaon or Garhwal amongst the ordinary hillmen, and is very similar to the Tibetan practice noted above, which is also found among the Eastern Bhotias.

At the pyre a head bone is kept to be thrown into the holy lake of Mansarowar, or into the Ganges, and until the opportunity for doing this may come it is put aside with some gold in a small brass box in the hollow of a tree or under a stone. All the mourners present at the cremation bathe, and on their return are purified with cow's urine according to the practice of orthodox Hinduism. A death in a village is considered unlucky, and people avoid undertaking any particular ceremonies from which they hope that success will ensue.

As is to be expected, we find that some of these Hinduised Bhotias still worship Tibetan deities; for instance, the Nikhurpas worship the god Dhurma.

This deity is specially sought after in the rainy season when the people have tired of a long spell of wet weather, and hope by propitiation of the god to effect

THE ROAD BELOW MILAM ←To Almora

a change in the climatic conditions prevailing. Two poles are fastened in the ground; to the top of one is fixed an iron or brass trident surmounted by a yak's tail, and to the top of the other an image of a man's head. Throughout the ceremony of worship music is played and finally a goat is slaughtered. Meanwhile the devotees are anxiously awaiting the moment when the god will manifest himself by taking possession of one of the throng. Suddenly some man is seized by the religious frenzy and rushing forward drinks the blood of the goat, and in this ecstatic state dances round the poles, and finally climbing the pole which holds the idol he imprints a bloody kiss on the mouth of the deity. A temple with rooms has now been built in honour of Dhurma: this is a new departure, for hitherto he owned no habitation built by men's hands.

Similarly at Burphu and Tola the Tibetan god Lhamsal is worshipped. The people fell a large tree, and carrying it to an open space fix it in the ground and make it firm with three ropes. Strips of cloth of every description are then fastened to every portion of it, and yaks' tails are tied in different parts of the tree. After these preparations the people sing and dance round the tree for three days on end. Persons who have had a son born to them are specially devoted to the worship of this god, and once a year offer a goat and liquor.

One of the most remarkable deities worshipped in Garhwal is the god Ghantakaran, or the Bell-god. It is common to find a large bell, sometimes one and a half feet long, suspended to a cross-bar supported by two uprights on the top of some lofty mountain. The lonely goatherd, or the zealous devotee, rings the bell when passing the spot. The Bell-god is very specially worshipped for nine days in the month of Magh, and in this special and remarkable service there are associated with him three other gods, viz., Kailas, the Tibetan deity Kumer and the deity Nanda Devi. The last-named is the loftiest mountain in the British Empire, and is situated in Bhot, and the first is the sacred mountain near Mansarowar Lake. The annual adoration takes place at Pandukeshar in Garhwal Bhot, and the ceremonies are specially interesting as they afford

→Our camp

RILKOT ON THE WAY TO ALMORA FROM MILAM

an instance of the religious fervour, or ecstasy, which seizes the devotee and makes him act as though goaded by a mania. An iron tripod is made red hot in a furious fire, which is zealously fed by the crowd. The men who are particularly favoured by the manifestation of the gods are Duryals of one family, living in

Pandukeshar. At this present time Gobind Singh is the favourite of Nanda Devi, Dhurma of Kailas, Meharban Singh of Kumer and Debu of Ghantakaran. Only the gods Kailas and the Bell-god manifest themselves. When the religious excitement is at its highest the two favourites of these gods suddenly rush down to the river and bathe, and dripping with water they rush towards the scorching fire. The crowd with cries of "Behold the god!" rub butter on the hands of the one who is devoted to the Bell-god, and he immediately raises the red-hot tripod and inverts it over his head and puts it back, while the other leaps into the flames and leaps out again. This is the ceremony as described to me by an eye-witness. The deity Acheri is worshipped everywhere. When any one has sore eyes, or a lingering illness, the goddess has to be appeased and her influence removed, and this is effected in one of two ways. Either a brass dish is put on an earthen pitcher and is beaten until the affected person begins in a frenzy to dance, and indicates what particular sacrifice will find favour with the deity, or a dooly is made with sticks and cloth and is worshipped with cakes and lights, after which it is carried to some lonely spot and left, the hope being that the malevolent influence is left with it.

The low caste Bhotias, called Dumras, are composed of blacksmiths, drum-beaters (dholis—from dhol = a drum), carpenters, basket-makers, tailors, shoe-makers and others. They only intermarry amongst themselves and their practices throughout Bhot are similar, bearing a general resemblance to Darma customs. In the funeral ceremonies (Dhurung), which they practise on the lines of the Darma Rajputs, they generally use a buffalo, which in some places they

RAI BAHADUR KISHEN SINGH MILAMWAL

SURVEY OF INDIA

THE PUNDIT "A.K." OF TIBETAN EXPLORATION, 1869–1893.

AT PRESENT LIVING AT MILAM

finally chase and kill with stones, sticks and knives, and in others, like Chaudans, they call in their fellow castemen from the next village and exhort them to kill the victim, and insist that death must be with one blow, otherwise, if the animal dies by a torturing death, they threaten that on a future occasion they will also torture in their turn the funeral victim of the other village. The Dhurung in Mana is only practised below Joshimath, and persons go that distance to perform it. The Dumra Bhotias do not give gifts to Brahmans, or in any way encourage them; in fact, they consider the sister's son to be the family priest, and so dispense with their services altogether.

After having lived at an altitude of 15,000 ft. for many weeks it was a curious experience to descend to Milam in British territory a little over 11,000 ft., but there can be no doubt that it was a much pleasanter change than the reverse which occurred when on our outward journey we were leaving British territory and going from Garbyang to our first high camp. Men who suffered severely from mountain sickness at the commencement of our trip entirely got over the effects as we marched from day to day in the higher altitudes of Tibet, and at the end of our journey no complaint of this kind was ever heard. At our first high camp at Sangcham, which was only 14,000 ft., many men were very seriously ill and were conveyed to Tibet with the greatest difficulty, but these very same men walked over the Balchh Pass, over 18,000 ft., on our return journey without the slightest inconvenience. It is plain, then, that one can become thoroughly accustomed to the high elevation.

The Milam valley running with the Gori river, which later meets the Kali at Askot, is very beautiful, and the delightful charm of tree forest, which commences some miles further south, is a strong contrast to the treeless wastes of Tibet. The track follows a fairly easy align-

THE LATE NAIN SINGH, C.I.E., SURVEY OF INDIA, THE PUNDIT "A." OF TIBETAN EXPLORATION, 1856–1876, WHO LIVED AT MILAM
He died fourteen years ago

ment, but, although this is in its favour, one could not help realising that the insuperable difficulties of the Untadhura and other passes are such as to entirely put this road out of the question for purposes of an Imperial Tibetan trade route. However much money were spent in improvements, there could never be any permanent road over the mountains as the material of the hill sides is of a crumbling nature, on which it would be impossible to effect any lasting impression. The traders of Johar are singularly courageous and

THE BRIDGE AT TEJAM ON THE WAY TO ALMORA
Alexis and Henri

intrepid and deserve every credit for the way in which they cope with appalling difficulties of climate, avalanches and elevation; but the fact remains that, in the face of many very much easier passes into Tibet, it is not in accordance with business principles to waste money in this quarter when it could be far better spent elsewhere.

As we descended further into India we found evidences

THE MEETING OF THE WATERS AT BAGESHAR ON THE SARJU RIVER

THIS IS A VERY HOLY SPOT, TWENTY-SIX MILES FROM ALMORA, WHERE OUR MEN SHAVED THEIR BEARDS, GROWN IN TIBET, AND BATHED, A LUXURY NOT APPRECIATED IN TIBET

of severe rainfall in the country immediately at the foot of the lofty snow ridges. Bridges had been swept away, fields inundated, rivers had formed lakes owing to heavy landslips, hamlets had been buried and there were reports of loss of life of men and cattle. And yet so effectual had the barrier of the Himalayas been, that literally hardly a drop of this excessive rainfall had reached the adjacent lands of Tibet, only a few miles distant as the crow flies.

In Tibet we had been singularly free from flies, except at the Mansarowar Lake, where they were a perfect plague, and also from all kinds of insect life, but we encountered all the pests usual to Indian hill life in the rains as we descended. The most terrible of all these pests is the leech, which is found actually in myriads in certain localities in the higher hills during the rains. So bad were they even on the roads at certain places of our march that one could see them in hundreds, like thin wire threads, on the path and the grass, wriggling with anxiety to find a victim. Men walking with bare feet were continually stopping, and would pick off three or four at a time, and this would occur every few minutes. The feet of the coolies were covered with blood, and a careful watch had to be kept on the horses' feet, otherwise some tiny thread-like leech would take hold and, before discovery, would have grown to an enormous size bloated with the poor beast's blood.

As we returned to the beautiful woods of India and saw pretty hamlets nestling in fertile valleys, and looked again upon a country full of houses and a visible population of men, women and children tending their fields or herding their flocks, we could not but compare this homely sight with what we had just left behind on the other side of the great barrier of the

Himalayas, where desolation is written boldly over a treeless landscape, where, with few exceptions, cultivation is unknown, and a nomad population living

THE BAZAAR AT BAGESHAR

The first we came to on our homeward journey, where our men revelled in all the luxuries of life, much appreciated after their long trip

in tents is so scattered over the barren wilderness that the traveller can travel for days and see no human being, while the absence of houses makes desolation more desolate; and we felt that, however pleasant our trip, the return home was good.

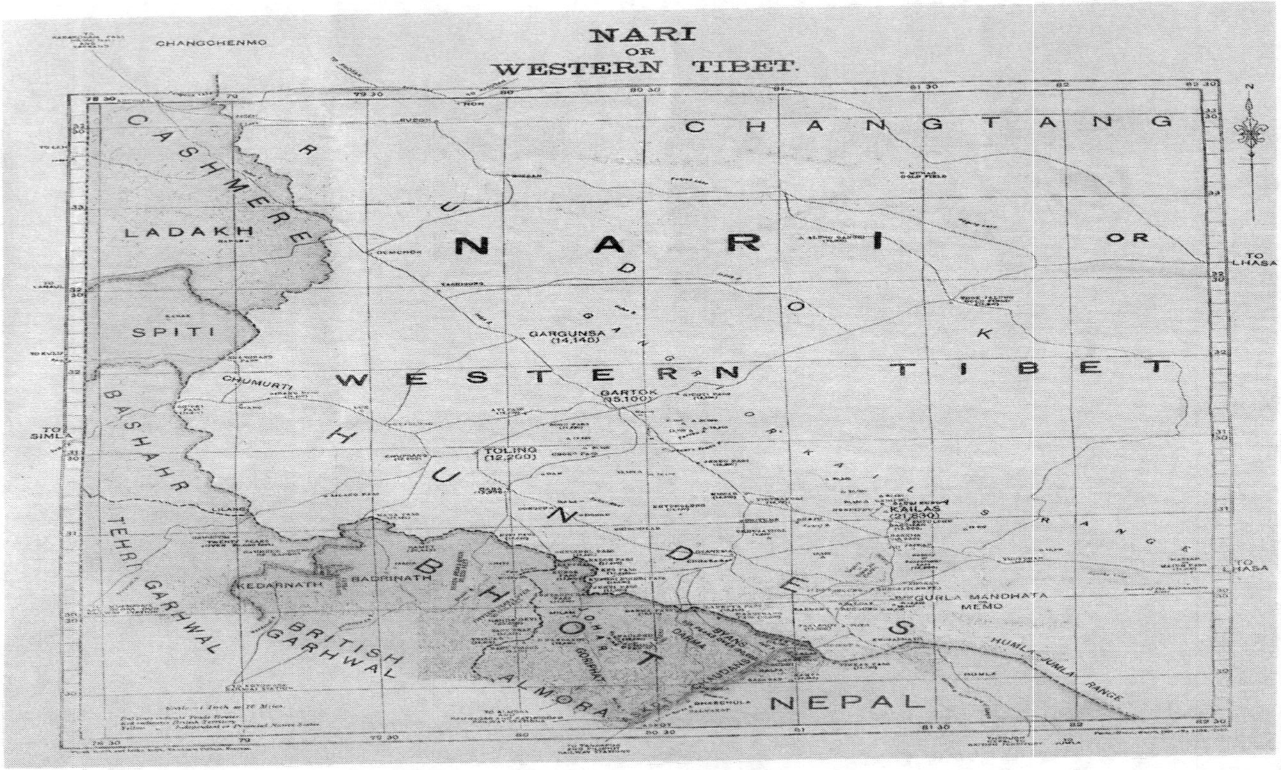
NARI
OR
WESTERN TIBET.
CHANGCHENMO
CHANGTANG
NARI
OR
WESTERN TIBET
NARI KHORSUM
HUNDES
BHOT
CASHMERE
LADAKH
SPITI
BASHAHR
CHUMURTI
GARGUNSA (14,140)
GARTOK (15,100)
TOLING (12,200)
KAILAS RANGE
KAILAS (21,830)
GURLA MANDHATA
MEMO
HUMLA-JUMLA RANGE
NEPAL
ALMORA
BRITISH GARHWAL
TEHRI GARHWAL
BADRINATH
KEDARNATH
JOHAR
DARMA
BYANS
CHAUDANS
GORIPHAT
TO SIMLA
TO LHASA
TO LHASA
LILANG
Scale—1 Inch = 16 Miles.

INDEX